BALD AMBITION

BALD AMBITION

A CRITIQUE OF KEN WILBER'S
THEORY OF EVERYTHING

JEFF MEYERHOFF

INSIDE THE CURTAIN PRESS

There is such a thing as intellectual tragedy.

STANLEY CAVELL

Contents

FOREWORD

Integral philosophy, as developed by Ken Wilber, is not only a system to be promoted and applied to our daily lives, but also a hypothesis to be validated and even challenged by specialists in various fields of science. In that area, not many initiatives have been taken. Since Jeff Meyerhoff offered his summary of his manuscript, *Bald Ambition*, in the summer of 2003 to IntegralWorld. net, the response has been predictable: sporadic comments, mostly cynical and dismissive, with an occasional appreciative remark. Apparently, "Green" postmodern critiques of a "yellow" integral model—to use the color-coding language of Spiral Dynamics—can be put aside as irrelevant.

This habit, so engrained among Wilberites, should be broken. Personally, I found Meyerhoff's text refreshing and stimulating, especially for those who, like me, have internalized Wilber's way of seeing the world over the years. I may not go along with all of his conclusions, but in the spirit of a healthy dialectic I approve the effort. This is how the game of science and philosophy should be played. This could be the start of a true Wilber debate.

Actually, what Meyerhoff has done, and what very few have even tried, is go back to Wilber's sources—among these are: Jean, Piaget, Jürgen Habermas, Charles Taylor, Jacques Derrida, and A.O. Lovejoy—and offer his own interpretations. In good postmodern fashion, he has attempted to "contextualize Ken," as the title of Andy Smith's review of this book aptly reads.[1] He has also analyzed Wilber's story of the Kosmos with the help of Hayden White's model, to better spot any blind areas and hidden values in

1 Andrew P. Smith, "Contextualizing Ken: A Review of Jeff Meyerhoff's Bald Ambition," http://www.integralworld.net/smith20.html.

the system. To many Wilber fans, the integral philosophy is taken to be an objective description of reality. Meyerhoff argues there's more subjectivity here then we might care to know.

Given the often-heated nature of discussions about the validity of Wilber's proposals, Meyerhoff's writing in *Bald Ambition* is remarkably composed and restrained. He does not focus on one field of study only—as many Wilber critics seem to have done—but offers the wide spectrum of the Wilber corpus, covering holon theory, psychology, epistemology, sociology, history, philosophy, methodology, and mysticism. Of special interest, given Meyerhoff's interest in the relationship between biography and philosophy, is his psychoanalysis of Wilber's beliefs, a chapter that makes extensive use of Wilber's own autobiographical statements. His book ends with an alternative approach to the problem of intellectual differences.

Several publishers turned down the manuscript of *Bald Ambition*, for unfortunately at the time of its writing, there wasn't a market yet for this type of literature. Therefore, integralworld.net serialized *Bald Ambition*, to make it known to a wider audience. Fortunately, the book is now also available in hard copy. Given the fact that the integral field has seen the growth of more academic approaches to Wilberism, it will surely find its readers.

Frank Visser

Webmaster integralworld.net
Author of *Ken Wilber: Thought as Passion*
May 2010

BALD AMBITION

INTRODUCTION

Ken Wilber's reputation includes everything from laudatory assessments that describe him as "the Einstein of consciousness" to derogatory dismissals that label him a New Age pseudo-scientist. His true merit lies somewhere between these extremes—and determining where is one of the goals of this book.

In the 1970s and '80s, Wilber established himself as a leading theorist of transpersonal psychology by integrating prominent western psychologies and eastern spiritualities into a spectrum of consciousness. In the '90s, he amassed an impressively diverse array of scholarship in the natural, social, and spiritual sciences to create an integral synthesis of knowledge, which he only half-ironically refers to as a "theory of everything." The first eight volumes of Wilber's collected works have been published, and his books have been translated into dozens of languages. A variety of thinkers engaged Wilber's work in the volume *Ken Wilber in Dialogue*.[1] Academic recognition has come from Charles Taylor, Michael Zimmerman, and Robert Kegan, and in the form of a book-length survey of his work.[2] The growing disenchantment

---

1 Donald Rothberg and Sean M. Kelly, eds., *Ken Wilber in Dialogue: Conversations with Leading Transpersonal Thinkers* (Wheaton, IL: Quest Books, 1998).
2 Frank Visser, *Ken Wilber: Thought as Passion* (Albany: SUNY Press, 2003).

with postmodern and poststructural thinking makes Wilber's integral synthesis look more attractive to those outside and inside academia.

Wilber is also a savvy propagandist of his work. Several web sites are now devoted to integral theory.[3] He, along with leading scholars, has founded Integral Institute, which promotes research from the integral perspective, offers integral consulting services, and, with John F. Kennedy University, offers a degree in integral theory. While his theory predicts a developmental transcending of the postmodern culture now ensconced in academia, Wilber knows that intellectual hegemony comes not just from the strength of the better argument but also from getting a younger scholarly generation to cudgel for his views and gain a foothold in academia. Wilber's growing popularity, networking, influence, and reputation make it a good time to evaluate his views.

Over the course of this book, I closely examine Wilber's scholarly sources and arguments, and offer a response from a strongly formulated critical, rational, postmodern, and spiritually informed position. I examine the major areas Wilber weaves together in his integral synthesis and demonstrate the problems and strengths of his arguments, methods, use of sources, and underlying philosophy.

Wilber has complained many times about critics misrepresenting his work.[4] In order to avoid misrepresentation I have tried to formulate his theory as strongly as possible. His magnum opus, *Sex, Ecology, Spirituality*,[5] is the main source of my interpretation, but I also draw from older and newer versions of his theory to elaborate his vision.

---

3 Examples include: integralworld.net, kenwilber.com, wilber.shambhala.com, integralinstitute.org, and integral-review.org.

4 See Ken Wilber, "Do Critics Misrepresent My Position?," at wilber.shambhala. com.

5 Ken Wilber, *Sex, Ecology, Spirituality*, (Boston: Shambhala Publications, 1995) will be referred to as *SES* throughout the book.

Chapters of this book are devoted to analysis of Wilber's views of philosophy, integral theory, methodology, the character of the natural world, individual and social development, mysticism, western history, and postmodernism. The areas of male/female relations and ecology have been examined by others and will not be examined here.[6]

Wilber's integral synthesis is an evolutionary-developmental theory that tries to connect the subject matters of the natural, social, and spiritual sciences. Using a model derived from the new sciences of complexity, he describes an evolutionary process in which self-organizing physical, biological, and human social and individual systems aggregate into increasingly complex forms to create novel, emergent evolutionary properties. The Big Bang set in motion a cosmic evolutionary process of aggregation, integration, and emergence. Subatomic particles aggregated into atoms which then aggregated into molecules, creating the stars, planets, and the other physical contents of the cosmos. On Earth, molecules aggregated into more complex forms, allowing the emergence of living matter, or organisms; this began a gradual biological evolution creating more complex and diverse forms of life. Emerging from this biological evolution were human beings and our unique form of consciousness. Human beings are a living embodiment of the inclusive complexity of the cosmos. Inclusive because within each of us are atoms within molecules within cells within tissues within organs within the body. Each level of existence both transcends and includes all lower levels forming a natural hierarchy within the still more encompassing purview of human consciousness.

Human consciousness continues this developmental process both individually and socially. Wilber uses the work of Jean Piaget and other developmental psychologists to chart the course of

---

6 See Michael Zimmerman, "A Transpersonal Diagnosis of the Ecological Crisis," *ReVision*, 18(4) and "On Transpersonal Ecology," *ReVision*, 19(2). Also P. Wright, "Gender issues in Ken Wilber's transpersonal theory," *ReVision*, 18(4) and "Difficulties with integrating the feminine," *ReVision*, 19(2).

individual development. He combines this with Jurgen Habermas's model of social evolution to describe a parallel development of society through history. Rationality is presently the most
advanced developmental stage of consciousness widely embodied
in the people and societies of the industrialized West. Transcending the rational is possible, according Piaget, Lawrence Kohlberg,
and Abraham Maslow, each of whom studied and theorized
higher stages of consciousness. Wilber uses these authors and the
spiritual sciences of disciplined introspection described in mystical literature to argue for a further unfolding of increasing consciousness. In contrast to mainstream western intellectual opinion, the mystical practices and literature of both the East and the
West constitute a rigorous, detailed, and empirical description of
the contents and the development of consciousness through the
disciplined use of contemplative and meditative practices. This
literature claims that there are levels of consciousness beyond, but
inclusive of, rational thought that provide an even greater integration of matter, life, and mind. Wilber creatively integrates this
work into his larger evolutionary synthesis.

To construct his integration Wilber uses the scholarship of academia. He bypasses the ongoing debates in the fields of study he
integrates by using what he calls the *orienting generalizations* in each
field. As the participants within each field debate the relevant issues over which they disagree, they also presuppose background
points of agreement, or orienting generalizations. In each field
of knowledge, Wilber culls this already-agreed-upon background
knowledge and constructs his integral synthesis.

This integral synthesis takes the form of a map of knowledge.
Within this map Wilber finds a place for the natural, social, and
spiritual sciences, which study different sides of individual and
social entities. Each individual and social entity has both a subjective, or interior, and objective, or exterior, side. For example,
phenomenology studies individual human subjectivity, or the interiors of individual consciousness; the history of consciousness

studies the consciousness, or subjectivity, of social groups through time; physics studies the individual and social exteriors of matter, such as sub-atomic particles and galaxies; demographics studies the exterior, or objective, aspect of human social aggregates. Each established science gives us information about a part of the larger whole that Wilber's model encapsulates.

Wilber's method and model also attempt to respond to and integrate the contemporary extreme postmodern relativism that sees no way to rank differing worldviews and sciences, and has left contemporary knowledge and society directionless and fragmented. Wilber's model strives to preserve the unique truths of disparate disciplines while integrating them within a hierarchical model that identifies the natural evolutionary tendencies that characterize the development of matter, life, mind, and spirit. In this way his integral vision is an advance over postmodern relativism and the fragmented specialization of the contemporary academy.

This book examines his work in two ways. First, I make good on my claim that Wilber does not actually use the method of orienting generalizations, by providing evidence in most of the subject areas he discusses—the natural sciences, developmental psychology, social evolution, western history, postmodernism, and mysticism—that his orienting generalizations are highly debatable and have widely varying degrees of validity. By examining his sources, such as Piaget, Habermas, Charles Taylor, Jacques Derrida, A.O. Lovejoy, and the fields in which they participate, I show the extensive and contentious debates surrounding the supposedly already-agreed-upon knowledge that Wilber uses to construct his integral framework.

But showing that the pillars of his integral framework are not the orienting generalizations of the major scientific disciplines is not the same as showing that they are false. So, second, I examine the validity of the arguments Wilber derives from his sources in each of the major areas he discusses. The focus here is on the evidence for his assertions, the logic of his arguments, and the assumptions and problems of evolutionary and developmental models.

After considering the evidence from academia, my critique of Wilber's synthesis examines his methodology. I demonstrate that there is a difference between Wilber's description of his method and the method he actually uses, and that further the method of orienting generalizations is necessarily unworkable. In a section on philosophy, I explicate Wilber's unstated philosophical assumptions and show how they are both problematic in themselves and prejudiced against differing philosophical commitments which, because they contradict Wilber's assumptions, are excluded from his inclusive synthesis.

After demonstrating the problems with Wilber's sources and arguments, I then present a different path available to those who esteem both rationality and self-development. That path explores the psychological underpinnings of belief and shows how that exploration can alter truth and objectivity, and has the potential to create more successful debate and self-knowledge.

I then illustrate this examination of the psychological causes of belief by asking why Wilber constructs his particular system. If, as I have shown, it does not fit the facts, and so does not derive its existence from what is the case, from where does it come? Using Wilber's journals and other sources I examine the psychological causes of his particular take on reality and the psychological purposes it serves. This provides insight into how intellectual blind spots operate and what perspectives get left out of his synthesis as a result. A conclusion assesses the positive and negative aspects of Wilber's thinking, and suggests where the integral conversation might continue from here.

CHAPTER 1

HOLARCHY

The core of Wilber's integral theory is his description of the structure and patterning of matter, life, mind and spirit: the Kosmos. This chapter comprises explication and analysis of three important aspect of Wilber's philosophy: holons—the theory's fundamental ontological concept; the twenty tenets—the Kosmos's basic patterns and structures; and the four quadrant model—which divides and arranges the elements of the Kosmos according to their natures and the disciplines that study them.

HOLONS

Wilber arranges all that exists, whether matter, life, mind, or spirit, in a special hierarchical relationship called a *holarchy*. The relative position of everything in the holarchy is determined by its level of developmental advance. All matter, life, mind, and spirit—the Kosmos—has evolved from the Big Bang, aggregating into successively more complicated arrangements, which create new emergent properties as the developmental process unfolds. Atoms aggregate into molecules, molecules into cells, cells into organisms. Each new emergent stage in the evolutionary process "transcends and includes" what came before it and exhibits new properties.

"Transcends" is used here in the sense that new properties emerge that had not been seen before. "Includes" is used in the sense that the newly emerged entity is constituted by its developmental predecessors and provides a new whole in which those predecessors now exist. A human being is made up of atoms within molecules within cells within tissues within organs within a mind that can transcend and embrace them all within consciousness. The resulting hierarchy is not the common top-down arrangement one normally thinks of but a concentric arrangement with each higher stage constituted by and embracing all the lower stages. In this way, the higher entities don't simply dominate the lower but are inextricably bound up with all below and all above. Each entity has an integral part to play and so the kinds of knowledge that illuminate these parts—physics, chemistry, biology, psychology, spirituality—must be preserved and integrated into a new synthesis of all knowledge.

According to Wilber, everything in the Kosmos is simultaneously a part and a whole; a part of some larger whole and a whole to its smaller parts. He uses Arthur Koestler's term *holon* to describe this part/whole quality of all things. Since the structure of parts within wholes is different from the usual top-down, pyramidal structure, Wilber terms his model a holarchy instead of a hierarchy.

Before examining Wilber's concept of the holon, we can ask about the institutional legitimacy, and so fitness to be an orienting generalization, of his conception of nature. The sources for Wilber's understanding of nature are the new sciences of complexity as summarized by Ervin Laszlo and Erich Jantsch. He writes that these are "the new sciences dealing with these 'self-winding' or 'self-organizing' systems . . . known collectively as the sciences of complexity," which he calls "the evolutionary systems sciences."[1] In scanning the literature on the sciences of complexity we find that not only don't these new sciences have orienting

1 *SES,* pp. 14–15.

generalizations, they are hardly even well defined disciplines. For example, M. Mitchell Waldrop begins his book *Complexity*, which is an upbeat report on the new sciences, by writing:

> This is a book about the science of *complexity*—a subject still so new and so wide-ranging that nobody knows quite how to define it, or even where its boundaries lie . . . because complexity research is trying to grapple with questions that defy all conventional categories.[2]

Similarly, in *Coping with Uncertainty: Insights from the New Sciences of Chaos, Self-Organization and Complexity*, Uri Merry, who is also favorably disposed toward his subject, writes:

> It must constantly be kept in mind that science is only at the onset of this journey and on the brink of applying this New Science to human affairs. The bulk of the work and its application is still ahead. Some of what the trailblazers write and describe may later be found to not exactly be in focus, some may be completely off course, and some may be pure speculation. . . . At the same time some findings may be scientific breakthroughs of great consequence. Only time will tell.[3]

Though Merry published his book two years after Wilber's *SES*, the state of the new sciences of complexity was no more settled.

John Horgan, in his critical book *The End of Science*, quotes physicist James Yorke, who coined the term *chaos*, saying, "complexity seems to refer to 'anything you want.'"[4] Seth Lloyd, of MIT and the Santa Fe Institute, e-mailed Horgan his thirty-one different definitions of complexity. These thirty-one definitions, Horgan thought, actually amounted to forty-five definitions. Interestingly,

---

2 M. Mitchell Waldrop, *Complexity*, (New York: Touchstone, 1993), p. 9.

3 Uri Merry, *Coping With Uncertainty*, (Westport, Conn.: Praeger, 1995), p. 14.

4 John Horgan, *The End of Science*, (Reading, Mass.: Addison-Wesley Pub., 1996), p. 196.

none of the twenty-eight names of scientists associated with the new sciences of complexity that Lloyd lists appear on Wilber's list of ten scientists whose differing works he fits under the umbrella term *complexity*.

The works of Ervin Laszlo and Erich Jantsch contain interesting grand synthesizing visions, but to say that they represent the already-agreed-upon knowledge of the natural sciences and so qualify as the orienting generalizations that Wilber needs to validate his system is inaccurate.

Similarly, Wilber uses the work of Paul MacLean as an illustration of how the human brain has evolved in a transcend-and-include fashion from the evolutionary early reptilian brain, to the paleo-mammalian brain, to our higher neo-mammalian brain. These "facts" appear to support Wilber's holarchical transcend-and-include approach. Yet when the research is consulted, we find a vigorous debate about the validity of Paul MacLean's work. A recent entry in this debate is a monograph that tries to counter the critiques of MacLean's work and reestablish its stature.[5] The introduction to the monograph laments that "in mainstream academic neuroscience . . . [MacLean's] work has been largely overlooked or ignored."[6]

Wilber does not use the orienting generalizations of the natural sciences, but that doesn't mean that his understanding of the structure of the Kosmos is wrong. Next we will examine the essential structure of Wilber's Kosmos to see how internally and factually consistent it is.

This material, while technical, is highly important for Wilber's system because it describes the ontology and essential structure of the Kosmos. If it doesn't work, there are essential flaws in the system, and it cannot be asserted to be a coherent depiction of the Kosmos.

---

5 Gerald A. Cory and Russell Gardner, eds., *The Evolutionary Neuroethology of Paul MacLean*, Westport, Conn.: Praeger, 2002).

6 Ibid., p. xxxi.

The motivation for such an ambitious project lies in the strong intellectual and societal trends that it is designed to counter. Wilber's integral theory tries to unite three problematic domains: the diverse natural scientific disciplines, which are characterized by an enormous specialization and division of scientific labor; the pluralism and relativism of the social sciences and the humanities; and the hitherto neglected and suspect mystical sciences. This specialization, fragmentation, and neglect can call forth the desire for a meaningful integration of knowledge. The attempt may seem preposterous, but the stakes are so high, and developments in the sciences of complexity so suggestive, that a claim from thoughtful people such as Laszlo, Jantsch, and Wilber that it can be done deserves examination.

In *SES*, Wilber says that all holons follow twenty tenets or rules. This understanding, later revised with Fred Kofman,[7] now explains that while all holons have a part/whole nature this partialness/wholeness differs for the four different kinds of holons that exist. These four types are: individual holons, social holons, artifacts, and heaps. To be an individual holon,[8] a holon must have: some kind of localized subjectivity, interiority, or consciousness; a defining pattern (i.e., not just be an amorphous lump); a unified exterior (i.e., be identifiable as one contiguous unit). Examples of individual holons are an atom, a molecule, a cell, and a person.

In contrast to the individual holon, the social holon has a *non*-localized or *inter*-subjective interiority or consciousness. We can think of the zeitgeist or group-mind as a consciousness that is not located in an individual. Also in contrast to the individual holon, the social holon has a *non*-unified exterior. We think of the social holon as a connected grouping of individual units. As in an individual holon,

7 Fred Kofman, "Holons, Heaps and Artifacts," at integralworld.net, January 2001.

8 More precisely, individual aspect of a holon. Each holon has four aspects: individual interior and exterior, and social interior and exterior, but Wilber refers to individual holons for ease of reference.

the parts that make up the social holon must have a defining pattern (i.e., they cannot just be a random lump). Lastly, the individual holons that aggregate to create the social holon must have a common affiliation. Examples of social holons are galaxies, planets, families, societies.

Artifacts aren't mentioned in *SES* and Wilber later noted the omission.[9] They are (insentient) holons that are created by individual or social holons. What distinguishes them from the sentient holons is that they have no interiority, whether localized or non-localized. Like sentient holons, they do have a defining pattern but, unlike sentient holons, it is imposed from without rather than arising from within. Examples of artifacts are computers, language, beaver dams, and anthills.

The fourth type of holon—like the artifact, insentient—is a heap. Heaps are just random accumulations of stuff. They have no interiority and no defining pattern. Examples are a pile of rocks or a mountain of trash.

The partialness/wholeness, or *holarchic*, arrangement of each of the four types of holons is different. The parts of individual holons are constituents or elements of the senior individual holon. They have much less freedom within the senior individual holon than the parts that make up a social holon do. The individual holons that constitute a social holon are not bound elements of the social holon but *members* of the social holon. The word "members" connotes the looser affiliation that the parts of the social holon have as compared to the parts of an individual holon, which are more tightly bound to the senior holon. Artifacts are made up of the individual pieces of which they are constructed. The difference between artifacts and sentient individual and social holons is that the defining pattern is assembled from without and not enfolded

9 Wilber, "On Critics, Integral Institute, My Recent Writing, and Other Matters of Little Consequence: A Shambhala Interview with Ken Wilber, Part II," at shambhala.com. Fred Kofman explains artifacts in "Holons, Heaps and Artifacts."

from within. Heaps don't have a defining pattern; their parts are parts accidentally, not because of an organizing consciousness within or without.

To enter the holarchic, holonic, and four quadrant debates is to enter a thicket of intricate argumentation. Wilber's four quadrant model, and Wilber and Kofman's reformulation of the holon, have left fundamental inconsistencies, which able commentators have identified, and tried to sort out and correct. The corrections array themselves on a spectrum. In the middle is Wilber's problematic model. At one end is the work, mainly, of Gerry Goddard and Mark Edwards, who, after defining the problems with Wilber's model, set out to save the model by multiplying the categories and quadrants and redefining and clarifying key terms. At the other end of the spectrum is Andrew P. Smith, who, acknowledging the same problems, has constructed a one-scale model of hierarchy in contrast to Wilber's four quadrant model. While Goddard and Edwards opt for a clarification, reworking, and expansion of Wilber's model, Smith offers a different model containing much of the same content. Since this is a book about Wilber, I will describe his model and then evaluate important parts of it using the work of his commentators.

Wilber described the structure of the Kosmos in *SES*, but problems later discovered necessitated revision.[10] The revised understanding fixes some problems, but, as is usual with large classificatory schemes, creates new ones. At first, these revisions appear to create the neat, consistent classificatory scheme described above, but closer examination reveals questions and contradictions that cause fundamental problems with the scheme. These problems have been identified by the commentators on Wilber's system mentioned above who publish their work at integralworld.net.

There are two interesting ironies surrounding this flourishing debate at integralworld.net that also serve to confirm two criticisms

---

10 Wilber, "On Critics" in section entitled Holons, Artifacts and Heaps; and Kofman, "Holons, Heaps and Artifacts."

I make of Wilber. One of my central criticisms of Wilber's work is that he does not show enough respect for the intellectual debates that provide the evidence supporting his theory of everything. An ironic confirmation of this condition is that Wilber's work has spawned the type of responsible intellectual debate that I claim he does not respect. To double the irony, Wilber is again not respecting this flourishing debate of his own making.[11] That debate is conducted like a proper academic debate in which participants propose understandings, cite evidence, engage in dialogue, consider alternative interpretations, answer criticisms from colleagues, and contend with anomalies. Wilber is outside this debate, yet unlike conventional academic debates, which don't mention him, the contributors here appreciatively acknowledge his contribution and see themselves as building upon, working out, and correcting his insights. Wilber does respond to some critics,[12] but usually to those whose criticisms are more manageable than those who are finding fundamental problems with the core of his system and his application of it. His latest position is that he will not respond to critics who are not in a dialogue with him personally.[13] On the one hand, this is understandable since he would like to develop further his integral theory, but on the other hand, this doesn't make sense, since it will hinder the development of his own theory. The criticisms of these critics are so cogent and essential that I think it would serve him well to work with these critics as part of his process of correcting and developing his work.

The second irony regarding this debate spawned by Wilber's work is that it confirms my claim that Wilber does not use the orienting generalizations of academia. Here we see Wilber's work, supposedly based on the agreed upon, orienting generalizations

11 Andrew P. Smith subtitles one of his essays, "Further Monologues with Ken Wilber."

12 See for example, *Ken Wilber in Dialogue*.

13 Wilber, "A Suggestion for Reading the Criticisms of My Work on Frank Visser's 'World of Ken Wilber' Site," at integralworld.net, March 2004.

of knowledge, creating a debate in which the fundamentals and the details of his work are questioned and countered by contending parties that have differing viewpoints regarding this material's theoretical concepts and facts of the matter.

Mark Edwards, Gerry Goddard, and Andrew P. Smith have written criticisms of Wilber's old formulation and Wilber and Kofman's new formulation of holons that have gone unanswered by Wilber and Kofman.[14] I suspect it has gone unanswered because remedying the problems would require a wholesale reformulation of Wilber and Kofman's conception of holons. Smith begins his critique by showing that the distinction between individual and social holons doesn't hold up. The four criteria that are supposed to distinguish a social from an individual holon are that the parts of the social holon have: a common affiliation; a patterned mode of interaction; a non-localized consciousness; and a non-unified exterior. But, as Smith points out, individual holons, such as atoms, molecules, cells, tissues, and organs, have, like social holons, parts that share a common affiliation and a patterned mode of interaction. The third criterion—a non-localized consciousness—is unverifiable to our ordinary consciousness and methods of verification. That leaves the fourth criterion: a non-unified exterior. It is not clear what this means, but if it means that social holons do not have definite boundaries in space, or that social holons do not closely cohere, it can be argued that this distinction does not succeed. Social holons, such as human societies, have identifiable physical boundaries just as do molecules, tissues, and cells. In both cases the boundaries may be changing and fluid. Close coherence or physical contact can sometimes be found in human society, while atoms have bonds of various strengths and distances. While the distinction between individual and social holons seems self-evident at first, a further examination reveals that it is arbitrary; things placed in one category can shuffle back and forth between

14 Andrew P. Smith, "Why It Matters: Further Monologues with Ken Wilber," at integralworld.net, December 2001.

categories. According to Smith's own division between individual and social holons, molecules and tissues are social holons not individual holons as in the Wilber/Kofman model.

Smith believes that a viable distinction can be made between individual and social holons, and offers one in his own "one-scale model."[15] In contrast, Mark Edwards, who has written a seven-part tribute, critique, and reformulation of Wilber's model, extensively criticizes the validity of the Wilber/Kofman distinction between individual and social holons. His alternative dispenses with the Wilber/Kofman revisions and simply develops the model set out in *SES* by placing holons within their "parental holarchy," or evolutionary line, to determine whether they are individual or collective holons. For Edwards, a toddler is an individual holon because it evolves from a fetus into an infant and then into a child and then an adolescent. In a critique of Edwards' stronger distinction between individual and collective holons, Andrew Smith points out that it is now difficult to see how these supposedly integrated individual and collective holons are related.[16]

A central concern of Wilber and Kofman is that Wilber's earlier formulation of the relationship between individual and social holons could be construed as justifying a totalitarian control of a social holon over the individual holons that constitute it. If a social holon has the same control over its individual holons that an individual holon has over the constituent holons that compose *it*, their conception of human societies would be one in which individuals would have no will of there own. Wilber and Kofman go to great lengths to explain that individual holons are a developmental advance over the previous developmental stages of the holons that compose them. For example, the cell is a developmental advance over the earlier stages of atom and molecule. Similarly, the social

15 Andrew P. Smith, "All for One and One for All," at integralworld.net, February 2001.

16 Andrew P. Smith, "The Pros and Cons of Pronouns," in section entitled Edwards' Intrinsically Social Individual, at integralworld.net, July 2003.

holon, of which individual holons are members, is not a developmental advance over the individual holons that compose it but a developmental advance over the temporally previous incarnation of *that* social holon. Kofman uses the example of a herd of elephants, which is a developmental advance over, not a single elephant, but a herd of evolutionarily prior woolly mammoths.

Wilber and Kofman's new formulation is wrong for two reasons. One, as with the distinction between individual and social holons, it doesn't hold up to scrutiny; and two, it suggests a confused view of how science works. Wilber and Kofman use a few examples to show that individual holons have more control over their constituent holons than do social holons over the individual holons that constitute them. Wilber says that when an individual moves his or her arm all the cells within the arm have to move, too. No social holon has this degree of control. But if we think of a different example, a different picture of the relation between holons emerges. Most humans would rather not age, get sick, and die, but because that is what their holons contribute to, that is what humans, the senior holons, are subject to. Likewise, Wilber tries to demonstrate the looser bonds between social holons and their members by observing that society can remove a member by putting him or her into jail; this is in contrast to an individual human holon that cannot simply remove a constituent part of itself, such as a vital organ. Yet prisoners are still a part of society, and even societal exiles from the U.S. would still refer to themselves as Americans. Looked at in this way, one can never escape the social holons of which one is a member. So when Wilber writes that "constituent elements have their agency subsumed by senior individual holons, but members retain a much larger degree of relative autonomy within the social holon,"[17] he's correct only if the right examples are used.

Smith and Edwards have described the many ways that social holons have control over individual holons. Edwards asks,

17 Wilber, "On Critics," in section entitled Social Holons.

How many people go out in public without some level of
conventional dress, what percentage of individuals con-
form with social conventions on public behavior, public
laws, putting out the garbage, cleaning snow off pave-
ments, mowing the lawn, paying rates, going to school,
learning to read and write, living in a house, speaking to
the neighbours (or not as the case may be), having a hair-
cut, etc., etc. Collective agency is ubiquitous and compelling.[18]

A second problem arises because of a mistaken view of science.
Wilber and Kofman criticize systems theorists because, they say,
these theorists construct hierarchies that subordinate individual
holons to social holons to the same degree that senior individual
holons subordinate their constituent holons. For the individual human holon, say Wilber and Kofman, that is tantamount to totali-
tarianism: total control by the social holon of which it is a member.
But what if the facts fit that description of the world better than
Wilber and Kofman's politically correct version? Here is an instance when it is important to distinguish clearly between science
and morality. For example, if we find that the non-human animal
world lives by survival of the fittest, we, as creative human beings,
can still choose to live another way. Our political and moral life is
not bound by the discoveries of science.

Smith describes the Wilber/Kofman definition of heaps as "im-
precise, even misleading,"[19] and notes that most planets and Gaia,
both of which Wilber classifies as social holons, fit the Wilber/
Kofman definition of heaps. Heaps, Smith contends, are not "a
random assortment of holons," as defined by Wilber and Kofman.

18 Mark Edwards, "Through AQAL Eyes, Part 5: Matter, Membership and Mu-
tuality," in section 6. Collective Agency and Governance, at integralworld.net,
May 2003.
19 Andrew P. Smith, "The Spectrum of Holons," at integralworld.net, January
2001.

Instead, "most heaps have a uniform composition."[20] Smith then puts heaps on a spectrum of development with social holons, seeing them as a less developed stage of an emerging social holon. Edwards, by contrast, reformulates the notion of heaps to bring them back into the holon fold. He notes that whether a "heap" is a heap depends on the eye and expertise of the beholder.

> This is especially true of the division between the "heap" category and other holons. One researcher might see puddles, sand dunes and piles of dust as belonging to the category of "heap," but that might only be due to a lack of knowledge of the developmental dynamics involved in those types of entities and environments. To specialists on aquatic, geological, or desert environments, the seemingly inert and randomly assembled entities such as puddles/ponds, sand dunes/beaches, or piles of dirt/rocks may each be regarded as a complete holonic ecosystem in themselves.[21]

The Wilber/Kofman definition of artifacts is probably the most problematic because when it is applied to all cases that meet its definition it turns everything into an artifact or a hybrid. By focusing on particular examples of artifacts like tools, computers, nests, and beaver dams we think we understand what artifacts are and how they differ from sentient holons. But Kofman states that

> enzymes can create artifacts, bringing molecules together to create a third molecule. The cell itself creates molecules all the time. In fact, the cell creates its own physical components; it recreates itself through a process called 'autopoiesis.' If one looks at the mitochondria, the ATP it produces is an artifact. If one switches up to consider the level of the cell, the ATP and other artifacts of mitochondria are

20 Ibid.

21 Mark Edwards, "Through AQAL Eyes, Part 1: A Critique of the Wilber-Kofman Model of Holonic Categories," in the section entitled The "Heap" Category of Entities, integralworld.net, June 2002.

included as constitutive elements. At the same time, the cell itself produces something (like bile in the liver) as an artifact. But this bile is a constitutive element of the organism.[22]

Acknowledging the artifactual quality of reproduction through natural processes opens the door to seeing that, as Smith writes, "following Kofman's definition leads to the conclusion that everything is an artifact" because:

> if a molecule created by an enzyme is an artifact, it's very difficult to say what is and what is not an artifact. Is the enzyme molecule itself an artifact? It's created by the agency of a gene, working with some other holons in the cell. Is the gene an artifact? It was created by the agency of another gene, which duplicated itself. What about the whole cell? It was created by the agency of some other holon."[23]

It is not only these biological processes that are artifactual; language and thought are artifacts, and there is no human society without them. So according to the Wilber/Kofman definition, human beings, as products of genes, the birth process, and social conditioning are artifacts.

Whether it is the revision of his ideas in *SES* or the original ideas themselves, it is evident that his definitions of the holon has fundamental flaws. All is not lost though. We have the curious situation in which Wilber's commentators and would-be interlocutors are now writing more reliably about, and applying more consistently, Wilber's own system than Wilber himself is. Because there are able thinkers reworking the fundamentals and details of his system, it may be that a holarchical model can become a useful tool for understanding the Kosmos.

---

22 Fred Kofman, "Holons, Heaps and Artifacts."
23 Smith, "Spectrum of Holons."

Wilber states that all individual and social holons follow the twenty
tenets. These are the "'laws' or 'patterns' or 'tendencies' or 'habits'" that "all known holons seem to have in common."[24] Tenet 1
states that *"Reality as a whole is not composed of things or processes, but of
holons*. Composed, that is, of wholes that are simultaneously parts
of other wholes, with no upward or downward limit."[25]

Contrary to this tenet, though, there are entities that are not
simultaneously parts and wholes at all. Smith writes that

> atoms and cells are capable of an independent (auton-
> omous) existence outside of higher forms of life. While
> some atoms exist as components of molecules, they may
> also be found as free forms of matter not bonded to each
> other. Likewise, cells can exist as unicellular organisms as
> well as components of organisms.[26]

One might reply that even these autonomous entities have to exist
somewhere and so are parts of *some* larger whole. But this type of reasoning will not work, because the whole that they are a part of is
actually a heap. Smith observes that at the physical and biological
levels of existence there are types of holons that are inert.

> There are *inert* atoms (such as helium), which form no
> chemical bonds with other atoms and which therefore can't
> become integrated into molecules. . . . There are *prokaryotes*,
> which like inert atoms do not bond or associate with one
> another, and therefore do not form multicellular organ-
> isms. . . . there are *invertebrates*, mostly asocial organisms

---

24 *SES*, p. 34. Wilber refers to the "twenty tenets," but only uses twelve numer-
als. Sub-parts of tenets two and twelve could total twenty depending on how you
divide them.

25 *SES*, p. 35.

26 Andrew P. Smith, "A One-Scale Model of Holarchical Existence," at geoci-
ties.com/andybalik/myarticles.html, July 2000.

that live most or all of their lives in isolation from others of their species."[27]

Smith argues convincingly that the collections of these inert holons correspond to the definition of heaps rather than that of social holons, and so are not a part of a larger whole that the definition of a holon requires. This directly contradicts tenet 1. Smith also notes that "evolutionary development of the hierarchy is a profoundly *selective* process; while an immense variety of holons are produced at each level of existence, only a very small proportion of them continue to develop into higher levels of existence."[28] This fact shows the selectivity of Wilber's mapping of the Kosmos, which emphasizes "only a very small proportion" of it. That small proportion being the one that leads to humanity.

A different critique of the first tenet, and of Wilber's use of the holon concept in general, has been made by other Wilber commentators.[29] The criticism is that by defining what the essential quality of all things in the Kosmos is, Wilber has contradictorily objectified the Kosmos in an effort to integrate it. Since Wilber's integral holarchic conception must include everything, a tenet that pronounces a way in which reality is beyond every other conception of reality reduces the Kosmos to this one way of viewing, when the whole point of his integral theory was to avoid reductionism and include all other established views. Sympathetic critics such as Mark Edwards, Gerry Goddard, and Brian Eddy feel the holon conception is valid if defined differently than Wilber defines it. In general, they argue that seeing the Kosmos in terms of holons should be understood as a *way* of seeing the Kosmos; as an interpretive device that creates a large-scale integration and sense of the Kosmos.[30]

27 Ibid., p. 8.

28 Ibid., p. 8.

29 See papers by Gerry Goddard, Brian Eddy, and Mark Edwards at integralworld.net.

30 Mark Edwards, "Through AQAL Eyes, Part 1." Wilber may have been in-

Tenet 2 states that "Holons display four fundamental capacities: self-preservation, self-adaptation, self-transcendence, and self-dissolution [later renamed and redefined as self-immanence]."[31] Self-preservation describes a holon's ability to maintain its identity over time. Wilber contrasts this with a holon's self-adaptation, which describes its ability to react to and be a part of its environment. Wilber says that these forces "are in constant tension . . . the more intensely a holon preserves its own individuality, preserves its wholeness, the less it serves its communions or its partness in larger or wider wholes (and vice versa: the more it is a part, the less it is its own whole)."[32] So the two forces are opposed. Yet there are examples where the two forces are not opposed, and where more self-preservation produces more self-adaptation. A democracy is a social holon that thrives when individuals and the groups that constitute it participate more or are more a part of the democratic process. In participating more they are also asserting themselves more. When they assert themselves more they become more a part of the democratic whole; when they don't assert themselves they are less a part, and the democratic holon is weakened.

Likewise, successful plants are those that adapt to their environments best. Plants that are more a part of their environment, and draw needed nutrients from it, best maintain their identities over time. Here, the greater the adaptation the greater the self-preservation.

Wilber mentions as an example of the "constant tension" "the battle between self-preservation and species-preservation"[33] But it is commonly understood in evolutionary biology that species preserve themselves because the individual members do all they can

---

fluenced by this critique, because in the latest version of his theory he abandons regarding the holon as the metaphysically primary entity and instead asserts a "post-metaphysical" theory whose basic category is the perspective.

31 *SES*, p. 40.

32 *SES*, p. 45.

33 *SES*, p. 45.

to preserve *them*selves. In that way, the members with the greatest survivability survive, ensuring a greater chance of species-preservation.

A larger issue regarding this tenet hinges on the relationship between the qualities this tenet describes—agency and communion—and the definition of individual and social holons. It has been extensively discussed by Goddard, Smith, and Edwards, and there are fundamental, unresolved questions about it. One question raised in this debate is how to define agency and communion as aspects of the holon different from the individual and social aspects. If agency is the holon's ability to persist through time, isn't that synonymous with its individuality? And doesn't the communing or adaptive part of a holon describe its sociality? How are these to be distinguished? None of the commentators mentioned here now believe a single four quadrant model can map all the aspects of holons.

The other two capacities all holons have are those of self-transcendence and self-immanence. A holon transcends when it becomes a new whole with new emergent properties. In becoming a new whole, the holon transcends upward. Corresponding to this is the new holon's immanent, downward embrace of all the nested holons that compose it.

Andrew Smith makes a compelling argument for the redundancy of these latter two categories. He observes that self-adaptation or communion—making greater connections with other holons and the environment—*is* the process of transcendence, since this is how new emergent properties occur. Likewise, immanence, or the downward embrace of all the holons within the senior holon, is another way of describing the identity of the holon; so greater self-immanence just is greater self-preservation or maintenance of the holon's identity.[34]

34 Andrew P. Smith, "God is Not in the Quad," Sec. 6, integralworld.net, August 2002.

This tenet also raises the issue of defining transcendence and dissolution. In describing the process of holarchical unfoldment, Wilber writes that

> normal or natural holarchy [is] . . . the sequential or stage-like unfolding of larger networks of increasing wholeness, with the larger or wider wholes being able to exert influence over the lower-order wholes. And as natural, desirable, and unavoidable as that is, you can already start to see how holarchies can go pathological.[35]

Here, value-laden terms like "normal," "natural," "desirable," and "unavoidable" are used in a way that implies value-neutral processes. Distinguishing "natural" processes from "pathological" ones requires some value-laden worldview and is not a neutral, scientific description of natural processes.

Wilber gives the example of groups that claim transcendence but appear from the outside to have too much communion.[36] One can think of so-called cults like David Koresh's Branch Davidian Christian sect from Waco, Texas, or the suicidal Heaven's Gate group in California. While the participants would say their group is transcendent, outsiders would say the opposite. Who is right? It depends on the viewer's values. Cults are notoriously hard to define. One person's cult is another's New Religious Movement (as they are referred to in academia). At various times, Zen groups, Quakers, and the early Christians were referred to as cults. When dealing with humans, values are always inserting themselves when we would like to have value-neutral descriptions.

Tenet 3 states that we get novel emergence through self-transcendence. This means that the interactions of similar kinds of entities cause properties not previously found in those entities to emerge.

35 *SES*, p. 22.
36 *SES*, p. 46.

This emergence is *self*-transcendent or *self*-organized in that it occurs predominantly because of the entities within the system rather than from a cause outside the system. For example, the interaction of atoms produces molecules, which have properties not found in atoms. An important result of this process for Wilber is that it runs counter to determinism and reductionism. The emergence of new properties means unpredictability, and that means processes that are not deterministic. So a higher-level process or entity cannot be reduced to a lower-level process, because the reduction will always leave out the emergent property not contained in the lower-level process.

It is certainly true that there are new properties that emerge from the interactions of similar, lower-level entities, but it's not clear what the word *emergence* describes. It may just be a place-holder for a process we don't yet know how to explain. When we do explain the details of the process of emergence, then we will be able to trace the causal determinants of that process.

Although Wilber states that "*Social holons* emerge when individual holons commune,"[37] this is a misstatement because he doesn't want to argue that it is the communing of individual holons that produces the novel emergence that occurs through society. Why? Because then he would have to claim that social holons transcend and include the individual holons that compose them, and he doesn't want to claim this, because he fears that this gives the social holon too much power over the individual holons that are its members. Wilber instead contends that social holons display emergence relative to earlier incarnations of the same social holon. Fred Kofman uses the example of a herd of elephants. The herd is not the senior holon to its individual elephant members; it is senior holon to the now extinct woolly mammoth herd and all prior evolutionary incarnations. This seems odd. Of course the elephant has new characteristics relative to the woolly mammoth, but does this constitute "emergence?" And while an elephant is

37 Wilber, "On Critics."

certainly different from a woolly mammoth, is the elephant herd a novel emergence over the woolly mammoth herd? Perhaps elephant herds have lost emergent properties that woolly mammoths had. How could we know?

On the cosmological level we find another inconsistency. According to Wilber's evolutionary chronology, stars, which are made up of atoms, are temporally prior to planets, which are made up of molecules; therefore, on Wilber's scale of social development, planets are a transcendence and inclusion of stars. Yet it's obvious that the important emergent properties of stars are not included within planets; the assertion of a developmental transition here doesn't make sense.[38]

Another problem arises for Wilber when he asserts that "social holons emerge when individual holons commune." If this were true, then a society, being an emergent property of communing individual holons, would be higher on the developmental hierarchy than the individual holons that compose it. Wilber's model is constructed around the premise that a holon has individual and social aspects that are at the same developmental level. The idea of society being a novel emergence over its individual members is the basis of Andrew Smith's critique of Wilber's holarchy and four quadrant model.

Tenet 4 states that holons emerge holarchically, which means that each new emerging whole embraces the parts that came together to create it. This is true for some holons and not for others. It is true for molecules that do embrace the atoms that come together to create them, and for cognitive developmental stages that incorporate prior stages. It is not true for other holons, such as types of human social development where prior social structures, like the stronger kinship and social relations in some tribal life, are lost.

As in tenet 2, a problem arises here when Wilber says, "The point, of course, is to tease apart pathological hierarchies—where

38 Andrew P. Smith, personal communication.

one holon usurps its position in the totality—from normal holarchies in general, which express the natural interrelations between holons."[39] The problem with the use of medical sounding terminology like "pathological" and "normal," and biological terminology like "natural," is that it hides the value judgments inherent in determinations of what is natural, normal, and pathological. Wilber describes pathology as occurring where "one holon usurps its position in the totality." But is one's use of power a usurpation or a beneficial self-assertion? It depends on your values and interests. When a meteor wiped out the dinosaurs, was that a pathological usurpation and a setback for evolution or a normal holarchic event? Defining good and bad holarchies is a moral decision. Words like *pathological*, *normal*, and *natural* mask this fact.

Tenet 5 states that "*Each emergent holon transcends but includes its predecessor(s)*. Each newly emergent holon . . . *preserves* the previous holons themselves but *negates* their separateness or isolatedness or aloneness. It preserves their being but negates their partiality or exclusiveness."[40] Yet Smith notes that

> in a cell, all of the lower holons can exist as both free (i.e., not components of the next higher stage) as well as bonded forms (in which they are components of the next higher stage). . . . some atoms exist free in cells (e.g., sodium and calcium ions), while others exist as components of small molecules. Some small molecules, in turn, exist free (individual amino acids), and some as components of polymers.[41]

On a higher level, "An organism . . . contains cells that are not parts of cell units (gametes; red and white blood cells); cell units

39 *SES*, p. 50.
40 *SES*, p. 51.
41 Andrew, P. Smith, "One-Scale Model of Holarchical Existence."

that are not parts of tissues, tissues that are not parts of organs, and so on."[42]

There are also counterexamples in the human world. Wilber uses the example of Hawaii. It was an independent nation but was subsumed within the United States, becoming a part of a larger emergent whole. Its being was preserved, but its separateness was negated. Poka Laenui, President of the Pacific Asian Council of Indigenous People, has a different view of what she calls the "Colonization in Hawaii."[43] She quotes U.S. President Grover Cleveland on the topic:

> By an act of war, committed with the participation of a diplomatic representative of the United States and without authority of Congress, the government of a feeble but friendly and confiding people has been overthrown. A substantial wrong has thus been done, which a due regard for our national character, as well as the rights of the injured people, requires we should endeavor to repair.[44]

But it wasn't repaired. The natives were forced to assimilate and were later annexed.

Another example comes from Wilber's own developmental social sequence. He draws a line in which human social development evolves from tribes to tribal/villages to early state/empires. Each step is a new emergent holarchic arrangement. But has the being of tribes and villages been preserved in the later social arrangements? What we have seen is the destruction of tribal and village life and the irretrievable loss of those cultures.[45] It's mistaken to

42 Ibid.

43 Poka Laenui, "Colonization in Hawaii," *Fourth World Bulletin*, Vol. 2, No. 3, July 1993.

44 Ibid.

45 See John H. Bodley, *The Powers of Scale* (Armonk, New York: M.E. Sharpe, Inc., 2003).

think that "the *basic structures and functions* were preserved and taken up in a larger identity."[46]

Tenet 6: *"The lower sets the possibilities of the higher; the higher sets the probabilities of the lower."*[47] For example, the laws of physics describe what is possible in the lower, physical world. The higher-order holon's range of possibilities is set by the laws acting on them through the lower-order holons that compose them. In contrast, the probable occurrence of any of these possibilities is determined by the higher aspects of the holon. The senior holon has a directing function that occurs within the range of possibilities given by the lower aspects. This sounds true, but the words *possible* and *probable* are elastic enough to be reversed. Isn't it true that the genes within an organism determine the probability of that organism getting cancer or not? Isn't that an instance of the lower—the genes—establishing probabilities for the higher—the organism? And don't humans create new possibilities for lower holons by combining them in new ways, as in genetic engineering? Does it seem more appropriate to call these novel creations probabilities or new possibilities?

Tenet 7: The greater the number of evolutionary levels contained within a holon the greater its depth. The greater the depth of a holon the less the span or number of that type of holon in existence. For example, atoms have less depth then molecules. Because atoms compose molecules there will always be more atoms than molecules.

Tenet 8: *"Each successive level of evolution produces GREATER depth and LESS span."*[48] As a correlate to tenet 7, each new emergent feature is said to produce more depth. The greater the depth the less the

46 *SES*, p. 52.
47 *SES*, p. 54.
48 *SES*, p. 56.

amount of holons at that level of depth. So a molecule will have greater depth than the atoms that compose it, but the atoms have greater span.

These two tenets do seem to be true; although they are true by definition. A higher holon is created by the aggregation of lower holons, so there will always be less of the higher holons than the lower holons that constitute them.

Tenet 9: *"Destroy any type of holon, and you will destroy all of the holons above it and none of the holons below it."*[49] This is a very important tenet for Wilber because he sees it as a foolproof way of determining which holons are higher and which lower in the developmental hierarchy. This allows him to rank all holons according to their level of developmental advance in a neutral way that applies equally to all holons. Tenet 9 is a thought experiment that determines which holons are higher and which lower in the developmental hierarchy. A typical developmental sequence is atoms to molecules to cells to organisms. Imagine that all holons of any one type in the sequence were destroyed. What you will find is that all holons higher in the hierarchy are also destroyed, while all holons lower than the destroyed holons survive. So if we destroy all cells, all organisms and every holon higher is also destroyed, but all molecules and atoms and everything lower still exists. By doing this for every type of holon we have a neutral, value-free way of ranking every holon in a hierarchy. Wilber states that "this rule works for any developmental sequence, for any holarchy . . . there are no exceptions."[50]

Andrew Smith has used some subtle argumentation to demonstrate that this rule undermines Wilber's entire attempt to rank holons when applied consistently. Wilber uses the destruction rule to not only rank holons as higher and lower but also to show that holons are on the same level of development. If two holons are

49 *SES*, p. 61.
50 Wilber, *A Brief History of Everything* (Boston: Shambhala Publications, 1996), p. 32.

on different developmental levels they are called *asymmetric*; if they are on the same developmental level they are called *symmetric*. Specifically, he asserts that individual and social holons have separate lines of development and should not be ranked on the same developmental scale. The destruction test bears this out. Apply the destruction test to both individual cells and the population of all cells and you find that "you cannot have cells without a society (population) of other cells, and you cannot have a population of cells with no cells at all—nothing exists alone without an environment of the similar."[51] Smith agrees but notes that this is only true for "unorganized and undifferentiated" populations.[52] If we apply the destruction rule to complexly organized human societies we find that society, contrary to Wilber's claims, is developmentally more advanced than the individuals that compose it. If human beings were all eliminated, human society would cease to exist. Conversely, though, if society is eliminated, human beings could still exist. We could each be a Robinson Crusoe. Therefore, society is developmentally higher than individuals. But Wilber's entire four quadrant model assumes that the individual and the social are two sides of the same developmental coin, one no more advanced than the other for each given level. He argues strenuously against those who conflate the two.

Smith does provide a possible reply for Wilber. Wilber divides human societies according to their developmental levels. For example, modern humans have a certain type of brain structure that is reflective of their use of reason and membership in nation-states. Modern humans' mental, societal, and brain developments are superior to medieval humans' mythic consciousness, their early states and empires, and their brain structure. Wilber could argue that if we destroy the modern society, then we destroy the modern individual (and vice versa) because a modern individual is defined as an individual that lives in a modern society. Wilber does

51 *SES*, p. 83
52 Smith, "One-Scale Model of Holarchical Existence."

assert that the destruction of a societal type causes a regression in its members to the less advanced developmental level. So the destruction of the individual means the destruction of the social and vice versa. Therefore they are on the same level of development. It appears Wilber is saved. But here is where Smith undermines Wilber's entire developmental model through consistent application of the destruction rule.

If we are going to distinguish between types of human beings based on their developmental achievement—rational, mythic, magic, etc.—then we should be consistent and apply the same logic to all holons. Smith notes that cells are not all alike. Cells found in organisms are quite distinct from cells that exist outside of organisms. Applying the destruction test now gives you a different result. Destroy all organisms and all cells of the kind found in organisms will all be destroyed and vice versa, because these kinds of cells can only exist within organisms. According to the destruction test this means that cells within organisms and the organisms that transcend and include them are on the same developmental level; this contradicts Wilber's developmental sequence. The same reasoning can also be used for atoms and molecules. This is one reason that Smith concludes that "the principle of asymmetry that Wilber uses to determine ranking in the hierarchy is rendered useless."[53]

Other applications of the destruction test contradict Wilber's contentions. According to his four quadrant model, the social organization of families is on the same developmental level as that of the individual developmental achievement of a limbic system; they are two sides of the same holonic coin. Yet when we perform the destruction test and "break up families . . . organisms do not suddenly lose their limbic systems,"[54] indicating that families are a higher developmental level than the limbic system.

53 Ibid.
54 Ibid.

Tenet 10: "*Holarchies coevolve.*"[55] By this Wilber means that individual and social holons always develop together. In Erich Jantsch's formulation, microevolution and macroevolution are inseparable. Individual holons require their environment in which to develop, while the environment requires the ongoing development of the individual holons to continue its development.

Regarding the evidence for this tenet, Smith notes, a "very problematic aspect of the Jantsch/Wilber framework is that in attempting to demonstrate a coevolution of macro and micro, it glosses over much data that don't easily fit."[56] The first atoms arose 300,000 years after the Big Bang, but their supposed macroevolutionary environment didn't arise until 600 million years after the Big Bang.[57] Additionally, a strong argument can be made that the relationship between, on the one hand, physical relationships such as (macro) stars to (micro) atoms and (macro) planets to (micro) molecules, and, on the other hand, biological relationships such as (macro) environments to (micro) organisms is so qualitatively different that tenet 10 cannot be said to hold for both.[58]

Tenet 11: "*The micro is in relational exchange with the macro at all levels of its depth.*"[59] This means that each micro and macro level of development remains interrelated no matter how deep the holon. For example, a human holon's physical body must remain in contact with the physical aspects of the earth; the same is true for the biological and mental levels.

In contrast to this tenet, Smith notes,

---

55 *SES*, p. 63.

56 Andrew P. Smith, "Wilber's Eight-fold Way," at integralworld.net, May 2003.

57 Ibid.

58 Gerry Goddard, in "Consciousness and the Holonic Infrastructure," April 2003, and Smith in "Wilber's Eight-fold Way," raise numerous issues with macro-/micro- coevolution.

59 *SES*, p. 66.

There are other kinds of holons in the micro or biological pathway that are ignored by Jantsch and Wilber, and
which also have no corresponding holon in the macro or
stellar pathway. For example, small molecules like amino
acids, and macromolecules like proteins are far more
complex than very simple molecules like water and car-
bon dioxide, and can't possibly be lumped together with
the latter. They have many emergent properties that the
latter lack, and they did not exist on the primordial earth.
They evolved considerably later.[60]

This means there are molecules on the micro level whose relational exchange is with the macro level of Gaia and not the planetary
level as Wilber suggests, violating tenet 11. Smith goes on to question the degree and quantity of relationality between many macro
and micro entities, stating,

It's misleading to suggest, for example, that superclusters,
clusters, or galaxies are associated with particular sub-
atomic holons. We can only say that stars are associated
with some elements, and that planets are associated with
(a very few, and very simple kinds of) molecules. Beyond
these two points, a correlation is not evident.[61]

Tenet 12 states that *"evolution has directionality."*[62] It is, perhaps, the
most important and most problematic of all the tenets. Tenet 12
has five parts, each with different criteria of directionality.

The first indication of evolution's directionality is increasing
complexity. And while cosmologists seem comfortable speaking
of an increase in complexity from the Big Bang to the present,
in biology it is highly debatable whether you can speak of an increase in complexity. Richard Dawkins states that "many people

---

60 Smith, "Wilber's Eight-fold Way," in the section entitled Erich Jantsch and
Holonic Pluralism.
61 Ibid.
62 *SES*, p. 67.

think that they know what they mean by simple, and its opposite, complex, but there have been few attempts to define these
terms precisely."[63] He, somewhat ironically, describes a possible
method of comparing levels of complexity. To compare the relative complexity of two creatures, first write a book about each that
describes them in comparable levels of detail. Then compare the
lengths of the two books. The longer book describes the more
complex creature. Dawkins says that this "thought-experiment of
the two books enables us at least to agree over what it is that we
disagree about. This may not seem like much, but in the field of
phylogenetic controversy it is a major achievement."[64]

Dawkins's glibness may detract from the validity of his point,
but Michael Ruse, in his sober and thorough study, subtitled *The
Concept of Progress in Evolutionary Biology*,[65] concurs. He concludes
that "more recent work, for instance on measures of complexity,
simply shows . . . that there is just no good reason to think that
complexity is a necessarily ever-increasing product of the evolutionary process."[66] And, more generally, he writes, "My key point
is that progress is not in evolutionary thinking today because of
pure epistemic factors."[67] In other words, the lack of an epistemic
criterion for progress is why the idea of progress does not play a
role in evolutionary biology.

Still, although evolutionary biologists cannot defend it, it may
just seem right that life started with the simplest of organisms and
progressed steadily to complicated life. Stephen J. Gould makes a
strong argument against this thinking. He observes that since life

---

63 Richard Dawkins, "Progress," in Evelyn Fox Keller and Elisabeth A. Lloyd,
eds., *Keywords in Evolutionary Biology*, (Harvard: Harvard University Press, 1994),
p. 265.

64 Ibid., p. 266.

65 Michael Ruse, *Monad to Man: The Concept of Progress in Evolutionary Biology* (Cambridge,: Harvard University Press, 1996).

66 Ibid., p. 535.

67 Ibid., p. 536.

starts with simplicity, any change will generate some complexity (since life cannot evolve to be simpler then the simplest), but that increasing complexity is not a necessary or even common evolutionary occurrence. Many biological organisms find their adaptive success in becoming simpler after a more complex beginning. Regarding the evidence for the "macroevolutionary reformulation of life's history," Gould points out that the "initial research has found no departure from the random model, and no overall preference for increase in complexity in studies that tabulate *all* events of speciation."[68] What Wilber does is take one species—humans—and arrange all of evolution as if leading to it.

Wilber also contends that this process of increasing complexification holds for human social life; so primitive tribes should be less complex than modern industrialized societies. Yet the sociologist Anthony Giddens notes that "there is simply no discernible correlation between linguistic complexity and the level of material 'advancement' of different societies," and that "some features of social activity found in oral cultures, such as those associated with kinship institutions, are exceptionally complex."[69]

The second indication of evolutionary directionality is increasing differentiation and integration. This tenet can be seen as a corollary of the complexity tenet above. As entities evolve they differentiate and then form new integrations. The integration of increasingly differentiated parts could be a criterion of increasing complexity. But, as described by Gould above, there is an abundant amount of organisms that have found their evolutionary success in a process of simplification not complexification. He quotes a *New York Times* reviewer reporting on two studies of evolutionary complexity: "In two of the first studies to measure these trends, based on mammals' backbones and fossil shells, researchers say

68 Stephen J. Gould, *The Structure of Evolutionary Theory* (Cambridge: Belknap Press of Harvard University Press, 2002), p. 901.

69 Anthony Giddens, *The Constitution of Society* (Berkeley: University of California Press, 1984), p. 241.

they have been unable to detect any overall evolutionary drive toward greater complexity."[70]

In the area of human social evolution, Charles Tilly names the idea of increasing differentiation as one the "pernicious postulates" of nineteenth-century social theory. He acknowledges that "many significant social processes do involve differentiation," but goes on to observe that the converse is true: "Many social processes also involve dedifferentiation: Linguistic standardization, the development of mass consumption, and the agglomeration of petty sovereignties into national states provide clear examples."[71] He concludes that "we have no warrant for thinking of differentiation in itself as a coherent, general, lawlike social process."[72]

Surprisingly, Wilber also tries to show that Jacques Derrida and Michel Foucault are "on board" regarding differentiation as an ever increasing evolutionary process. But the quotes he uses to prove his contention don't show that Derrida and Foucault have any belief in a directional evolutionary process. The spirit of Derrida's and Foucault's poststructuralism is captured better by David Hoy when he writes that "not only do Foucault and Derrida give up humanism's belief in epistemological progress, they also give up its belief in social-historical progress, which is . . . probably [the] most important feature of the critique of humanism."[73]

The third indicator of evolutionary progress is increasing organization and structure. I don't see how this is distinguished from increasing complexity, which, as indicated above, is problematic.

The fourth indicator of directionality is increasing relative au-

70 Carol Yoon, "Biologists deny life gets more complex," *The New York Times*, March 30, 1993, quoted in Stephen J. Gould, *Full House* (New York: Three Rivers Press, 1996), p. 212.

71 Charles Tilly, *Big Structures, Large Processes, Huge Comparisons* (New York: Russell Sage Foundation, 1984), p. 48.

72 Ibid., p. 48.

73 David Hoy, "Jacques Derrida," in Quentin Skinner, ed., *The Return of Grand Theory in the Human Sciences* (Cambridge: Cambridge University Press, 1985), p. 49.

tonomy. This is unclear as Wilber defines it. He first says that "it simply refers to a holon's capacity for self-preservation in the midst of environmental fluctuations."[74] This sounds like degree of survivability; yet if that were the case then, as Stephen J. Gould colorfully put it, "we might do ourselves in by nuclear holocaust, but prokaryotes will probably hang tough until the sun explodes,"[75] suggesting that greater survivability lies with the prokaryotes. Wilber then appears to change course two sentences later when he writes, "This does not mean greater permanence or concrete stubbornness."[76] He then settles on saying that "relative autonomy simply refers to a certain flexibility in the face of changing environmental conditions,"[77] and gives the example of a fox that can vary its internal temperature relative to external conditions, whereas a rock cannot. Yet one can argue the opposite. The rock flexibly alters its temperature while the fox is constrained by having to keep its temperature within a benign range. Or think of a fire raging through a forest. The fox dies or is driven from his home while the rock remains. The rock flexibly adapts to changing environmental conditions. Wilber needs a more stringent definition of relative autonomy.

His example of increasing relative autonomy for humans' intellectual productions is also problematic. He contends that new perspectives on human social life from Freud, Marx, Heidegger, Foucault, and others force us to rise above limited perspectives. "Each time we identify a deeper context, our relative autonomy actually increases, because in identifying with a deeper perception, we have found a wider freedom."[78] Or, we have found more confusion and fragmentation because to plumb the depths of

---

74 *SES*, p. 71.
75 Stephen J. Gould, *Eight Little Piggies* (New York: W. W. Norton & Co., Inc., 1993), p. 323.
76 *SES*, p. 71.
77 *SES*, p. 71.
78 *SES*, p. 73.

these perspectives, to actually be a Heideggerian or a Marxist, is to adopt a large, orienting vision of the world which includes an understanding of why other visions are not as good as one's chosen vision. Each would have its own critique of the other, and all would criticize Wilber's synthesis. They, like Wilber, would acknowledge certain truths in other perspectives and, again like Wilber, weave those truths into *their* vision of the world. These differing perspectives on human life won't fit neatly into Wilber's map if we see the world from their perspectives.

The fifth indicator of directionality is increasing telos. Wilber contends that inherent within the physical, biological, and mental processes are goals that holons tend towards. "The end point of the system tends to 'pull' the holon's actualization (or development) in that direction, whether the system is physical, biological or mental."[79] Contradicting this for biological processes, James Lennox, in his article on teleology, terms Wilber's idea of the endpoint's pull on the system "backward causation" in which "the future goal state causally influences the events leading up to it." According to Lennox this is one of three "illicit features [that] discussions of teleology among biologists and philosophers of science during the last forty years" have tried to avoid.[80] They try to avoid explanations using backward causation, because "this violates standard scientific conceptions of causation and causal explanation, according to which causes precede their effects and a phenomenon is explained by citing its causes."[81]

Even a biologist who is one of the innovators of the new sciences of complexity upon which Wilber relies, heralds this new perspective by saying:

79 *SES*, p. 74.

80 James G. Lennox, "Teleology," in *Keywords in Evolutionary Biology*, p. 331.

81 David J. Buller, "Function and teleology," from the *Encyclopedia of Life Sciences* (Macmillan Reference Ltd., 1997) at www.soci.niu.edu/~phildept/Kapitan/teleology.html.

The "new" biology is biology in the form of an exact science of complex systems concerned with dynamics and
emergent order. Then everything in biology changes. Instead of the metaphors of conflict, competition, selfish
genes, climbing peaks in fitness landscapes, what you get
is evolution as a dance. It has no goal. As Stephen Jay
Gould says, it has no purpose, no progress, and no sense
of direction. It's a dance through morphospace, the space
of the forms of organisms.[82]

The difficulties that biologists have with speaking unproblemati-
cally about the telos of biological life are shared by social theorists
about the telos of social life. While individuals have goals, and
various social theorists speak of social systems as goal-directed,
this doesn't make it so. To buttress a goal-directed view of society,
Wilber conveniently refers to Hegel, Marx, Freud, and Habermas,
all of whom have teleological systems, while dismissing non-teleo-
logical theorists because, as he assumes we all agree, "any decent
theorist is an omega-point [teleological] theorist."[83] Of course, this
casual remark excludes *in*decent social theorists like Durkheim,
Nietzsche, Weber, and Foucault, whose theories aren't teleological. In addition, Wilber tries to pass Derrida off as a teleological
theorist in order to get a poststructuralist imprimatur. He appears
to quote Derrida in support of his position, but when we check
the quote's citation, we find it is Harold Coward's gloss on Derrida and not Derrida himself who is being quoted.[84] To see social
systems as goal directed is a value-laden choice of social theorists,
not a fact of social life. It is this moral component that makes it
such a vexing question in both the biological and human sciences.
    Determining the goal of evolution is so difficult because of the
part that values play in the determination. Early in *SES* Wilber

82 Goodwin, Brian, "Biology is Just a Dance," in John Brockman, ed., *The Third
Culture*, online at www.edge.org/documents/ThirdCulture/zb-Pt.4Intro.html.
83 *SES*, p. 78.
84 *SES*, p. 77.

suggests that by determining evolution's own natural tendencies the fact/value distinction can be resolved. He writes that "we are inextricably involved in judgments that are hierarchical . . . to consciously join these judgments with the sciences of holarchy . . . the result [is] that values and facts are no longer automatically divorced," and "we are now in a position to realign facts and values in a gentler embrace, with science working with us, not against us."[85] One immediate problem with this rapprochement between facts and values is that it flies in the face of the fact-value gap which is a long-standing problem in philosophy. A second, bigger, problem has to do with Wilber's contention that much scientific evidence in many diverse fields points to the same holarchic processes and so demonstrates that nature's own goal has been discovered. As I have shown for the life and human sciences, there are fundamental disagreements about whether there is a neutral goal that can be determined at all. In the physical sciences, the idea of a goal of nature is only used metaphorically, because the entities they deal with are not considered to have intentions.

As this chapter shows, there are many anomalies and contradictions that show the twenty tenets do not describe the "'laws' or 'patterns' or 'tendencies' or 'habits' . . . all known holons seem to have in common," as Wilber contends.

THE FOUR QUADRANTS

Wilber maps the evolutionary unfolding of matter, life, mind, and spirit from the Big Bang to the present day and beyond. To understand his conception, picture x and y axes intersecting at right angles. The point of intersection represents the Big Bang. Concentric circles radiating out from the point of intersection represent the stages of evolution, with each widening ring a chronologically later and more advanced level of holonic development. Each

85 *SES*, p. 31.

holon has four aspects, represented by the four quadrants created by the intersecting x and y axes. The upper right quadrant is the exterior of the individual holon's development (e.g., an atom, a cell, a brain). It is what you see on the surface or exterior of the individual holon. The lower right quadrant is the exterior aspect of the holon's social development (e.g., galaxies, families, the nation state). The upper left quadrant is the interior, or subjective, side of the individual holon's development (e.g., sensation, impulse, cognition). This we have to intuit or interpret, since it is inside of or interior to the holon. Finally, the lower left quadrant is the interior, or inter-subjectivity, of the holon's social development (e.g., magical, mythical, or rational worldviews). Each successive wave of evolutionary development transcends and includes all the stages that precede it. For example, the individual animal subsumes atoms within molecules within cells within the brain. Each higher level provides a wider context in which the lower levels exist.

Since the four quadrants, holons, and the twenty tenets are interrelated, Edwards's, Goddard's, and Smith's criticisms of the latter two have implications for the former. The four quadrant map, as originally drawn in *SES*, depicted the four different aspects of each holon. Each holon had an individual, social, exterior, and interior aspect. Yet Wilber routinely referred to individual and social holons, not individual and social aspects of holons. This may seem to be a minor linguistic shortcut, but, as I'll demonstrate below, Wilber's commentators have shown in great detail how this semantic slip reveals what is crucially problematic about Wilber's four quadrant model, causing Andrew Smith to conclude "that the four-quadrant model, in its original form, is dead."[86] Adding to this confusion regarding individual and social holons and individual and social aspects of some third thing called "a holon" is another aspect of each holon described in tenet 2, which is its characterization as being somewhere on the self-preservation/self-adaptation or agency/communion spectrum. Depending on how

[86] Smith, "Wilber's Eight-fold Way."

these terms are defined it is not clear how to distinguish between agency and individuality on the one hand, and sociality and communion on the other. If agency and communion are interpreted as another set of aspects of each holon, does that require further axes and quadrants in order to map the character of each holon? This question has led Edwards and Goddard to construct multiple, and more complicated, maps, and Smith to reassert the effectiveness of his one-scale model of holarchy.

Smith's criticism of the distinction between individual and social holons makes the separation of the upper right and lower right quadrants fall apart. The details of this criticism have been described already;[87] Smith's conclusion is that "the criteria that Wilber and Kofman provide for distinguishing individual and social holons are useless. Some of these criteria either fail to make the distinction at all—as shown by the fact that they apply to some of their listed examples of individual holons ("molecules, cells, organisms") as aptly as they do to social holons; others can't be applied at all."[88]

Edwards agrees that the Wilber/Kofman revisions are mistaken, but unlike Smith thinks them unnecessary since the original four quadrant model and holon definitions in *SES* can be retained as long as they are applied consistently. This more consistent application, however, requires creating two four quadrant models in order to do justice to both individual and social holons, each of which has four aspects.

Smith also points out an interesting contradiction in Wilber's four quadrant division. He notes that Wilber, like most holarchic thinkers, observes that the Kosmos unfolds from matter to life to mind to spirit. Mind emerges from life, yet on every level of Wilber's four quadrants mind and life are present together. Do we conceive of the rational mind as emerging from the brain, and therefore a higher emergent development, or do we see it as the

87 See Holons section, above.
88 Smith, "All for One and One for All," at integralworld.net, Feb. 2001.

individual interior aspect of the individual exterior brain, both on the same developmental level?

This asymmetry between the exterior brain and the interior mind is also found among individual and social holons. The cells of the brain demonstrate a relatively high degree of interactive or social connection, more so than lower invertebrates, which are on a higher developmental level than cells. According to Wilber's four quadrant model, the sophistication of social interactions should be greater for the lower invertebrates than for the relatively lowly cell, but it is not.[89]

The relationship between the mind and the brain is a contentious issue in a number of fields. Wilber has decided that they are two aspects of a third thing, the holon. But if his model is supposed to integrate as many other theories as it can, isn't it prejudiced against many other ways of understanding the mind/brain relationship? Since no consensus in cognitive science or the philosophy of mind has been reached regarding the status of consciousness, his map, which takes a definitive stand on the mind/brain relationship, cannot include the orienting generalizations or truths determined by these fields of study.

The four quadrant division is an *ontological* division. It describes the essential kinds of things in the Kosmos. On top of these ontological divisions, Wilber overlays *methodological* and *epistemological* divisions. The methodological division assumes that each of these four aspects of the holon needs a particular method of knowledge acquisition. They are different kinds of things and so require different methods to know them. The epistemological division assumes that these four quadrants have differing criteria of validity.[90]

Wilber claims that the characteristics of the exteriors (the right hand side) and the interiors (the left hand side) of the holarchy each

---

89 Smith, "Different Views: Intersubjectivity, Interobjectivity and the Collapse of the Four-Quadrant Model," at geocities.com/andybalik/Hargens.html.

90 Wilber, *A Brief History of Everything*, Chapter 6.

requires a distinct methodology in order to be understood. The elements on the right hand side have in common that the object of inquiry is on the exterior and can be read off the surface. We can all share in looking at a cell, a brain, a village. The left hand side is different because the object of inquiry is subjective, and internal contents must be interpreted to be known. So Wilber is overlaying the ontological division of the interior left hand side and the exterior right hand side with a methodological division. The exteriors require structural and functional methodologies used in the natural sciences and applied to the social sciences and humanities. The interiors require a hermeneutic methodology in order to interpret meaningful content. But in contrast to Wilber's claims, there are quite a few examples of right hand methods used to illuminate left hand objects of inquiry. Claude Levi-Strauss used structuralism to study the myths and worldviews of the lower left quadrant in a scientific way. Piaget, who Wilber relies upon greatly to construct his model of individual development, used structural methods and psychological experiments externally verifiable to describe interior worlds. Daniel Dennett makes arguments regarding human subjectivity using scientific research and tries to dispel the illusion of our subjective sense of consciousness or the "Cartesian Theatre." Emile Durkheim studied suicide using right hand methods and gained insights into society's mental life, the lower left quadrant. Buddhism and phenomenology use a subjective empirical inspection, or a "reading off," of the contents of consciousness similar to the empirical methods of the natural sciences. Buddhist practitioners are given the hypothesis that all the contents of consciousness—thoughts, emotions, and sensations—are impermanent, and then use the mindful experiencing of those contents to either confirm or deny this hypothesis.

Reversing this, there are hermeneutic (interpretive) left hand methods that are used to study the right hand side. Qualitative sociology is used to study the village, the family, and the city. These qualitative methods are not used just to determine the cultural (lower left) aspect of these social groupings but also to understand the kind of social structure present—a lower right (exterior) aspect. More fundamentally, Wilber's original distinction between the exterior-objective of the right hand side and the interior-subjective of the left hand side breaks down because the social exteriors he describes are constituted not just through objective viewing like an atom or a cell but through the subjective meanings that the participants in the villages and families give them as well. In some primitive tribes the mother's brother—who we would call the uncle—is regarded by the child as his or her father. What constitutes "the family" here? In many households there is no father or there are two mothers. Are they families? It depends on how we define "family." This is not an objective determination but one that must include how the participants subjectively regard each other. So the two quadrants in this case are inextricably bound. Right hand, scientific, structural-functional researchers occlude this subjective element because it confuses their neat methodology. Wilber reproduces this occlusion by taking for granted the right hand researchers *stated* method of inquiry.

We see now that the methodologies used to study the different quadrants do not follow Wilber's ascriptions. In fact, the use of differing methodologies in differing domains is one way those methods of study stake out new areas of inquiry. The territories are always being redrawn depending on the success or failure of the contending methods. Epistemological, political, and popular success determines the ever ongoing re-mapping that Wilber is trying to fix. He is assuming that there are natural kinds in the world and that they are divided according to his neat four-part division; that they have different essences requiring different methods of study. The philosopher and cognitive scientist Brian Cantwell Smith describes the way new sciences are describing and explaining aspects of the subjective realm:

> Neuroscience is ablaze with excitement about elucidating the phenomenology of consciousness . . . mathematical

> models are being developed of such basic notions as or-
> der, autonomy and self; evolutionary accounts are offered
> of altruism, tribalism and belief; computational models
> traffic in meaning and interpretation. . . . Not since the
> nineteenth century has "natural science" been restricted
> to the physical.[91]

Wilber wants to integrate the subjective and objective sides of reality, but he also wants to preserve the domain of subjectivity by
what he contends are inappropriate encroachments by the natural
sciences.[92] To integrate these new types of inquiry he would have
to redraw his four quadrant map.

   On top of the ontological and methodological distinctions, Wilber overlays an even more problematic epistemological division.
He states that the differing quadrants have differing criteria of
validity. The right hand (exterior) side uses propositional truth;
the upper left (individual interior) uses sincerity or truthfulness;
and the lower left (social interior) uses justness or moral fitness.
Yet it's clear that to study all quadrants we need the validity of
propositional truth. The developmental sequence that Wilber describes as constituting the upper left quadrant, based on Piaget's
and Wilber's developmental models, is much more dependent on
propositional truth than truthfulness and sincerity. Additionally,
the judging of sincerity is not only dependent on empathizing and
interpreting an individuals depths; a big part of our determination of people's sincerity is whether we think they are lying. This
we determine, in part, by whether what they tell us is proposition-
ally true and logically consistent. Likewise, the determination of
justness in a society requires propositional truths such as income
distribution, changes in real wages over time, and the shape of the
social structure, all of which refer to social exteriors.

91 Brian Cantwell-Smith, "God, approximately," W. Mark Richardson et al.,
eds., *Science and the Spiritual Quest* (New York: Routledge, 2002), p. 209.
92 *SES*, pp. 146–149.

The central criticism of the structural-functional approach in sociology, which supposedly determines value-neutral propositional truths of the right hand exteriors, was that it was unwittingly value-laden, an aspect of the knowledge of the left hand interiors. Hayden White argues that to even write a narrative history of an objective social entity like a state or war-making necessitates a value-system or moral stance.[93]

Instead of having one map in which we fit three overlapping classifications—objects of inquiry, methods, and validity claims—we actually have three that don't overlap. In addition, the distinctions that create each of these three maps don't stay in their respective categories. Generally, Wilber writes as if the four aspects of all holons are ontological divisions of the Kosmos, but he also argues that the division between the four quadrants is an historical, and so changing, achievement. Seeing it as an historical achievement, he could allow the ontological, methodological, and epistemological integrations and mergers that I describe; but if he did this he would have to call into question the very divisions upon which his four quadrant model is based.

---

93 White, Hayden, *Metahistory* (Baltimore: Johns Hopkins University Press, 1973).

CHAPTER 2

INDIVIDUAL CONSCIOUSNESS

Of all the areas of knowledge that Wilber explores, he is most knowledgeable about individual consciousness. An evolution in his thinking has made his theory of consciousness the most usefully descriptive part of his entire integral synthesis. This is due to his extensive research in this area, his use of the current scholarship, and his responding to the criticism his theory of consciousness has received. This improvement in his theory comes with a cost, however, because the evolution in his thinking has been motivated by an unacknowledged contradiction. This contradiction is one manifestation of a larger contradiction in Wilber's thinking that he is trying to reconcile. The larger contradiction is between a model inclusive of the findings of academia and other sources, on the one hand, and the diversity of those findings, on the other. Here it appears as a tension between a unified, goal-directed, developmental model and a diverse, semi-independent model that "has no overall linear sequence whatsoever."[1] This chapter consists of an overview of his model, an examination of the scholarship used to validate it, and an evaluation of its validity.

1 This surprising statement can be found in the introduction to the second edition of *SES* on p. xvii and in *Integral Psychology* (Boston: Shambhala Publications, 2000), p. 17.

THE MODEL

Wilber's theory of consciousness is a developmental theory. This means that individual consciousness, when unfolding normally, grows in progressive, qualitative shifts. The three main parts of consciousness in Wilber's model are: the basic waves or levels of development, the developmental lines or streams, and the self-system. The basic waves or levels are structures of consciousness that unfold in an age-related, irreversible order and gradually form the necessary conditions for all conscious experience. As development unfolds, each prior level of consciousness is superseded and incorporated into a new whole organized by the higher level. A brief summary of the basic levels will convey a sense of them. As infants we start out on the *sensorimotor* level. Our consciousness is unformed and we are very much physical as opposed to a mental beings. Our main task is "differentiating the *physical* self from the *physical* environment."[2] The infant is most noticeably a tactile being. The *emotional-sexual* level builds on and incorporates the sensorimotor level as the infant now tries to "*differentiate its feelings* from the *feelings of others*."[3] Next, *representational mind* incorporates the earlier stages, including the inchoate mental images of the young child. "The rep or preop mind can form symbols and concepts, and thus *represent* not only things but classes, but it cannot yet *operate* on or coordinate those representations."[4] Operating upon mental representations requires the incorporation of rules and roles so that the mind can perform operations on the representations. This *rule/role mind* operates on the world, but still lacks the capacity to reflect on itself or "think about thinking."[5] With the arrival of *formal-reflexive mind* the individual can imagine possibilities and think about thinking. These levels represent the first

2 *SES*, p. 211.
3 *SES*, p. 215.
4 Wilber, *Eye to Eye* (Garden City, New York: Anchor Books, 1983), p. 272.
5 Ibid., p. 273.

half of Wilber's developmental spectrum. The higher levels of consciousness will be discussed in later chapters.

These basic levels of consciousness manifest in different ways. The mind has many different lines of development, such as cognition, morality, affect, will, aesthetics, and interpersonal skills, to name a few. The basics levels provide necessary but not sufficient conditions for the development of the various lines. For example, one could be at the level of rule/role mind, but, because of detrimental environmental influences, be behaving with a primitive type of morality. While the necessary level of consciousness is present, the sufficient conditions for advanced morality are not present. Each line then follows a semi-independent developmental path. For example, one can be well developed spiritually, moderately developed interpersonally, and poorly developed morally depending on natural talents and environmental influences. T. S. Eliot was well advanced on an artistic line of development, and yet maintained a morally retarded anti-Semitism. A spiritual teacher could be supremely advanced on a spiritual line and act immorally in his sexual relations. Each of our many lines of development could be mapped as to its level of development, with no two people having identical psychic maps.

The basic levels of development are permanent structures in contrast to the transitional structures which constitute the lines of development. The basic levels develop in a cumulative way according to the universal developmental sequence of transcending and including previous levels. The capacities we developed at earlier levels are integrated within the newly arisen higher level of development. In contrast, lines of development are formed from transitional structures, which are transcended when a new higher structure is in place. Wilber offers the comparison between Piaget's and Kohlberg's developmental sequences. For example, Piaget's level of sensorimotor development doesn't disappear at higher levels; otherwise we wouldn't have the basic capacities to deal with matter, sensation, and perception that we develop at the sensorimotor level. Conversely, when we reach Kohlberg's conventional level of development on our moral line we don't simultaneously act from the preconventional moral level we have already superseded.

The third part of consciousness is the self-system. There are many parts of the self-system. The two main parts are the *proximate* self and the *distal* self. The proximate self is our subjective self-sense, our sense of *I*. The distal self is our self as an object. When we view our bodies as an object to ourselves, our proximate self is regarding our distal self. What parts of us are proximate and distal keeps changing. When, through meditation, we begin to view our own thoughts as *not I*, where previously we just thought we were our thoughts, we have changed what is proximate and what is distal within our *overall* self. Our overall self is the combination of the proximate, distal, and larger, ever-present Witnessing Self, which coexists in each of us. As with overall development, "the overall self does *not* show a sequential or stage-like development."[6] Curiously though, Wilber says that the proximate self does show a stage-like development as it navigates through the basic levels of development. "Each time the self (the proximate self) encounters a new level . . . it first *identifies* with it and consolidates it; then disidentifies with it (*transcends* it, de-embeds from it); and then includes and *integrates* it from the next higher level. In other words, the self goes through a *fulcrum (or a milestone) of its own development*."[7] If a part of the proximate self does not de-embed from the particular line of development to which it is identified it can become stuck there and form what Wilber calls a subpersonality. "*Each of these subpersonalities can be at a different level of development in any of its lines . . . a person can therefore have facets of his or her consciousness at many different levels of* morals, worldviews, defenses, pathologies, needs, and so forth."[8]

6 Wilber, *Integral Psychology*, p. 34.
7 Ibid., p. 35.
8 Ibid., p. 100.

This summary of Wilber's theory of consciousness focuses on issues relevant to my discussion of his model later in the chapter. The model is centrally indebted to the developmental model of Jean Piaget, although Wilber uses a variety of scholarly sources, including Lawrence Kohlberg and the cross-cultural psychologist John W. Berry. Since Wilber makes much of the scholarly consensus backing his model, I will now examine the strength of that backing in the psychological literature.

THE SCHOLARSHIP

Wilber presents his model as if the consensus of scientific opinion supports it, but this is not the case. By tracking down his sources, revealing in them what Wilber does not mention, and exploring more fully the disciplines he uses, I will show that Wilber's version of individual development is not a valid generalization of scientific findings.

To validate his model, Wilber exaggerates the level of agreement in the scientific community regarding the claims he makes. He speaks of using "orienting generalizations," or the "already-agreed-upon" knowledge, in the sciences. He makes statements like, "The evidence is virtually unanimous,"[9] and "Summarizing the existing research . . ."[10] This gives the reader the impression that he has culled the "simple but sturdy" knowledge of psychology. But in going back to his sources and investigating others, I have found a great deal of ongoing disagreement about Wilber's "already-agreed-upon" knowledge.

Robert Siegler, a well-known developmental psychologist, has formulated his own approach to cognitive development, in part because the "neo-Piagetian, theory-based, and information-

---

9 *SES,* second edition, revised introduction, p. xv.

10 Wilber, "Waves, Streams, States, and Self," *Journal of Consciousness Studies,* Vol. 7, No. 11/12, November-December 2000, Sec. 1, p. 4.

processing approaches" current today "have proved to be inconsistent with a great deal of data."[11] He notes that

> there is no dominant theory of cognitive development. The limitations of the major theories in the area—Piagetian, neo-Piagetian, Vygotskian, information processing, social learning, ethological, and neo-nativistic—are sufficiently large and apparent that none of them can claim the adherence of anything like a majority of investigators. In all likelihood, the greatest number of developmentalists see themselves as eclectic, borrowing concepts from many theories, but not being entirely comfortable with any one of them.[12]

Siegler constructs a model that does away with levels, or waves, and focuses instead on individuals' strategy choices.

In 1991, Michael Chandler and Michael Chapman published *Criteria for Competence*. They introduce their collection of papers in developmental psychology with an overview of the field. They write:

> Each wave of incoming research delivers a new flotsam of increasingly divergent claims about almost any developmental milestone one might care to mention. For example, recent evidence can be found to indicate that children are able to reflect or deduce or behave intentionally somewhere between the ages of 5 months and 15 years of age, depending on which authority one happens to read. . . .

> Clearly something is seriously amiss. How could research into questions as fundamental as when persons first acquire a sense of self or learn to reason transitively yield up answers that are seemingly so far apart? How can it be that experts who hold to such radically different views appear

11 Robert S. Siegler, *Emerging Minds* (New York: Oxford University Press, 1996), pp. 10–11.
12 Ibid., p. 20.

to be so unruffled by this same divergence of opinion? Where is the collective embarrassment one might reasonably expect in the face of such wholesale disagreement? . . .

The problem appears to be getting progressively worse rather than better.[13]

Alison Gopnik and Andrew Meltzoff write that "in the wake of the collapse of Piagetian theory, cognitive development has been a bit of a mess, with almost theories, half theories, pseudo-theories, and theory fragments floating about in the sociological ether."[14] They also write:

Recent empirical work in infancy and early childhood has led . . . to the rejection of the central tenets of Piaget's theory: cognitive development does not depend on action, there are complex representations at birth, there are no far-reaching domain-general stage changes, young children are not always egocentric, and so on.[15]

Regarding moral development, Wilber says that "Kohlberg was able to suggest a six-stage scheme of moral development, a scheme that research so far has found to be largely invariant and universal."[16] Yet the four scholars, sympathetic to Kohlberg, who collaborated on a "Neo-Kohlbergian Approach" do so to counter the "numerous suggestions in the academic literature that Kohlberg's approach to morality was so fundamentally wrong-headed and flawed that researchers in morality are better off starting

13 Michael Chandler and Michael Chapman, eds., *Criteria for Competence* (Hillsdale, N.J.: L. Erlbaum Associates, 1991), p. viii.

14 Alison Gopnik and Andrew Meltzoff, *Words, Thoughts and Theories* (Cambridge, Mass.: MIT Press, 1997), p. 49.

15 Ibid., p. 2.

16 Wilber, *Integral Psychology*, p. 81. Wilber adds in a footnote (p. 234 n. 12) that "Kohlberg's stage six is an ideal limit, and not an actual stage."

anew."[17] While they disagree with this assessment, they note that "some critics regard his work as outmoded, beyond repair, and too faulty for anybody to take seriously."[18] After acknowledging the problems with Kohlberg's stage-staircase model and his interview techniques, they state, directly countering Wilber's contention above, that

> Kohlberg eliminated Stage 6 from his scoring system for lack of finding empirical cases of Stage 6 thinking. Furthermore, there is little evidence for Stage 5 scoring in Kohlbergian studies from around the world (Snarey, 1985). Gibbs (1979)—a co-developer of the scoring system—even proposed that true Piagetian stages of moral judgment stop with Stage 4. The lack of empirical data for Stages 5 and 6—post conventional thinking—is a serious problem for Kohlberg's enterprise, because he defined the stages from the perspective of the higher stages. The seriousness of this problem is underscored by the fact that virtually every critic in the book *Lawrence Kohlberg: Consensus and Controversy* (Modgil & Modgil, 1986) find the absence of Stages 5 and 6 to be a fatal flaw.[19]

Wilber does cite legitimate sources to validate his belief in Kohlberg's model, but he neglects to inform his readers of other sources that validate the opposite view, leaving the reader with the impression that his view is the consensus in the field.

It is not only alternate sources that can be cited to contradict Wilber's assertion of scholarly consensus, his own sources when examined closely yield a different picture than the one he presents.

Wilber now calls the basic levels of development *waves*, and the lines of development *streams,* following the usage of Howard Gardner et al. in their 1990 article. He cites and quotes this article

17 James Rest, et al, *Postconventional Moral Thinking* (Mahwah, NJ: L. Erlbaum Associates, 1999), p. 1.

18 Ibid., p. vii.

19 Ibid., p. 22.

several times as evidence for his claims about the universality of the basic levels. And the parts of the article Wilber cites do support his contentions, but the quotes are carefully selected, and a return to Gardner et al.'s article reveals evidence that runs counter to Wilber's model.

I will examine the Gardner article because it is where Wilber got his new wave and stream terminology and because he uses it more than other sources in the latest version of his developmental theory in *The Eye of Spirit* and *Integral Psychology*. It is indicative of Wilber's use of sources in general; sources upon which, at his level of abstraction, he is wholly dependent.

Gardner et al. first describe four waves of development that span the years 2 through 7. Relative to Wilber's macroscopic model, this is a microscopic description of the waves of development, and Wilber inserts it within his more general model. Gardner et al. then speculate on the character of development beyond the age of 7 and name the three developmental stages *preconventional* (2-7 yrs.), conventional (7-12 yrs.), and *post conventional* (12 yrs. and beyond). Wilber, seeing the Kohlbergian terminology he likes, adds enthusiastically, "Add post-postconventional, and we are in full accord!"[20] But the character of the development described by Gardner et al. is different from Wilber's description. According to Gardner et al. the passage from 7 to 12 years is caused not by some inborn developmental unfolding but because "the agenda of the culture comes much more to the fore."[21] Gardner et al. quote Alison Lurie to illustrate the shift from the preconventional to the conventional stage. She writes that "encouragement of imaginative creation is often quietly replaced by encouragement of what have begun to seem more important traits: good manners, good marks, good looks; athletic and social success; and a willingness

20 Wilber, *Integral Psychology*, p. 218.
21 Charles N. Alexander and Ellen J. Langer, eds., *Higher Stages of Human Development* (Oxford: Oxford University Press, 1990), p. 89.

to earn money mowing lawns and babysitting—traits that are believed to predict adult success."[22] Additionally, the beginning of
the conventional stage coincides with the start of schooling and
one of the main tasks of the school system is to rein in children's
creative imagination and train them to be able to sit still and be
quiet for long periods of time while they are taught what society
thinks they should know.

The beginning of adolescence sees the youth rebelling. This in-
augurates the postconventional stage, in which the adolescent tries
to free himself or herself from the conventions imposed during the
conventional stage. Oddly, though, this developmental sequence,
which Wilber uses as a confirmation of his model, Gardner et al.
say, is "an idealization, and most particularly so in its final strokes."
They say this because "most adolescents, at least in our society,
never achieve sufficient mastery of skills, knowledge of a domain,
or awareness of self to be able to make innovative products."[23] So
we have a developmental theory which does not describe "most
adolescents."

That a developmental theory is referred to as an "idealization"
may seem odd for a descriptive science like developmental psychology, but it is not. In the book *Developmental Psychology*, three
well-known scholars acknowledge the distinction between "the
facts of psychological growth" and the idealization called "development." Jerome Kagan, referring to Bernard Kaplan, describes
"a reasonable and useful distinction" between "the facts of psychological growth which Kaplan chooses to call ontogenesis, and the
sequence that describes how children approach the metaphysical
ideal each theorist believes children should grow toward, which
he calls development."[24] Sheldon White concurs, stating that "one
should sharply distinguish development as an ideal process from

22 Ibid., p. 89.

23 Ibid., p. 92.

24 Richard M. Lerner, ed., *Developmental Psychology* (Hillsdale, N.J.: L. Erlbaum
Associates, 1983), p. 232.

ontogenesis as an actual one."[25] And Kaplan, the most radical of the three, writes that "*development does not lurk directly in the population(s) studied but resides fundamentally in the perspective used.*"[26] This is why Gardner et al. say "the symbolic waves are a psychologist's convention (and invention)." The impression Wilber gives when he uses developmental psychology research is that this is the truth of individual growth as confirmed by psychological science.

Gardner et al.'s developmental model differs in other ways from Wilber's. In Wilber's model the basic levels are the only aspect of consciousness that develops holarchically. This means that, unlike the transitional structures of consciousness, the basic levels all remain active and integrated within the currently dominant level of consciousness. Gardner et al.'s model is described as "non-hierarchical" by the editors of the collection in which it appeared. To attain the post conventional stage and to make innovative adult creations a return or "shift back" to the preconventional stage is required. Gardner et al. state that "the trajectory of creative development, unlike most other developmental trajectories, is nonlinear."[27] This sounds more like Michael Washburn's model, which describes a necessary return to earlier developmental stages in order for growth to occur. In Gardner et al.'s model of individual creative development, if there is no reappropriation of the child's creative imagination there will be no creative innovation in adulthood. This is why the editors of *Higher Stages of Human Development* say "the authors [Gardner et al.] recognize significant differences between creative development and the spheres of cognitive development studied by Piaget and Kohlberg."[28]

Gardner et al.'s waves also have an unusual elasticity that stretches the notion of developmental levels to new proportions. They contend that "our studies of symbolic development suggest

25 Ibid., p. 237.
26 Ibid., p. 196.
27 Alexander and Langer, *Higher Stages of Human Development*, p. 91.
28 Ibid., p. 13.

that each of the waves has its own developmental history."[29] That
means that a wave—such as the first one, called event structuring
by Gardner et al., in which the child learns how to place events in
a logical sequence like, "Mommy, go, store"—can have its own developmental history, which, the authors say, can be "as lengthy as
an individual's life."[30] Thomas Pynchon is an example of someone
whose development of event structuring grew throughout his life
and resulted in original contributions to narrative. It is an interesting idea and does describe innovations like Pynchon's, but don't
waves now have the property of streams? Event structuring, which
is a particular developmental level that is superseded by the next
wave, called topological or analog mapping, can also continue on
its own developmental course. In an effort to make developmental
theory match the facts of psychological growth the theories become more convoluted. Wilber could say these are the details that
have to be worked out in all the areas of knowledge his model encompasses, but at some point the "facts of psychological growth"
start to break the bounds of the developmental models designed
to organize them.

Other sources Wilber uses to validate his contentions become
problematic when examined. In a recent restatement of his psychological model[31] he defends the idea that there are universal levels of consciousness by quoting John Berry et al., who authored
the book *Cross-cultural Psychology*. Wilber introduces the quote with
the phrase "Summarizing the existing research," and then quotes
Berry et al. agreeing with his view that cultural differences in development are under-girded by universal or basic structures of
consciousness. It appears to be a strong confirmation of Wilber's
view. But, when we go back to the book from which it was tak-
en, we learn that Berry et al. are using one particular framework

29 Ibid., p. 95.
30 Ibid., p. 95.
31 Wilber, "Waves, Streams, States, and Self."

that "derives from earlier models proposed by Berry, where it was called an 'ecocultural model.'"[32] They distinguish this approach, which they label *universalist*, from two others current in cross-cultural studies called the *relativist* and the *absolutist*. The relativist denies cross-cultural universals, and the absolutist denies much of a role to culture. "The *universalist* position adopts the working assumption that basic psychological *processes* are likely to be common features of human life everywhere, but that their *manifestations* are likely to be influenced by culture."[33] What Wilber cites as a summary of the existing research is actually one perspective within an ongoing debate.

Wilber gives the impression that there is broad agreement on the reality of cross-cultural levels of development, but we learn in his source for this contention, *Cross-Cultural Psychology*, that "the status of the concept of development is a much debated theoretical issue."[34]

In another standard text edited by John Berry and others, *The Handbook of Cross-Cultural Psychology*, non-developmental approaches to comparing cultures are discussed. In the sub-discipline known as *cultural psychology* we find "the rejection by many of the universalistic notion of a 'psychic unity of mankind.'"[35] Michael Cole, one of the leading cultural psychologists, in his book *Cultural Psychology*, reviews work in cross-cultural psychology on perception, intelligence, and memory, and concludes: "Assuming that my assessment of these three examples more or less characterizes accomplishments in other psychological domains, the marginality of cross-cultural research to mainstream psychology is not difficult to understand. Its substantive offer-

32 John W. Berry et al, *Cross-Cultural Psychology* (Cambridge: Cambridge University Press, 1992), p. 11.

33 Ibid., p. 258.

34 Ibid., p. 236.

35 John W. Berry et al., *Handbook of Cross-Cultural Psychology* (Boston: Allyn and Bacon, 1997), pp. 353-354.

ings appear modest, and the evidence on which they are based is suspect."[36]

Richard Shweder is a leading advocate of cultural psychology. From his perspective, "the main discovery of cross-cultural psychology . . . is that many descriptions of mental functioning emerging from laboratory research with Western-educated populations do not travel very well to subject populations in other cultures."[37] He then gives a number of reasons why "in general psychology, cross-cultural psychology has diminutive status, and why its research literature tends to be ignored. Not surprisingly, developmental psychology—the study of age-graded differences in performance on psychological tests and tasks—has suffered a similar fate, and for similar reasons."[38]

These views from within and outside of developmental psychology contrast sharply with Wilber's confident assertion that "after almost three decades of intense cross-cultural research, the evidence is virtually unanimous: Piaget's stages up to formal operational are universal and cross-cultural."[39] These scholars who work outside the developmental model are quite skeptical of the universal, cross-cultural assumption, but because their perspectives do not support Wilber's model they are ignored.

Wilber needs to be able to include all the true parts of these scholars' works because of his metaphysical assumption that the world is one and all accurate descriptions of it, because they are about the same one world, should, in principle, fit together into one great description. But some recent thinking in philosophy has adopted a different understanding of what we can know. This alternative thinking suggests that because one's perspective partially

36 Michael Cole, *Cultural Psychology* (Cambridge, Mass.: Belknap Press of Harvard University Press, 1996), p. 68.

37 Richard A. Shweder, *Thinking Through Cultures* (Cambridge, Mass.: Harvard University Press, 1991), p. 84.

38 Ibid., p. 86.

39 Wilber, *SES*, second revised edition, p. xv.

affects the appearance of the world, we can speak of many worlds that are not all reducible to one world. A milder version of this argument is that there may be one world, but we can never know it, because we cannot escape our temporal, spatial, historical, and linguistic embeddedness. The developmental psychologist Bernard Kaplan has described the strong version of this perspectivism:

> It is preposterous to expect any perspective, except that of G - D, to account for, or explain, these different species of facts, generated by different theories, as if these "facts" were theory neutral. To constitute a life-span developmental psychology in terms of a catalogue, or telephone book, of facts garnered from every perspective, utilizing every method, and examining the functional relations between every variable and every other variable in not only a vain endeavor; it is an inane one.[40]

Confronted by a welter of diverse and conflicting facts and theories, Wilber assumes that they can all be integrated into one big synthesis. But if "what are taken as facts by those adopting one perspective may well be invisible to those who are wearing other spectacles" so that "different theories will yield 'different facts'"[41] then one big theory of everything can never be accomplished. Furthermore the believers of a purported synthesis will have to work overtime and employ a great deal of cognitive dissonance not to see the facts and theories that don't fit into their integral embrace.

How are we to decide which metaphysical assumption to make? Is it one big world or many worlds? In the end it will probably be one's temperament that determines what assumption one adopts, but it is still possible to test individual attempts at a big synthesis and see if they hold up. In contrast to Wilber's depiction of the basic agreement in the world of developmental psychology,

40 Lerner, *Developmental Psychology*, p. 197.
41 Ibid., p. 197.

I adduce several contrary sources that present a much different picture of the state of developmental psychology.

Sheldon White, a Harvard psychologist, studied developmental psychologists, and his research suggested an interesting dichotomy in the field. He found that developmental psychologists divide into two groups over the question of "what they are all doing together."[42] He names their two views the "Bewildered" and the "Paranoid." I will quote his description of the two views at length because they are quite startling and informative. The Bewildered see the field in this way:

> 1. *Developmental psychology is not seriously unified. It is a political convention, not a field. Many people do research with children under the tent of developmental psychology, studying everything from evoked potentials to single-parent families from a great range of basic and applied viewpoints. In the journals and conventions shared by developmental psychologists, people give one another miscellaneous political and intellectual support, but it is a mistake to think of all this heterogeneous activity as in any serious way constituting a common intellectual discipline.*

> 2. *Developmental psychologists work with the trappings of scientific analysis, but in truth they are working with feeble or empty stuff. You can't really do science unless you explore the effects of some independent variables. The independent variable of the developmental psychologist, age, is empty. Developmental psychologists endlessly document age effects through their longitudinal designs and cross-sectional designs, but any high school senior can tell you that age doesn't cause anything. Age is a dimension in which things happen—biological variables, environmental variables. Those are the causes. When you say that such-and-such happened with age, you say almost nothing.*

> 3. *Developmental psychologists find with monotonous regularity that children get better at everything with age. Sometimes they seem to find*

42 Ibid., p. 235.

cases in which children's performance worsens with age, but then they explore those cases and—aha!—what the older children do really is better after all. Developmental findings are largely nonnutritious and boring.[43]

The Paranoid view is an almost point by point description of Wilber's view of developmental psychology and science in general. Even the meaning White intends by the designation "Paranoid" applies to Wilber for, as White says, he uses "Paranoid not in the sense of everyone-is-out-to-get-me but rather in the sense of I-am-the-King-of-the-world."[44] White describes the Paranoid position thusly:

1. *Developmental psychology is only superficially the study of children. Really, you are studying many things that go beyond childhood but whose nature is clarified by the patterning of age changes in children's behavior.*

2. *The proper and only way to approach behavior is through the study of development.*

3. *Time series phenomena in evolution, organizational change, history, geology, cultural practices, the history of science, etc. show interesting and useful communalities. At the same time, psychopathology, neuropathology, social dissolution, and other forms of human disorder may be usefully interpreted as reversions in universal human organicist patterns of growth.*

4. *The study of developmental psychology yields values. It takes you from is to ought.*[45]

43 Ibid., pp. 235–236.
44 Ibid., p. 236.
45 Ibid., pp. 236–237.

The glibness in White's summaries may be mistaken for a lack of seriousness and validity, but he cites the five studies he did that provided the evidence for his formulations. White also notes that the Paranoid view, which describes Wilber's view, is the "minority" position in the field.[46]

AN EVALUATION

Having investigated the evidence behind Wilber's synthesis, I will now examine the model itself. Unlike my opinions of Wilber's overall model, which are decidedly critical, my view of his latest theory of consciousness is mixed. On the one hand, Wilber retains the universal levels of development that unfold in a progressive, cumulative developmental sequence. On the other hand, he has opened his model up, loosened its rigid linearity, and allowed it to be more usefully descriptive. This last effort has led to a less goal-directed model. The tension comes because this move to a less goal-directed model conflicts with his desire to show that there is a direction to development and a way of ranking levels of advancement. In Wilber's terminology, the hierarchical elements in which "rule or governance is established by a set of priorities that establish those things that are more important and those that are less" is in tension with the heterarchical elements in which "rule or governance is established by a pluralistic and egalitarian interplay of all parties"[47] By balancing these two elements, he has both improved his model and accentuated the implicit tensions within it.

Tensions appear in Wilber's attempt to describe the hierarchical and heterarchical elements of his theory of consciousness. The tone with which he tries to elucidate the differing parts of consciousness demonstrates the degree to which he is trying to shake the criticism that his model is a rigid, linear, stepladder of

46 Ibid., p. 235.
47 *SES*, p. 16.

development: "It is not that these levels are set in stone"; "This does not mean that all, or even most, of the important aspects of development are hierarchical."[48] On the heterarchical side, he asserts that, "overall development follows no linear sequence whatsoever."[49] And within levels, heterarchy, or the pluralistic play of egalitarian aspects of consciousness, is in the majority with hierarchical elements in the minority. Hierarchy, on the other hand, is seen in the relationship between levels. For example, if you analyze a person's aesthetic stream of development you would see a hierarchical unfolding from level to level. So, as mentioned earlier, each person would have a distinctive psychograph that described their level of development on each stream. This is the opposite of the rigid, ladder-like structure Wilber disclaims. Yet how can Wilber judge overall development if *"a person's overall development follows no linear sequential sequence whatsoever?"*[50] He needs to judge overall development because his larger theory of everything is directional and goal-directed. This attachment to hierarchical rankings is shown in the many judgments he makes about individuals' and societies' levels of development. He needs to be able to rate who is more advanced than whom, but how can he if there is no overall linear sequence whatsoever? He could reply that he finds people's "centers of gravity," as he does when assessing a society's level of development. But how would it work? Which semi-independent streams are rated as more important than others? Imagine an unscientific psychograph of a "primitive" person. He or she may be highly advanced artistically, low on cognition, highly attuned sensorily, have well-developed interpersonal skills to be able to live in a closely knit community that would drive a Westerner crazy, have a mid-level moral development towards outsiders, and have a high spiritual attainment. How does one average all of those

48 Wilber, *Integral Psychology*, p. 30, 31.
49 Ibid., p. 30.
50 *SES*, second revised edition, p. xvii.

together to determine the level of advancement relative to a modern person?

To rate individuals as more or less advanced requires a value scheme. Wilber contends that his value scheme arises from the developmental patterns we see in the physical, biological, human, and spiritual sciences. This is a fallacy since developmental psychology is essentially value-laden. Development is not something simply read off from life that either matches the way things are or not. Wilber writes as if it is. ("I will be telling the story [of the Kosmos] as if it were simply the case.")[51] He further suggests that it is the scientific backing behind his map that allows him to derive semi-objective values: "We are now in a position to realign facts and values in a gentler embrace, with science working with us, not against us."[52] Science provides the "simple, but sturdy" knowledge we need in order to know how the Kosmos operates. Yet two important scholarly sources Wilber relies upon acknowledge the constructed and value-laden character of developmental models. The editors of *Higher Stages of Human Development* say on the first page of the book that "one's conception of the endpoint of development is fundamental, for it contains one's assumptions about the direction, possibilities, and dynamics of human growth. Moreover, all prior developmental stages will be viewed as progressive approximations of this goal."[53] This is why Modgil and Modgil, the editors of *Lawrence Kohlberg: Consensus and Controversy*, say that the lack of empirical confirmation of Kohlberg's higher stages of moral development is a "fatal flaw."[54] It is a fatal flaw because without the reality of the endpoint of development established, how can you judge whether subjects at lower levels are advanced or regressed?

The other source that Wilber relies upon is Howard Gardner et al. Gardner et al. refer to their developmental scheme as "an

51 *SES*, pp. ix–x.

52 *SES*, p. 31.

53 Alexander and Langer, *Higher Stages of Human Development*, p. 3.

54 Rest, *Postconventional Moral Thinking*, p. 22.

idealization, and most particularly so in its final strokes." The "final strokes" refer to the later stages.

There are some in developmental psychology who define the field in terms of its value-ladenness. Bernard Kaplan's definition of developmental psychology is, "*Developmental psychology is a practico-theoretical discipline, a policy discipline, concerned with the perfection (including liberation or freedom) of the individual.*"[55] Jerome Kagan acknowledges "the metaphysical ideal each theorist believes children should grow toward," but differs from Kaplan in preferring to emphasize "compassion, nurture, and love," and says "such a trio of final purposes places obligations on children and adults that restrict seriously the freedom Kaplan cherishes."[56] While Sheldon White says, "*Developmental psychology can be defined in terms of what self-proclaimed or officially canonized developmental psychologists do.*"[57] This is why Gardner et al. say that "the symbolic waves are a psychologist's convention (and invention)." These perspectives, from well-known developmental psychologists, undermine the impression Wilber creates that the developmental unfolding that psychology describes is a universal truth about humans.

Depending on the endpoint of development chosen, the behaviors that lead toward that endpoint will be deemed natural, healthy, or normal, and those that don't will be deemed unnatural, retarded, or pathological. This is why the idea of development is an "idealization." Progressiveness and regressiveness are such not because they abide by nature's own pattern but because they do or do not live up to the standard contained in the endpoint. We see this in one of Wilber's examples of growth: the development of an acorn into an oak. It is certainly a natural process of growth. But do most acorns become full-sized oaks? No. Is it somehow unnatural for them not to? No. In fact, it is an essential part of the natural process of growth that most acorns do not grow and develop into

55 Lerner, *Developmental Psychology*, p. 188.

56 Ibid., p. 232.

57 Ibid., p. 233.

oak trees; otherwise, the forest would be too crowded to support *any* oaks. If the acorns that don't become oaks, the seedlings that never make it to full-sized trees, and the deterioration and death that are the fate of all trees are just as natural as the developmental process of acorn to oak, why does Wilber focus so much attention on the growth from acorn to oak? It is not because the growth from acorn to oak is an exemplar of nature's process that tells us what process to value in general; it *is* because, for humans, the fully formed oak tree is what is of value. It gives us shade, beauty, and wood, so we tend to be interested in it. But it is no more natural for a tree to grow than for a tree not to grow, or for a forest to be wiped out by lightning. Wilber's interest in a particular kind of optimal development causes him to pick from nature one way of understanding its patterns and then elevate it to Nature's Way. Just compare the exceedingly natural pattern of birth, growth, decline, and death, which rarely, if ever, makes an appearance in Wilber's work. He is constantly extracting from nature a picture of life that is ever upward and onward, and tries to validate it as somehow being nature's own tendency. But all of nature's patterns are nature's tendencies, whether you label them growth, progression, regression, sickness, or health. These labels are reflective not of nature but of our all too human interests. Wilber does not show us how we *do* live and grow; he instead depicts *one* way we can choose to see life and growth.

Convincingly rendered alternative models provide an alternative vision of life and enable us to see Wilber's developmental model as one among many, having both positive and negative qualities. Michael Washburn's circular model of transpersonal development, in which we return to a lost source and see it for the first time, has more of the character of the birth, growth, death and rebirth vision.[58]

Wilber's model is strongly developmental because he has a strong idea of where humanity should go. This is why Bernard

58 Michael Washburn, *The Ego and Dynamic Ground* (Albany: SUNY Press, 1988).

Kaplan writes that *"development does not lurk directly in the population(s) studied but resides fundamentally in the perspective used."*[59] He presents his model of development as if it is what has been discovered by science and so is a reflection of what is, but all developmental models are value-laden and so they tell us different ways people develop depending on the psychologist's belief about how people should develop.

59 Lerner, *Developmental Psychology*, p. 196.

CHAPTER 3

VISION-LOGIC

Vision-logic is Wilber's term for the next, higher developmental stage of consciousness. It constitutes a transcendence and inclusion of the developmentally less inclusive *egoic-rational* consciousness which is the characteristic form of consciousness of the modern world of advanced industrialized countries since the Enlightenment.

Egoic-rational consciousness arises with the arrival of modernity and allows humans to consider other peoples' perspectives. Prior to this, the pre-modern, mythical consciousness required a belief in *its* absolute truth and the denial of alternative perspectives. This advance in consciousness is essential for the moral advance of tolerance because if we can consider the perspectives of others we can understand them better. Rationality has its limits, though; the perceiver can acknowledge differing perspectives, but cannot integrate them without reducing them to his or her own "truth." The rational person understands what the other believes, and simultaneously excludes it as wrong. The choice is between being a dogmatic defender of one's chosen view or a wishy-washy relativist who says any view is as good as any other.

Wilber claims that a solution to this problem is occurring through a shift in consciousness. We are moving from the dominance of egoic-rationality to a new consciousness and mode of being called *vision-logic,* or *integral-aperspectival.* This new consciousness allows us to step back and mindfully view the contents of consciousness. By gaining this ability to view rationality as a whole we can now transcend it. This transcendence is no mere detachment but a greater embrace in which the previously disassociated spheres of matter, life, mind, and spirit can be integrated. Humans can become qualitatively different beings. Instead of experiencing ourselves as an awkward mixture of a mechanical living machine and a seemingly immaterial consciousness, we can experience ourselves as an integrated whole of sensations, emotions, thoughts, and spirit, all held within a larger witnessing awareness. Wilber sometimes refers to this new mode of being as *centauric,* after the mythic beast that combined the human and the animal.

Wilber's conception of vision-logic has remained relatively consistent since his early account of it in *Eye to Eye* in 1983, although its fullest elaboration occurred more recently in *SES* and *Integral Psychology.* As a mode of cognition, vision-logic is not rooted in one perspective. It can range over multiple perspectives and differing domains of knowledge, seeing the interconnections, relationships, and analogies between systems of knowledge, and integrate these seemingly disparate systems. Differing kinds of knowledge—scientific, religious, poetic, experiential, rational—and their multifarious perspectives on reality are not pejoratively or invidiously compared—"Science is true, religion is bunk"; "The liberals are right, the conservatives wrong"—but considered and understood, with their truths culled and integrated into greater understandings and larger systems of knowledge.

Rational thinkers cannot affirm the truth of their perspectives without reducing opposing perspectives to their own, yet cannot find the justification for such a reduction using reason alone. They are stuck with the prospect of a fragmented culture in which there is no final arbiter of truth. Vision-logic or integral-aperspectival consciousness can solve this dilemma. With the emergence of vision-logic, consciousness grasps its own structure for the first time and so is transparent to itself. Wilber states that "so much of the verbal-mental-egoic dimension . . . becomes *increasingly objective*, increasingly transparent, to centauric consciousness,"[1] and notes that "this 'transparency,' according to Gebser, is a primary characteristic of the integral-aperspectival mind."[2] Vision-logic, he says, has "the capacity to go within and *look at* rationality [and] results in a *going beyond* rationality."[3] What consciousness now sees is its holonic nature; that there are "contexts within contexts within contexts forever."[4] In seeing this infinity of contexts, the integral-aperspectival mind is not tempted to reduce one perspective to another, as rationality does. The poststructural insight that no perspective is final is accepted and integrated, but the nihilistic conclusion that all perspectives are of equal value is rejected. The integral-aperspectival mind solves the riddle of relativism by preserving the truths of differing perspectives and integrating them into the great holarchy. Each perspective now has its proper place within the whole.

There are three ways that Wilber argues for the superiority of vision-logic: one, that the vantage-point itself is superior—the *means* of knowledge acquisition are better; two, that the knowledge gained from the vantage-point is better—it produces better *results*; and three, that developmental psychology has verified its existence—the *research* confirms it.

Mindfully observing consciousness can produce profound results, and it is a method neglected by most mind researchers.[5] Yet the power of this type of mental observation does not necessarily mean that it is a superior means of observation, only different. Different approaches to understanding mind and reason range

1 *SES*, p. 189.

2 *SES*, p. 187.

3 *SES*, p. 258

4 *SES*, p. 187.

5 For an exception see Francisco J. Varela, Evan Thompson, and Eleanor Rosch, *The Embodied Mind* (MIT Press, 1991).

from the detached rationality of cognitive science and the philosophy of mind to the subjective immediacy of phenomenology. All
deal with the upper left quadrant of Wilber's map and understand
the mind in differing ways. These other investigative methods use
rationality and self-reflection to understand the mind in ways different than the supposed disinterested witnessing consciousness of
vision-logic.

Mindful viewing of one's subjective consciousness does give an
experience of self-certainty regarding what is seen, but the criterion of experienced self-certainty is different from the criteria that
the rational inquirer uses. Since different methods and criteria of
validity are used, one cannot say that one is superior to the other.
That would require a meta-criterion to adjudicate the differences
between the two approaches. The mystic would say to the rational
inquirer that they have not done the mindful viewing necessary
to examine consciousness. The rational inquirer would say to the
mystic that their statements regarding the nature of consciousness or rationality are open to this or that criticism. For example,
the rational inquirer could contend that vision-logic doesn't really
stand outside of a thing called rationality; what it actually does is
offer a view from a unique, subjective, witnessing position of the
flow of reasoning and thought inside of one's own mind. Witnessing one's personal reasoning and flow of thought is not the same
as empirically studying reason itself. Should we adjudicate the difference using the experienced self-certainty of mystical inquiry or
do we use the results of a critical rational questioning? Which criteria we think superior is an existential choice, neither ultimately
rationally defensible nor ultimately demonstrable to all.

A central insight of the twentieth century's *linguistic turn* in the
social sciences and the humanities is an appreciation of the fundamental role that language plays in the existence of consciousness. The aforementioned fields of cognitive science and the philosophy of mind have focused on language as a presupposition of
rationality and consciousness. Wilber notes that Jean Gebser, the

pioneering theoretician of a potential integral consciousness, emphasizes the importance of language for our historical age. Wilber quotes Gebser stating that "Language itself is treated as a primordial phenomenon by recognizing its originating-creative nature."[6] But language and the linguistic turn are tricky things. Once you acknowledge the "originating-creative" nature of language for consciousness, it is hard (I would contend impossible) to escape it. Martin Heidegger and Hans-Georg Gadamer say language creates our unique form of *human* being, but they do not argue that there is any form of transparency available to man of the sort that Wilber implies. Jacques Derrida and others would argue that language can never be a transparent transmitter of reality, because its multiple and ever-changing words and meanings do not allow one to escape its confines. An intention to produce the most precise and permanent description of anything will always be undermined by the changing multiplicity of meanings that are inherent in language. There is no one-to-one correspondence between word and world.

Whether our capacity to view the internal contents of our minds allows us a transparent or unmediated viewing of those contents is quite a vexed question in the philosophy of mind. The apparent direct witnessing of the contents of our minds has been disputed by many in the philosophical tradition, including Wittgenstein, Gilbert Ryle, Wilfred Sellars, and Donald Davidson.[7] In a recent paper, the philosopher Ernest Sosa reviews the "various accounts of how beliefs can be *foundationally* justified through sticking to the character of the subject's own conscious experience at the time," and concludes that "none of these has been successful."[8] Simon

---

6 *SES*, pp. 189–190.

7 William Lycan has published two books that describe the variety of positions regarding the nature of consciousness from the perspective of the philosophy of mind: William G. Lycan, *Consciousness* (Cambridge: MIT Press, 1987) and William G. Lycan, ed., *Mind and Cognition*, (Malden, Massachusetts: Blackwell Publishers, 1999).

8 Ernest Sosa, "Privileged Access," in Quentin Smith and Aleksandar Jokic, eds.,

Blackburn, in his *Oxford Dictionary of Philosophy*, defines Wilfred Sellars's "Myth of the Given" as the "name adopted by Sellars for the
now widely-rejected view that sense experience gives us peculiar
points of certainty, suitable to serve as foundations for the whole
of empirical knowledge and science."[9]
    A convincing transcendent experience must still be put into
words to have the kind of interpersonal verification that Wilber
seeks. The criteria of verification within a mystical community,
such as a Buddhist monastery, may be clear-cut, as Wilber contends, but if one is inclined toward rational verification, the verbalized propositions are open to questioning and counter-argument
and drawn into inevitable debate.[10] The verbalized propositions
will assume their role as the vehicles of one perspective among
many.
    Vision-logic does not transcend and include other perspectives
and put them in their proper place. To place them, it must extract
the partial truths of differing perspectives, using the orienting generalizations of knowledge, and arrange them accordingly. But, as
I show throughout the book, the method of determining orienting
generalizations is not possible and not done by Wilber. Since Wilber does not use orienting generalizations, he does not have truths
according to that criterion. What he is claiming is not automatically
sanctioned by the relevant research in the natural and social sciences. Therefore, he must be using a perspective to determine what is
true and false. Yet he says that he is using integral-aperspectivalism,
which transcends perspectives. Wilber's solution to perspectivalism
doesn't work because integral-aperspectivalism *is* a perspective.
    Wilber contends that vision-logic incorporates the poststructur-
al insight of contexts within contexts, yet he leaves out the crucial

Consciousness: New Philosophical Perspectives (Oxford: Oxford University Press, 2003),
p. 289. Sosa does go on to "sketch…a positive view that seems more promising."
9 Simon Blackburn, *The Oxford Dictionary of Philosophy* (Oxford: Oxford University
Press, 1996), p. 253.
10 See the work of Steven Katz, et al. discussed in Chapter 4.

poststructural contextualization: the contextualization of oneself, the observer. Wilber reacts with such vehemence when confronting the relativists, and takes such repeated delight in exposing their alleged self-contradiction—they supposedly make the absolute statement that "all is relative"—because their alleged contradiction is his actual contradiction. His contradiction is that on the one hand he wants to claim that he is practicing a non-reductionistic, aperspectival synthesis of the partial truths of knowledge while on the other hand he is actually using an unacknowledged perspective and criterion of truth in order to decide what will count as truth. He uses the fiction of the orienting generalization, and its purported sanction of what he considers the facts, to promote as universal his highly partisan and selective vision of what is true for all.

This desire to both honor contextualization and transcend it causes Wilber to make confused assertions. He commends poststructuralism for saying that no perspective is final, but condemns it for saying that this means that no perspective is better than any other.[11] (As usual, no actual poststructuralists are quoted saying these things.) He then deploys the usual self-contradiction argument and says that because they make the absolute assertion that no perspective is better than any other they are committing a self-contradiction. What Wilber does not seem to notice is that even asserting that no perspective is final, as he and the poststructuralists do, involves one in a self-contradiction. For from what perspective can one assert that no perspective is final, and have it be absolutely true, than from a perspective that claims itself to be final. What could final mean here but the ultimate perspective?

Ironically, Wilber, who has personally had such a profound nondual insight,[12] is so locked into the paramount epistemological duality of absolutism vs. relativism that he cannot see beyond it. It causes him to say things like, "That all perspectives interrelate, or that no perspective is final (aperspectivism), does not mean that

11 *SES*, p. 188.
12 Wilber, *One Taste: The Journals of Ken Wilber*, (Boston: Shambhala, 1999), p. 80.

there are no relative merits among them."[13] Yet how does he determine relative merits except through his perspective, which he unwittingly disguises by thinking of it as a transcendent aperspective?

Finally, that Wilber's aperspective is a perspective is apparent from what follows his description of vision-logic: a defense of his view against the inevitable (but comfortably simplified) objections (i.e., other perspectives).

The superiority of vision-logic as a mode of knowing is dependent upon the arguments made for the validity of the integral synthesis as a whole. Wilber argues that vision-logic is superior because: it transcends and includes rationality; it is developmentally later, and so is more advanced; and it explains more, since it integrates all that has come before. In each instance, vision-logic's superiority is dependent upon the validity of the integral theory. When Wilber states that vision-logic sees that "consciousness is actually holonic" so that "its own operation [is] increasingly transparent to itself,"[14] he assumes that the holonic way of looking at consciousness is correct. Yet that is the burden of Wilber's work, which I show is highly problematic.

This attempt to validate the superiority of vision-logic through the results of the integral theory leads to a circular logic. Wilber's ability to create his integral synthesis is supposedly a result of his use of vision-logic. Vision-logic is that state of mind that allows the weaving together of the partial truths of other fields of study in order to create a synthesis of knowledge that the rational consciousness cannot accomplish. Yet the validity of vision-logic, as we have seen, is justified by the correctness of the entire integral synthesis, which, through its evolutionary-developmental perspective, makes sense of the welter of scientific knowledge currently available and gives vision-logic a favored place. Wilber writes,

13 *SES*, p. 188.
14 *SES*, p. 187.

> The aperspectival mind, in other words, is holonic through and through . . . every structure of consciousness is actually holonic (there are only holons), but vision-logic consciously grasps this fact for the first time, and thus finds its own operation increasingly transparent to itself (this "transparency," according to Gebser, is a primary characteristic of the integral-aperspectival mind).[15]

In other words, the key to Wilber's integral synthesis is the insight into the holonic nature of the Kosmos. This holonic nature is seen for the first time by vision-logic, which transparently sees its own operation because it sees the holonic nature of things, placing vision-logic beyond rational consciousness. So the fact that vision-logic sees holons within holons demonstrates its transparency to the nature of mind, because we know, through using vision-logic, that the nature of the Kosmos is holonic. It's like saying, "I know I'm right because I have the best faculty for judging rightness. How do I know it's the best faculty for judging rightness? Because it judges things rightly. How do I know it judges things rightly? Because it is the best faculty for judging rightness," *ad infinitum*.

If vision-logic's transparency to consciousness is evidenced by its ability to see the holonic nature of consciousness, then its validity is dependent upon Wilber's description of consciousness. Certainly, all describers of consciousness would claim that their view is the right one, so Wilber appears to be no different. However, he *is* different because he claims that his description of consciousness is the knowledge of everyone else's combined. Whereas most researchers assert the truth of their view within the context of the debate in which they are engaged, Wilber tries to assume a position above the debate through the device of the orienting generalization. This device makes it appear as if he is neutrally reporting the findings of all the members of the debate, and causes him to make grandiose claims, such as consciousness finally becomes transparent to itself through vision-logic.

15 *SES*, p. 187.

Wilber's unreliable reporting of the results of scholarly research is one central feature of my critique; this same problem arises, although less severely than usual, when he justifies vision-logic by citing scholarly research.[16] In developmental psychology, Wilber's vision-logic is called postformal thought. Scholars in the field use the term *postformal* to refer to a hypothesized stage of cognitive development beyond Piaget's formal stage of cognition.

Wilber refers to a number of researchers exploring vision-logic. A measured and knowledgeable survey of postformal thinking, written by Helena Marchand,[17] confirms Wilber's characterization of postformal thinkers as having a general consensus regarding, what Wilber terms, "the developmental space they portray."[18] She writes that

> it is possible to identify in the diverse descriptions of post-formal thought (cf. Kramer, 1983, 1989) some features which would be specific to this level: (1) the recognition and understanding of the relativistic, non-absolutist, nature of knowledge; (2) the acceptance of contradiction to the extent that it is part of reality; and (3) the integration of contradiction into comprehensive systems, i.e., into a dialectical whole (Kramer, 1989).

This statement confirms Wilber's claim that there is a broad consensus *within* postformal studies regarding what postformal theorists agree upon, but it says nothing about the status of the postformal concept *outside* of postformal studies in the larger discipline of developmental studies.

Michael Commons and Francis Richards are the postformal thinkers Wilber refers to most frequently. Commons and Richards

16 Frank Visser alerted me to the material in this section and the importance of examining it.

17 Helena Marchand, "Some Reflections on Postformal Thought," *The Genetic Epistemologist*, Vol. 29, Number 3, 2001, http://www.piaget.org/GE/2001/Ge-29-3.html#item2.

18 Wilber, *Integral Psychology*, p. 90.

divide the postformal stage into four increasingly advanced levels termed the systemic, the metasystemic, the paradigmatic, and the crossparadigmatic. In essence, each level uses the products of the previous level as its object of thought. For example, the person at the paradigmatic level will work with metasystems to create a new paradigm. Wilber believes he's at the highest or crossparadigmatic level: "I am presenting a cross-paradigmatic model."[19] However, while Marchand thinks Commons and Richards's work is the most worthwhile among postformal thinkers, she notes that it has not been confirmed by later empirical studies, a major drawback. She writes:

> The results obtained by Commons, Richards & Kuhn (1982) confirm such reconstructions in that which relates to the systematic, metasystematic, and paradigmatic stages (They did not find such results at the transparadigmatic level). However, these results were not confirmed in studies carried out by various researchers who studied the relationships among formal thought and systematic and metasystematic thought (Demetriou, 1990; Kallio, 1995; Kallio & Helkema, 1991; Kohlberg, 1990). For these authors, systematic thought would be identical to that designated by Piaget as "consolidated formal operations" (i.e., Formal B) and, thus, could not be considered postformal.[20]

And in her conclusion, the whole area of postformal thinking does not fare well. Marchand concludes that

> given the heterogeneity of theories about thought beyond the formal level, and given the inconclusiveness of the research carried out so far, it is not possible, for now, to determine the true nature of the type of thought referred to as postformal. This being the case, and it being nec-

19 Wilber, "Waves, Streams, States and Self," n. 4.
20 Marchand, "Some Reflections."

essary to defend the requirement that any scientific and epistemological theory must be based on underlying presuppositions such as conceptual clarification, parsimony, and simplicity, it seems preferable to abandon the term "postformal" (except, possibly, in the case of the conceptualization put forth by Commons and coworkers) and to speak simply of adult cognition, or adult thought. [21]

Of course, Marchand's view is not the last word, but, at the very least, her conclusion, so contrary to Wilber's confident assertions, indicates that there are grounds for a healthy scholarly debate. Since the postformal scholarly literature is supposed to validate vision-logic, this disagreement brings its nature and existence into question.

Other problems arise for vision-logic as a social-historical phenomenon, as opposed to an individual, cognitive phenomenon. As with all holons, vision-logic has an aspect in the lower left or intersubjective quadrant. Vision-logic is purported to be a qualitative shift in social consciousness on the scale of the magical, mythical, and rational socio-historical shifts. Yet what distinguishes these categories as massive historical shifts is that they each provide new criteria of validity for knowledge as described in Michel Foucault's well-known portrayal of differing historical eras' regimes of knowledge. [22] Wilber makes an invidious comparison between the methods of knowledge acquisition in pre-modernity versus those of modernity. The pre-Enlightenment Renaissance period used appeals to authority and metaphorical association to gain and validate knowledge claims. This method contrasts with modernity's use of empirical evidence, experimentation, and the standards of rationality. If the shift to vision-logic is of the same order of magnitude as the shift from the medieval to the modern, then vision-logic must have its own new criteria of valid knowl-

21 Ibid.
22 Michel Foucault, *The Order of Things* (New York: Vintage Books, 1973).

edge. Wilber does describe criteria of valid knowledge claims, but, as I argue in Chapter 8, they are not a new criterion of knowledge. So no new criterion of knowledge is offered that would distinguish vision-logic from the standard rules of rational argumentation and establish it as a new stage of social-historical development.

The purported epistemological difference between egoic-rationality and vision-logic has been used by Wilber to forestall criticism of his integral synthesis. Recently, Wilber has claimed that you need to have attained a certain level of consciousness to really understand his theory. He writes, "nothing that can be said in this book will convince you that a [theory of everything] is possible, unless you already have a touch of turquoise [higher consciousness] coloring your cognitive palette."[23] So I, at the first or second level of vision-logic (the green level[24]), simply can't fully understand Wilber's theory which is at the fourth level of vision-logic (turquoise) because my cognitive development is not advanced enough. I still see a relativistic world of multiple perspectives and can't transcend that consciousness and see the interconnections and patterns between perspectives, the holarchical nature of things. It's similar to a scientific rationalist at the egoic-rational stage (orange) having a debate with a religious fundamentalist at the mythic level (blue).[25] The person at the lower level just can't understand the higher-level person's thinking. As Wilber says about these "cross-level debates":

> This is why developmental studies in general indicate that many philosophical debates are not really a matter of the better *objective* argument, but of the *subjective level* of those debating. No amount of orange scientific evidence will convince blue mythic believers; no amount of green bonding will impress orange aggressiveness; no amount

23 Wilber, *A Theory of Everything*, (Boston: Shambhala, 2000), p. 14.

24 Wilber uses here a color code for the levels of development taken from Don Beck and Christopher Cowan's book *Spiral Dynamics: Masters Values, Leadership and Change*, (Malden, MA: Blackwell, 1996).

25 See chapter 5 for a description of these levels of consciousness.

of turquoise holarchy will dislodge green hostility—unless the individual is ready to develop forward through the dynamic spiral of consciousness unfolding. This is why "cross-level" debates are rarely resolved, and all parties usually feel unheard and unappreciated.[26]

This argument is problematic in a number of ways and has the potential, already partially realized in the Wilberian integral community, of stifling the free flow of ideas and causing exclusionary behavior. As stated above, Wilber's description of the problem is odd. He says he's talking about "philosophical debates," yet refers to "orange aggressiveness," "green bonding," and "green hostility" as if the discussants aren't asserting their views using rational arguments and rhetoric but instead bullying or hugging each other. Presumably, I would be labeled a green hostile. But I'm not trying to dislodge Wilber's turquoise holarchy with hostility; I'm making arguments, asking questions and producing evidence. How else would people have a rational discussion about their views? He also says that these debates "are not really a matter of the better *objective* argument," as if that can be determined objectively, independently of the debate itself. While it's true that debates often end in stalemate, there is a simpler explanation that I suggest below.

Any objectivity claimed for Wilber's arguments is fundamentally dependent upon the validity of the developmental levels that Wilber has adopted. If vision-logic or the postformal is not a separate stage of development, then there is no discrete, hierarchic difference in consciousness between people assigned to different levels. As I show above, there is much room for debate about the reality of a postformal stage. Even more, the citations in Chapter 2, on individual consciousness, show that there are well-established developmental psychologists who question, criticize, and have abandoned Piaget's and Kohlberg's developmen-

26 Wilber, "Introduction to Volume 7 of the *Collected Works*," in the section entitled The Jump to Second-Tier Consciousness, at http://wilber.shambhala.com/html/books/cowokev7_intro.cfm/.

tal models. More broadly, outside of developmental psychology, there are non-developmental psychologists who simply don't use a developmental model at all. As Wilber himself says, in a curious statement for someone who says he's relying upon the scholarly consensus for the validity of his integration, a version of the postmodern green meme, with its pluralism and relativism "has also made developmental studies, which depend on second-tier [higher stage] thinking, virtually anathema at both conventional and alternative universities."[27] This statement is so mistaken that I wonder if Wilber had a mental lapse when writing it, since Wilber also contends, in that very same piece, that the developmental models he uses have the *sanction* of mainstream academia. In addition, even a superficial survey shows that developmental studies are well ensconced in academe. But it does indicate, from Wilber himself, the embattled—as opposed to the consensual—situation of developmentalism. An embattled situation means that arguments and evidence against developmentalism have a strong foothold in academia, as shown in Chapter 2. This directly contradicts Wilber's frequent statements that the developmental models he's using are validated by the consensus in the field. So the validity of vision-logic—and developmentalism itself—is an open question.

Assuming vision-logic were a separate level of development, does it hold, as Wilber suggests, that those who have not achieved it can't understand the thinking of those who have, or can only understand it in a limited fashion? Andrew P. Smith is, with Mark Edwards, one of the best students of Wilber's work. He has constructed his own novel one-scale model of holarchy. To create such a model, according to Commons and Richards, requires taking intellectual paradigms as one's object of thought; this means that Smith is working at the highest, cross-paradigmatic level of vision-logic. So he has the requisite level of consciousness, according to Wilber, to understand his integral theory. Yet Smith has been so ignored by Wilber and his followers that he's resorted to subtitling

27 Ibid.

one of his essays: "Further Monologues with Ken Wilber." In addition, Smith's evaluation of Wilber's integral theory is done in the standard way: he describes the theory, asks whether it agrees with the facts, whether it's consistent, and whether it provides a solid explanation for what it purports to describe. Even I, a lowly, entry-level vision-logician, have read Smith's work, understand it, and have used it in my book and received a strong, positive review from Smith.[28] So Smith, a cross-paradigmatic thinker, has critically evaluated Wilber's work, using the standard modes of intellectual evaluation, so successfully that neither Wilber nor any one of his supporters has even tried to contradict him. Were Smith to be engaged, it would be an intra-level debate acceptable to Wilber and virtually required by Wilber's hero Jurgen Habermas in his conception of the ideal speech situation.

Smith's, Wilber's, and everyone else's use of the well-known tools of rational substantiation and evaluation raise the question of what special criteria of validity Wilber, or any cross-paradigmatic thinker, uses? Commons and Richards illustrate the highest level of postformal thinking—called crossparadigmatic or transparadigmatic thinking, the stage Marchand says Commons and Richards themselves could not empirically validate—with the great discoveries of Copernicus, Newton, Darwin, Planck, Einstein, and Godel. All of their revolutionary discoveries were validated by the standard criteria of scientific rationality: logic, consistency, evidence, experimentation, elegance. Where is the new criterion of knowledge that accompanies any shift in cognition of the scale that Wilber claims for vision-logic?

If it is not a difference in levels of consciousness, what causes the common occurrence of unresolved and unsatisfying intellectual debates? I propose that irreconcilable debates are caused by people adhering to differing criteria of validity. When I've had discussions with fundamentalist Christians and we disagree, I

28 Andrew P. Smith, "Contextualizing Ken: A Review of Jeff Meyerhoff's Bald Ambition at http://www.integralworld.net/smith20.html, Sept. 2004.

don't think I have a higher level of consciousness and that's why they don't agree with me; I think that because of their personality and life experiences they have decided that the ultimate criteria of validity is a literal reading of the Bible. I still think I'm right and they're wrong, but I also know there is no way to ultimately adjudicate the difference. They think that if I could take a leap of faith and surrender to the infinite love of Jesus Christ I would understand His Truth; while I think that if they would just look at the facts and the evidence and be reasonable *they* would understand what's true. Moreover, there are fundamentalists who understand science well enough to state the basics correctly—they just don't believe in it. We just believe different things and we each think ourselves right and the other wrong. As the book's epigram by Stanley Cavell says, "There is such a thing as an intellectual tragedy."

Wilber's argument here is so weak that another explanation has to be found for why he's asserting it. It seems like a transparent attempt to avoid criticism by devising a rationale that invalidates the criticizer. If, as he often laments, people don't understand his theory, the explanation lies in their not being cognitively developed enough to understand it. In addition, all the explaining in the world will not help because they are constitutionally unable to understand; therefore no attempt even needs to be made. And, any criticism the critic makes can be ignored because of the lower level of consciousness of the person making it. Wilber is committing the common fallacy of the *ad hominem* argument—the argument against the man.

In conclusion, the burden of Wilber's theory of everything is to use the perspective-laden scholarship of noted academics to construct a synthesis that transcends their interminable debates. While the witness consciousness of vision-logic may give the experience of transcending the rational mind, as soon as any insight gained from that perspective, or any defense of that perspective, is put into words it can be subject to rational debate. By entering

the realm of rational debate the tools of reason become opera-
tive. Debate participants use arguments, facts, rhetoric, logic, and,
most fundamentally, language. The twentieth century's linguistic
turn in the humanities and the social sciences has not, contrary to
Wilber and Gebser, led to a "transparency" of rationality and a
superior vision-logic but instead to the inescapability of language.
As soon as we think or speak or, as some would now argue, become
humanly conscious, we presuppose language. Vision-logic, and
the integral synthesis that justifies its status as an advanced form
of consciousness, is one perspective among many. It is doubtful as
a new type of socio-historical consciousness because it does not
have a new criterion of knowledge, which has been a fundamental
characteristic of earlier types of consciousness, such as the magical, mythic, and the egoic-rational. Debates within and outside
developmental psychology cast doubt on the reality of vision-logic
as a separate stage of development. Without the proper validation,
the use of levels of development as a tool to exclude particular
debate participants or to rationalize inferior argumentation can
be seen as a transparent attempt to avoid rational discussion, the
standard way of adjudicating differences between differing intellectual perspectives.

CHAPTER 4

MYSTICISM

Mysticism is the use of spiritual practices to directly perceive the nature of reality or God with an immediacy greater than that of the mind, the emotions, or the senses. Wilber wants to show that the knowledge gained through mysticism is valid knowledge, because essential aspects of his system rely upon its validity. He claims that the Kosmos has a spiritual nature and that its goal is to realize this nature through a developmental unfolding. This realization of the Kosmos's own essence occurs on earth through the development of humans, who, if their development unfolds naturally and fully, will collectively embody this spiritual essence. According to Wilber, some adepts have already realized reality's nature, Wilber himself being one of them. This insight brings with it the knowledge that all holons have a bit of this spiritual essence or consciousness. The progressive development from egoic-rational consciousness to vision-logic allows an aperspectival seeing of this larger integrated picture of our unfolding. Vision-logic has four spiritual stages that, Wilber contends, distill the essence of the spiritual paths of all authentic mystical practices.

The mystic gains certainty into the nature of reality through experience, but to validate this knowledge to the non-mystic requires rational argumentation. Wilber uses a variety of arguments to

validate mystical knowledge, but none, as they stand, are successful. While it would seem to be a good idea to legitimate the profound insights of mysticism to Western intellectuals, ultimately, I
think it a losing battle. Doing so requires that mystics and their de-
fenders use intellectual weapons, which, according to the mystics
themselves, cause the delusion that mystical practice dispels. Additionally, by their nature, rational arguments can never provide
the justification that mysticism needs to prevail. The linguistic turn
in twentieth-century thinking in the humanities and social sciences
has shown that absolute conclusiveness through argumentation is
highly doubtful. Mysticism, which claims knowledge of an absolute beyond language, will hinder its cause by trying to fight on a
linguistic terrain. It will always find itself drawn into a quagmire
of interminable debates that draws its practitioners further from a
way of being most conducive to realizing the insights that mystics
are advocating.

To validate mystical knowledge Wilber does three things: he
describes why mystical knowledge is as valid as any other form
of knowledge; he counters objections to mysticism's validity; and
he claims that there is a cross-cultural similarity between the core
insights of the world's major mystical traditions.

Against the view that mystical knowledge is not valid knowledge, Wilber describes the "three stands of any valid knowledge
quest."[1] Wilber asserts these three steps are: *injunction*, or telling a
person what to do to get the knowledge; *apprehension*, or the per-
ceiving of what is experienced through the injunction; and lastly,
communal confirmation, or checking what was perceived with others
who used the same injunction. This is an excellent response to
those who ignorantly assert that mysticism is just mental fuzziness,
but it is a problematic response if your goal is to validate mystical
knowledge to support a great synthesis heavily dependent on mysticism's validity as provider of Truth.

The problem becomes clear when we compare Wilber's "three

1 *SES*, p. 273.

strands of any valid knowledge quest" with the philosopher Richard Rorty's description of the scientific method. The example of Rorty is significant here because Rorty is accused by his opponents of being a relativist who, in Wilber's words, believes that "cultural productions are shifting conversations with no validity claims of their own."[2] In Rorty's article "Method, Social Science, Social Hope," he writes:

> If "scientific method" means merely being rational in some given area of inquiry, then it has a perfectly reasonable "Kuhnian" sense—it means obeying the normal conventions of your discipline, not fudging the data *too* much, not letting your hopes and fears influence your conclusions unless those hopes and fears are shared by all those who are in the same line of work, being open to refutation by experience, not blocking the road of inquiry. In this sense, "method" and "rationality" are names for a suitable balance between respect for the opinions of one's fellows and respect for the stubbornness of sensation.[3]

Sounds like Wilber's three steps. Rorty is saying that scientific inquirers follow the "normal conventions" or injunctions of their discipline, respect "the stubbornness of sensation" or what's perceived through apprehension, and "respect . . . the opinions of one's fellows," or use communal confirmation. Unlike Rorty, though, Wilber wants more certainty then a methodology like that can give. The method allows mystical inquiry and the knowledge it produces to take its place among other types of knowledge, but it says nothing about whether it represents what it says it represents: Reality, Truth, or the Absolute.

Whether mysticism delivers the Truth or is just one more way of knowing is a question that goes unacknowledged in *SES* but makes

---

2 *SES*, p. 559.

3 Richard Rorty, *Consequences of Pragmatism* (Minneapolis: University of Minnesota Press, 1983), pp. 194–195.

its presence felt. If, as Wilber writes, "social *practices*, or social *in-junctions*, are crucial in creating and disclosing the types of 'world-space' in which types of subjects and objects appear (and thus the types of knowledge that *can* unfold),"[4] then the injunctions help to disclose/create the knowledge. The use of "creating and disclos-ing" is a manifestation of an ambivalence in Wilber's thinking. On the one hand, he wants to be postmodern and up-to-date by as-similating the poststructural view that we *create* knowledge. On this view, our practices or injunctions are so powerful that they are the determiners of the worldspace in which various kinds of subjects and objects appear, and hence creative of the kind of knowledge that there can be. On the other hand, he also needs to have some way of asserting that his view is supreme, and not just one among many ways of creating knowledge, because he wants it to be above competing claims and act as the grand synthetic integrator of our fragmented world. For the latter reason he needs to preserve the idea that we *disclose* knowledge, which retains the older, modern, Enlightenment idea that we gain knowledge by uncovering what is already there.

In the section from which the last quote was taken, Wilber is arguing for an equality of validity between mystical insight and the natural and social sciences. To do so he emphasizes practices or injunctions and communal confirmation, because this allows mystical practice to have the same validity as these sciences. They all have the same three strands of any valid knowledge quest. The problem, as he realizes a few paragraphs later, is that the unseemly taint of relativism appears. If "communal confirmation" plays such a big role in verifying knowledge, then it can be argued that what the community says goes. This is one version of a relativist theory of truth in which it is the community and not objective reality that legitimates knowledge. Sensing the specter of relativ-ism, Wilber tacks away from relativism and back to absolutism by strongly emphasizing the disclosing part of knowledge acquisition.

4 *SES*, p. 274.

He writes that

> paradigms are first and foremost *injunctions*, actual *practices* (all of which have nondiscursive components that never are entered in the theories they support)—they are methods for disclosing new data in an addressed domain, and the paradigms *work* because they are true in any meaningful sense of the word."[5]

Here Wilber simply begs the big questions in the philosophy of knowledge. Are practices nondiscursive? Could one even understand and execute a practice without discourse or the meaningful understanding of what to do and why it is being done? Practices are only nondiscursive if you conveniently forget the discursive distinction between discursive and non-discursive. And what happened to their role in creating the worldspaces, the subjects and objects that inhabit those worldspaces and the resulting knowledge?

Do "the paradigms *work* because they are true in any meaningful sense of the word," or is it the other way around, they are true because they work? To say the former—they work because they are true—as Wilber does, suggests there is a hard, objective reality out there awaiting disclosure and validating those paradigms that work. Yet one can argue the opposite, that paradigms are true because they work; this is a Rortyan, pragmatic approach that suggests, paraphrasing Rorty, that "true" is a compliment we pay to certain sentences that work for us;[6] a defensible position, which emphasizes the creative role that our practices play in making knowledge.

Finally, what is that "meaningful sense of the word" *true* that Wilber is using? Philosophers have been debating that for centuries; it won't be solved by simply declaring that it exists.

---

5 *SES*, p. 275.

6 Richard Rorty, *Philosophy and the Mirror of Nature* (Princeton: Princeton University Press, 1979), p. 10.

This ambivalence between creating and disclosing is one manifestation of a deeper schism that runs through Wilber's system.
On the one hand he wants to acknowledge that language mediates
our knowledge of the world, that we only know things from within social-historical contexts, and that reductionism has hindered
knowledge acquisition. On the other hand, Wilber wants to be the
one who provides the neutral framework for all other knowledge,
wants there to be a way to know reality as it is, and wants to claim
that he knows the transcendent goal of all evolution. The schism
goes unacknowledged but pokes through Wilber's confident discourse.

In addition to validating mystical knowledge claims, Wilber also
tries to counter common objections to the validity of mystical
knowledge. Depending on his imagined audience, he does a good
or bad job countering those objections. One audience is the average intellectual or academic who is ignorant about mysticism
and believes it is synonymous with fuzziness, mysteriousness, or
religion. Wilber's responses to this group's naive criticisms are
effective. But there is a second, smaller audience of intellectuals
and academics who are knowledgeable about mysticism and can
carry on sophisticated debates about it. The effective responses
Wilber makes to the first, ignorant group are easily criticized by
the second, knowledgeable group. There are legitimate philosophical questions about the validity of mystical states due to
their purported ineffability, the difficulty of public verification,
and their non-rational and even paradoxical character. A better,
more sophisticated response is needed if the power Wilber claims
for mysticism is going to be demonstrated to those knowledgeable
about mysticism. This Wilber does not provide. In general, while
his counterarguments to the most common objections to mystical
knowledge—it's not knowledge; it's only subjective, and it can't be
put into words—prevail, they prevail against ignorant opponents
and so don't have the sophistication necessary to legitimate the

big intellectual synthesis Wilber is proposing. Here again we find Wilber's usual treatment of critics: caricaturing their positions and not quoting anyone in order to avoid the difficult problems that true critics would raise.

The first objection that Wilber tries to counter is the view that "mystical states are private and interior and cannot be publicly validated; they are 'merely subjective.'"[7] That's the entire statement of the critics' position that Wilber provides. I wonder what the critic means by "merely subjective." And isn't the question of public validation different from the question of subjectivity? Wilber doesn't notice these difficulties. He replies that if mystical states are "merely subjective" then they share that with all nonempirical forms of knowledge. Nonempirical forms of knowledge here mean the social sciences and the humanities as opposed to the empirical disciplines of the natural sciences where the objects of inquiry are naturally occurring things like rocks, protons, and cells. In the nonempirical sciences the objects of inquiry are man-made and don't naturally exist out there in the world. Without humans we wouldn't have equations, books, and mystical states, but humans are not necessary to the existence of rocks, protons, and cells. So mystical knowledge shares this trait of subjectivity or non-objectiveness with other forms of knowledge like mathematics, literature, and history, and can be accorded a similar validity.

While technically it's true that the objects of mathematics do not occur naturally in the world—there is no circle or root two out there in the world—the materials that mathematicians use exist out there in the world. When two mathematicians work on an equation they can write it down on paper and share what it is they are examining. This is not the case with mystical states; they exist within each mystical practitioner. Further, it's often stated that these states are ineffable, so the actual materials that mystical inquirers can share—the words or pictures representing the states—are, according to mystical inquirers themselves, a poor

7 *SES*, p. 266.

second to the mystical experience itself. Now you could, as Wilber does, claim that mathematical representations like equations and drawings are secondary renderings of some unrepresentable sub-jective creation, but it's not an issue when doing mathematics. In contrast, the ineffability of mystical states, and so their essentially private nature, is often considered one of their defining character-istics, and is a central issue in debates about the epistemological status of mystical states. The two mystical inquirers cannot look together at one mystical state that exists out there. There are al-ways two objects of inquiry, each within the subjective experience of the mystical inquirer.

Now, one could argue that the one mathematical equation on paper is actually two because it is seen through two perspectives, but this is a difference that doesn't make a difference and results in a radical perspectivalism that Wilber himself would want to avoid.

In literature the situation is similar. The object of inquiry is an objective thing existing in the world that two inquirers can share: a written work. Literary critics can persuasively argue they share the same object of inquiry and not two objects, as in mysticism.

The example of history seems different. Here you could argue two ways: that the objects of inquiry are the cultural artifacts of the past that have survived, and so are objectively present to the historical inquirers; or, you could argue that the object of inquiry is the past itself, which no longer exists, forcing historians to use the remnants of the past that have survived into the present. Further, you could argue that history is in worse shape epistemologically than mystical inquiry in that the mystic can at least have his or her object of inquiry present in the moment, whereas the historian's object of inquiry—the past—is gone forever.

The merging of two different points, and Wilber's too brief statement of the critic's objection to mystical knowledge makes the objector's point unclear. There is, on the one hand, the point about mystical knowledge being "private" or "merely subjective" (although it's still not clear what the critic's point here is), and, on the other hand, there is the contention that mystical knowledge "cannot be publicly validated." As shown above, if the point here is that public validation is dependent on the "objectiveness" of the object of inquiry in the outside world, there will be subtle differences in the different nonempirical disciplines. But public validation could be interpreted differently as referring to the degree of agreement between inquirers within and between disciplines. While mathematics may have a subject matter that, technically, is "subjective," and so isn't available publicly (i.e., no circle exists in the world) the public validation, understood as degree of agreement about the major questions in the discipline, is unparalleled among scientific disciplines. For the most part, mathematical theorems are either regarded as proved, unproved, or disproved. By this criterion of public validation, mathematics is superior to all other sciences. The same type of examination for degree of disciplinary agreement could be done in all areas of knowledge. Is this what Wilber means by his limited rendering of the critic's complaint that mysticism lacks public validation? We can't know, because Wilber states the objection in one sentence, cites no one, and says no more.

The second objection Wilber presents to mystical experiences is that "because they cannot be put into plain language, or into any language . . . [they] are therefore not epistemologically grounded, are not 'real knowledge'"[8] Here again it's hard to understand the critic's point. Wilber seems to be interpreting this as meaning that because mystical states are described as ineffable they cannot be rendered in any language, and are therefore not real knowledge. Wilber counters this by arguing that language works the same way for all phenomena described. He uses Ferdinand de Saussure's distinction between the *signifier*, the *signified*, and the *referent*. The signifier is the spoken or written word, the word in its material form. The signified is the immaterial meaning in the mind or the concept. The referent is the actual thing-in-world that is being

8 *SES*, p. 268.

represented by the sign (i.e., the signifier and signified combined). So you have the word (signifier), the meaning (signified), and the thing itself (referent).

Wilber argues that a sign like "dog" is structurally the same as the mystic's use of "emptiness," the only difference being the commonness of experiences of dogs and the rarity of experiences of emptiness. For both "dog" and "emptiness" there is the signifier, the signified, and the referent. All experienced phenomena, whether dogs or emptiness or anything else, have the same epistemological status, which can be captured equally well or poorly depending on the person's experience of the object and their facility with language.

There are two problems with this line of argumentation. First, is it the case that the referents of the words "dog" and "emptiness" are shared in the same way? Don't we commonly think of the referent "dog" as being the furry, four-legged thing out there in the world, and "emptiness" as being experienced inwardly, or, for some, an immaterial or trans-material essence of the world? Many people have experienced the same dog as referent or object in the world, but have two mystics ever shared the same internal experience of emptiness? Mystics may call their experiences the same, but how do we know they originated from experiencing the same referent?

One possible response to this would be to claim that emptiness describes the nature of everything and so the referent is shared. The problem with this is that the only way that two experiencers of emptiness could know they had the same experience was by sharing signs and not referents. Yet two people who made reference to a dog can share the same referent.

Wilber's strict philosophical point about the similar structure of all signs and referents has truth to it (if we forget the above point about the unshared referent), but this strict philosophical response to the critic's objection obscures a more common and relevant objection to mystical knowledge that distinguishes it from the knowledge of dogs, plants, or social life. It is that mystics them-selves commonly say that their experience is ineffable, that words do not capture it and it can never be captured in words by its very nature. Does this problem arise for biologists who study cells? Do they complain that "cell" just doesn't capture the cellness of the cell? No, it's a non-issue. Do sociologists say that "group" just doesn't capture the groupness of the group? They might, but it wouldn't be a philosophical discussion of whether a thing called "group" exists and whether it can be captured in words, it would be a more pragmatic discussion of whether this is the best termi-nology to use to grasp this social phenomenon. It's left to philoso-phers to debate whether words do represent something separate called "reality." And that is an open and hotly debated question. So the same question of whether mystical states can be put into language, plain or otherwise, is an issue different from other areas of knowledge and significantly problematic for the legitimacy of mystical knowledge.

Mystics talk about realizing the Truth, the Godhead, or Real-ity. Wilber writes as if what mystics say they know—the Truth—is what they know. "These are direct apprehensions or illumina-tions—in a word, *direct spiritual experiences* (*satori, kensho, shaktipat, nada, shabd,* etc.)."[9] He gives a cross-cultural argument, rather than a philosophical argument, for why mystics do know the Truth. He argues that all the major mystical traditions' ultimate insight is the same. This is a resuscitation of the perennial philosophy, which states that the core insight of all the major mystical traditions is the same despite the differing languages, methods, and rituals used by the different traditions. By studying the major mystical traditions, Wilber claims to have extracted the basic four stage developmental sequence that all mystics pass through on their way to the ulti-mate realization. Each stage is a transcendence and inclusion of the previous stage leading to the ultimate integration of the One and the Many.

9 *SES*, p. 276.

Wilber further claims that only people who have had the relevant experience gain the requisite meaning and then can use the corresponding signifier.[10] Yet people use the words "absolute," "emptiness," and "nirvana" sensibly without ever having experienced their referent. There are many scholars of mysticism who use these terms and are understood. So they do have the requisite signified or meaning. One could object that, yes, people use the words sensibly, but they do not have the experience itself. But how do we know if people have had the experience themselves except by their claim that they have and the rightness of the words they use to describe it? For example, a spiritual practitioner I knew who was working with an "enlightened" spiritual teacher felt he had a glimpse of emptiness. The teacher said he was mistaken. The student disagreed, left that teacher, and found another teacher who confirmed his experience. Did he know emptiness? Did his teachers know emptiness?

Wilber writes of "Shankara, Vedanta's greatest philosopher-sage (Ramana Maharshi being one of Shankara's many descendants), and Shankara's Nondual (Advaita) Vedanta."[11] Yet Steven Katz, professor of religious studies, writes that

> Shankara does not shrink from entering into heated polemics with his Buddhist opponents about the meaning of the ultimate experience, understood by him in a non-personal monistic way, or again with his more theistically-minded Hindu colleagues—and of saying that they are wrong! They do not understand! They do not have the ultimate experience! —only he and *his* students find the ultimate experience because only they are properly equipped to find it.[12]

10 *SES*, pp. 270–273.

11 *SES*, p. 639.

12 Steven T. Katz, "Language, Epistemology, and Mysticism," in Katz, ed., *Mysticism and Philosophical Analysis* (New York: Oxford University Press, 1978), p. 45.

It is for each of us to decide, based on whether we are convinced of the mystic's experience, whether the mystic is enlightened or not. Wilber exaggerates the ability of mystics to confirm each other's experiences of the Ultimate when he says, "Zen masters talk about Emptiness all the time! And they know exactly what they mean by the words."[13] But transpersonal psychologist Jorge Ferrer reaches a different conclusion about this aspect of mysticism when he surveys the perennial philosophy. He writes that "*the esotericist idea that mystics of all ages and places converge about metaphysical matters is a myth that must be laid to rest.*"[14] He argues that disagreement rather than agreement better characterizes the dialogue among mystics in different traditions and in the same traditions.

This line of argumentation presents another problem for Wilber. He says his own study of mysticism confirms that there is a common core to all legitimate mystical practices. Yet since there is no one person who has actually experienced the ultimate state from within all the major mystical traditions, and only someone who has could speak reliably about them, how can one be sure that the core of all the traditions is the same? In his book *Integral Psychology*, Wilber again combats the view that there is not a common core to mystics' supreme experiences. He writes that

> Daniel P. Brown's extensive work on the cross-cultural stages of meditative development deserves special mention as being the most meticulous and sophisticated research to date. . . . What he and his coworker Jack Engler found is that "The major [spiritual] traditions we have studied *in their original languages* present an unfolding of meditation experiences in terms of a *stage model*"[15]

The italics are Wilber's. He emphasizes "*in their original languages*"

13 *SES*, p. 271.

14 Jorge Ferrer, "The Perennial Philosophy Revisited," *The Journal of Transpersonal Psychology*, Vol. 32 (1): 7-30, 2000, p. 20.

15 Wilber, *Integral Psychology*, p. 131.

presumably because it strengthens the reliability of the conclusion. It does, but it also acknowledges that what we are comparing
when we compare mystical states is the verbal report of the state.
Any cross-cultural analysis must be a textual, not an experiential,
analysis.[16]

The contention that people who have an experience of the Ultimate have some advantage over those who have not in debates
about the cross-cultural similarity or dissimilarity of mysticisms
may seem convincing, but when examined more closely really has
no bearing on such debates. According to Wilber's journals, his
non-dual experience dates from the later '80s. He wrote *The Spectrum of Consciousness* in the late '70s, and in it made his argument
for the perennial philosophy. Does his not having had the ultimate
mystical experience invalidate his argument? No. Let's assume he
did have by that time a glimpse of the Absolute, would it have
lent more credence to his argument? No, because to argue that all
the major mystical traditions lead toward the same ultimate state
and to argue that it requires experiential knowledge to evaluate
this requires one person to have achieved the Ultimate through all
the different traditions. There is no one like that. Even having a
glimpse of the Ultimate through one tradition doesn't lend greater credence to one's perennial philosophy arguments, because, as
Wilber himself had to do in *The Spectrum of Consciousness*, one still
has to read the relevant mystical texts and show with words that
the major mystical traditions all point to the same goal. It's the
validity of the textual analysis that is the ultimate determiner of
correctness, whether you're the Dalai Lama, Steven Katz, or Ken
Wilber. This is why it's a losing battle for mystics to try to prove the
ultimacy of their insight using the tools of rational debate. And it
is why mystics say that one must transcend language and conceptuality to realize the ultimate insight.

---

16 I discuss the textual, as opposed to the experiential, aspect of this issue in
chapter 7.

CHAPTER 5

SOCIAL EVOLUTION

According to Wilber, human society is evolving in a sequence of stages from simpler to more complex social formations and worldviews. The developmental pattern of *transcend and include* is as true of human social history as it is of the physical and biological worlds and individual consciousness. I will summarize Wilber's view of social evolution, place his view and his sources relative to current academic opinion, and then evaluate the validity of his view.

The earliest human tribes were hunter-gatherers who foraged for food; they are associated with a cultural worldview termed *archaic*. Their primitive worldview is animal-like in that the sensory and perceptual structures hold sway. Humans, at this stage, are motivated by survival instincts and urges, and consciousness is "largely undifferentiated, global, fused, and confused."[1] The development of sensory and perceptual skills is crucial for further human development; these structures endure and are integrated into the next developmental stage. But the undifferentiated worldview is transitional and is surpassed in the next stage. This level of development would correspond to the infant at a pre-linguistic stage of development.

1 Wilber, *Eye to Eye*, p. 275.

The *magical* worldview transcends and includes the basic structures of the archaic view. Here symbols and images hold sway in consciousness. There is no clear delineation between self and community, or between the human and nature. Animism is one example of a worldview in which inanimate and natural objects have living spirits that must be appeased in order to live successfully in the world. An autonomous ego has not differentiated itself from the body and, what Freud terms, "a bodyego"[2] characterizes the magical self-identity. The communal identity is characterized through kinship and sharing common ancestors.

The *mythical* worldview arises as magical kinship groups coalesce into larger social groupings. A new basis for social cohesion arose with a new social consciousness that bound individuals not to a kinship group but to a role in society and a place within a larger order that had a connection to God through the ruler. The individual identity has the capacity for concepts and rules, but the formal rules for manipulating those concepts have not yet developed, and there is a tendency to accept the reigning order because of tradition and the mythology that the order is ordained by God. Greek, Roman, and Christian myths are examples of explanatory stories that characterize the consciousness at this stage.

As empire building occurred across the globe mythic societies met, dominated, or were subjugated by other mythic societies. A clash of mythic divine truths occurred. This prompted the need to justify divinely given truths, and so a new mode of consciousness arose that allowed people to now apply formal operational principles—reasoning—to the concepts and rules that characterized the mythic consciousness. The rational worldview arose and brought with it new ways of organizing and justifying the social order. A new way to maintain social cohesion arose that was not dependent on the mythic stories but on political philosophies that articulated the ideas of individual rights, the rule of law,

2 *SES*, p. 165.

and secular government. These attributes characterize modern, advanced, industrialized societies.

In *SES*, Wilber uses Jurgen Habermas as a source for most of this story of social development. Habermas is a great scholar, and his depiction of social evolution is a compelling one, but it is not a summation of the orienting generalizations of the field, as Wilber implies it is. In fact, just the opposite is the case. Michiel Korthals, who's favorably disposed to the idea of societal development, assesses the status of the idea in the collection *The Philosophy of Development*:

> The idea of societal development has often been connected with the idea of progress, for better or worse. Both ideas have met with severe criticisms, especially in anthropology and sociology, and it would be an understatement to say that in the present intellectual climate the very notion of a universal, progressive, cumulating development of society is not very popular."[3]

In reference to the part of Habermas's work most used by Wilber, Thomas McCarthy, a sympathetic interpreter of Habermas's work and someone Wilber respects and quotes, states:

> The critical queries to which Habermas's conception of social evolution gives rise are legion. They begin with questions concerning the status of the ontogenetic theories upon which he draws, for the work of Piaget, Kohlberg, and the others is itself fraught with difficulties relating to fundamental concepts (for example, 'stage'), to fundamental assumptions (for example, that ontogenesis follows a developmental logic), and to methodological procedures (for example, the extent to which these approaches incorporate a substantive, culturally rooted bias); and they

3 Wouter van Haaften et al., eds, *Philosophy of Development* (Boston: Kluwer Academic Publishers, 1997), p. 163. An exception to the overwhelming trend is Michael Horace Barnes, *Stages of Thought* (New York: Oxford University Press, 2000).

extend to questions concerning the applicability of onto-
genetic models to social systems.[4]

Charles Tilly, the great sociologist and historian of modern
Europe, includes stage theories in his list of "the four pernicious
postulates" held over from nineteenth-century thinking. His post-
mortem describes "the general abandonment of optimistic development theories in the face of political criticism, of empirical dis-
confirmation, and of the elaboration of counter-theories featuring
dependency and/or world-economic processes [all of which have]
hastened the discarding of stage theories."[5]

Wilber also neglects to mention the dissenting views of Habermas's own colleagues. William Outhwaite notes "the failure of
[Habermas's] Starnberg colleagues . . . to get anything useful out
of a Piagetian analysis of law,"[6] which would be an important
part of a theory that asserts the parallel development of individuals and societies. Wilber quotes approvingly Habermas's description of the movement from tribal-magical organizations to mythic
organizations and notes Habermas's collaboration with Klaus
Eder. But at the time of Wilber's writing, Klaus Eder, whose work
Habermas relies upon, had already abandoned Habermas's assertion of an automatic link between learning processes and social
evolution in order to focus on the empirical reality of historical
individuals and groups.[7]

There is ample evidence of the highly debatable character of
Habermas's work, but showing that Wilber does not use the orienting generalizations of academia is not the same as evaluating

4 McCarthy, Thomas, *The Critical Theory of Jurgen Habermas*, (Cambridge: MIT
Press, 1985), p. 261.

5 Charles Tilly, *Big Structures, Large Processes, Huge Comparisons* (New York: Russell
Sage Foundation, 1984), p. 41.

6 William Outhwaite, *Habermas: A Critical Introduction* (Stanford: Stanford University Press, 1994), p. 62.

7 Ibid., p. 62.

the validity of Wilber's assertions. I will therefore examine the validity of his conception of social development.

Wilber's characterization of the magic, mythic, and rational stages often veers into caricature. This is because he makes facts fit a particular theoretical mold in order to preserve his theory. The theoretical mold requires that each later stage be progressively better than all previous stages. For example, when describing the morality and cognition of mythic society he emphasizes the most intolerant and aggressive aspect of it. He then contrasts this with the egoic-rational stage's world-centric morality of toleration. Wilber writes that for mythic-members the fact "that others would not buy their God sends agonies of proselytizing fury through their souls; infidels are *intolerable*, and can actually be killed in order to save them."[8] Yet the historical record provides examples of mythic societies that did not find that "infidels are *intolerable*." In Charles D. Smith's *Palestine and the Arab-Israeli Conflict* we learn that beginning in 638 C.E, Palestine under "Muslim rule was generally unobtrusive, to the point that construction of new churches and synagogues was permitted. Friction among the religious communities and the official sanction of violence against one group or another were infrequent."[9] So too, the subsequent "Ottoman society was pluralistic, similar in its inclusion of different peoples and faiths to its Byzantine and Arab predecessors but on a larger scale."[10] Smith quotes Braude and Lewis's *Christians and Jews in the Ottoman Empire: The Functioning of a Plural Society*, in which the authors write that "for all their shortcomings, plural societies did allow diverse groups of peoples to live together with a minimum of bloodshed. In comparison with the nation-states that succeeded them, theirs is a remarkable record."[11] Here we have large-scale, mythic cultures

8 *SES*, p. 243.
9 Charles D. Smith, *Palestine and the Arab-Israeli Conflict* (Boston: Bedford/St. Martin's, 2001), p. 9.
10 Ibid., p. 10.
11 Ibid., p. 10.

in which the society was more religiously tolerant than the suppos-edly more advanced "nation-states which succeeded them." Con-trary to Wilber's assertions, religious intolerance is not a necessary attribute of mythic societies.

The last part of Wilber's quote above, which says, "infidels are *intolerable*, and can actually be killed in order to save them," is remi-niscent of the famous quote from an American military officer in Vietnam who said that they had to "destroy that village in order to save it." That war, managed by "the best and the brightest" members of the egoic-rational stage, is just one example of the proselytizing democratic fury that was used to justify horrifically destructive campaigns by Europeans and the U.S. throughout the Third World in the nineteenth and twentieth centuries. And re-garding democracy, the supposedly more morally primitive, tribal societies actually had more democracy than our advanced indus-trialized societies, if we define democracy as actual participation in the distribution of resources and group decision making. The anthropologist John Bodley notes that "when the scale of human societies increases, at least five things are likely to happen," one of which is that "democracy declines, because decision making becomes more cumbersome and more concentrated."[12]

Degree of violence is another way of comparing the relative moral superiority of differing types of societies. Comparative studies of warfare in human history let us make some general statements about the levels of violence of different historical ep-ochs. Since that is a debate in itself, I will choose a source that is more likely to support Wilber's position that the more primitive the society the more violent it is. Patrick Frank summarizes Law-rence Keeley's research by stating that "there doesn't seem to be much to distinguish the willingness to go to war among human societies of whatever level of organization."[13] Keeley, in his book

12 John H. Bodley, *The Power of Scale* (Armonk, New York: M.E. Sharpe, Inc., 2003), p. 66.
13 Patrick Frank, "Whence the 'Noble Savage,'" *Skeptic*, Vol. 9, No. 1, p. 55.

War Before Civilization, which is presented as countering the prevailing "pacification of the past now epidemic in anthropology,"[14] states that "the larger sample of ninety societies . . . indicated that the frequency of war increased somewhat with greater political complexity," and concludes this comparison: "obviously, frequent, even continuous, warfare is as characteristic of tribal societies as of states."[15]

In *SES* we so often hear of the "warm embrace," "the relations of self-esteem," the universalizing tolerance of the egoic-rational societies as compared to the domination and suppression of dissenters in the mythic cultures. Conversely, someone defending the opposite thesis would speak of the stability, social cohesion, and small village life of the mythic societies, and contrast that with the greed, alienation, world war, genocide, and eco-cide of the egoic-rational societies. When evaluating such large, diverse historical categories as the mythic and the egoic-rational a writer can make history do what he or she needs it to do to suit his or her ideological interests. Wilber wants there to be progressive social development, and to that end offending facts are ignored or stated in such a way that their import is diffused.

We see an example of diffusing the import of offending facts when Wilber describes the development from a mythological to a rational worldview. According to Wilber, the establishment of the modern state and the global market economy, while "grounded in universalistic reasons," was "still tinged, initially, by remnants of imperialism, which indicated not an excess of reason but a lack of it."[16] The words "tinged" and "initially" are needed to minimize the imperialistic depredations of the Third World that have been an integral part of the rise to prominence and worldwide dominance of First World powers, allowing them to extract the resources they

14 Lawrence Keeley, *War Before Civilization* (New York: Oxford University Press, 1996), p. 23.
15 Ibid., pp. 32, 33.
16 *SES*, p. 178.

need to maintain their high standards of living. The economist Rajani Kannepalli Kanth summarizes the high costs to the colonized by the exploitative practices of the colonial powers, their moral superiors according to Wilber.[17] The extensive literature on the underdevelopment of the Third World demonstrates that the rise to power of the Western industrialized countries was causally intertwined with the impoverishment of the Third World countries.[18] The colonialism and imperialism characteristic of egoic-rational societies in the nineteenth and twentieth centuries is conveniently ignored when Wilber compares the mythic and the egoic-rational.

Another example of diffusing offending facts occurs when Wilber acknowledges what humanity has lost over the centuries. He acknowledges "mythic-membership does indeed provide, or can provide, an *intensely cohesive social order*," but, we learn, that is "principally because it can export disorder and excommunicate unbelievers."[19] So, although "it will appear that the emergence of rationality was somehow a massive loss of cultural meaning and social integration," that "is only true from an ethnocentric (or mythic-membership) bias."[20] A bias, we may assume, to which Wilber, ensconced in a rational-egoic society, is not subject.

Biases are hard to spot, the more so for those who have them. Wilber's world-centric (rational membership) bias is glaring to anyone who can step outside of it. A few examples demonstrate his stunning lack of political self-awareness and manifest the larger moral and theoretical beliefs that skew Wilber's view of social evolution. Wilber writes of contemporary society:

> The transformation from mythic-membership to egoic-rationality (and its perils) is already open to China, Cuba,

17 Rajani Kanth, *Breaking with the Enlightenment* (Atlantic Highlands, N.J.: Humanities Press, 1997), pp. 2–3.

18 See classic articles by Paul Baran and Andre Gunder Frank in Rajani Kanth, ed., *Paradigms in Economic Development* (Armonk, N.Y.: M.E. Sharpe, 1994).

19 *SES*, p. 242.

20 *SES*, p. 242.

Libya, Iraq, North Korea, Serbia, and any other social holon that wishes to surrender its mythic "superiority" and join the community of nations governed by international law and mutual recognition, that wishes to cease dissociating and splitting off from the free exchange of planetary consciousness, that wishes to reintegrate into a common world spirit and collective sharing of reason and communication and vision.[21]

Is it a coincidence that each of these countries was, at the time of Wilber's writing, an unofficial enemy of the U.S. and demonized by the U.S. as an outlaw or "rogue" state? Another view, not so credulous when it comes to the information gained from our "free exchange" of ideas, understands that from the point of view of the international community, powerful military nations like the U.S., Israel, and others are the world's flouters of international law. Cuba, for instance, while politically repressive internally, has been a leader of Third World nations for decades, all the while bearing the brunt of the U.S.'s international-law-defying terrorism against it.[22]

Of course, as a good liberal, Wilber acknowledges that "the United States, Japan, and an ominously emerging 'fortress Europe' [?] . . . are still distorting supranational exchanges for their own particular interests" and that these distortions do "not prevent or relieve them from continuing to search for more reasonable and equitable exchanges with the world community."[23] "*Continuing* to search?" Is that what the world's most powerful nations have been doing? It is if you see the world with a First World bias. The Third World understands that the most powerful nations want exchanges that favor them, and the degree to which they get them is a measure of their power. If the U.S. doesn't like something that the

---

21 *SES*, p. 204.

22 See Noam Chomsky, *Rogue States* (Boston: South End Press, 2000), especially the chapter entitled, "Cuba and the US Government: David vs. Goliath."

23 *SES*, p. 204.

U.N. or World Court decides, they ignore it. Why? Because they have the power to do so. Beyond the myths of world-centrism this is how the real world works. And are "equitable exchanges" what the U.S. has been seeking through the International Monetary Fund and the World Bank. Former World Bank senior vice president and Nobel Prize-winning economist Joseph Stiglitz exposed the destructive policies imposed by First World countries upon the Third World for the wealthier countries' benefit.[24]

Even if the reader disagrees with my alternative take on international relations, it is clear that there is a different view and that the view one holds depends upon one's values or biases. Another example demonstrates even more startlingly Wilber's First World bias because it so flies in the face of his humanitarian impulse. He is trying to show that "in the noosphere, right makes might," and says that "a war fought in part for antislavery motives [i.e., the Civil War] would grind up as many men in single battles as were lost in all of Vietnam: 51,000 were killed in three days at Gettysburg alone."[25] This is accurate, except for the small matter of the 1.5 million Southeast Asians who were killed by the "right makes might" capital of the world, the U.S. Wilber goes on to inform us that Gettysburg was "fought because the nation was 'dedicated to the proposition that all men are created equal.'" "All men," except for the forgotten Southeast Asians who could be killed in their own countries and not be counted as part of the "men" who died in "all of Vietnam." It's a testament to the political biases embedded in the U. S. doctrinal system that a good person like Ken Wilber would not even see the bias in these examples.

Lastly, to illustrate how development occurs such that wholes become parts within larger wholes while retaining their basic integrity, Wilber uses the example of Hawaii. Before it became a state and a part of the United States it was a whole unto itself, with all the prerogatives of sovereignty. After statehood it was no

24 Joseph Stiglitz, *Globalization and Its Discontents* (New York: W. W. Norton, 2002).
25 *SES*, p. 389.

longer a sovereign nation, but it was preserved within the larger sovereignty of the United States. Fortunately, as Wilber writes, all of its "basic structures were preserved in the new Union; none of them were destroyed or harmed in the least."[26] And this is certainly true as long as we maintain Wilber's big view of history. Unfortunately, those native Hawaiians who suffered military occupation, colonization, economic exploitation, and de facto second-class citizenship may not have the requisite level of consciousness to understand the big picture as well as Wilber can.[27]

In all of these examples it is the yellow, brown, and black people of the Third World who are forgotten; and this by a non-racist man with good intentions. This bias determines the content of Wilber's developmental story. While it appears as if the movement from archaic to magical to mythic to egoic-rational is a developmental progression, this is only true if you have already decided that the egoic-rational stage should be the destination point. Wilber's analysis is made to sound like a neutral description of the traits these diverse types of consciousness and associated moralities exhibit, but it's actually, when shorn of its false value-neutrality, an analysis that asks the question: In what ways are previous worldviews not yet like ours? Or, to phrase it differently, given that we are morally and cognitively superior, what are they lacking and what kinds of changes are required for them to eventually become like us?

---

26 *SES*, p. 52.

27 Poka Laenui, "Colonization in Hawaii," *Fourth World Bulletin*, Vol. 2, No. 3, July 1993.

CHAPTER 6

WESTERN HISTORY

The second half of *SES* is devoted to Wilber's reconstruction of Western history. While Wilber's strong background in psychology and mysticism give his views in those areas authority, his lack of background in history undermines his effort to tell a convincing story of the West. In *SES* Wilber constructs his history of Western civilization, and his more specific history of Western modernity, in the same way. He finds an author whom he uses predominantly, extracts from that author's complex and nuanced work two opposing forces that drive history, and then reifies that duality into two conflicting "camps" that engage in a life or death struggle for supremacy. The strong duality is then ripe for Wilber's transcending resolution.

Wilber uses Arthur O. Lovejoy to validate his story of Western history as a whole. He acknowledges in a footnote that Lovejoy, being a rationalist with no sympathy for mysticism, is not "an authority predisposed to support my position."[1] So Lovejoy, because he "is a hostile witness," is not biased in favor of Wilber's position, and this lends extra credence to Lovejoy's validation of Wilber's story of history. He's right that Lovejoy would have no sympathy for Wilber's Kosmic story and that this does make him a better

---

1 *SES*, p. 628, n. 1.

source. But what Wilber neglects to discuss is how the biases of his other main sources influence their history writing and predisposes them to *support* his position. Charles Taylor, W.R. Inge, and Paul Tillich share with Wilber a belief in the importance of a spiritual connection to the Ultimate and a scholarship affected by that spiritual connection. Their particular perspectives help Wilber tell a story of history in keeping with Wilber's vision of the Kosmos.

Wilber relies heavily on one source for his reading of Western history as a whole, Arthur Lovejoy's *The Great Chain of Being*.[2] Lovejoy's book, however, does not provide enough support for Wilber's sweeping historical generalizations. Wilber's first chapter on Western history is headed by a misquotation, the nature of which reveals his overall aim. The chapter begins with the oft-quoted saying from Alfred North Whitehead that "the European philosophical tradition . . . consists of a series of footnotes to Plato."[3] I've just quoted Whitehead's actual words from *Process and Reality*, where they first appeared. Wilber, on the other hand, chooses to broaden the quote by substituting the phrase "the whole Western philosophic tradition"[4] for the more limited "European philosophic tradition." Shortly thereafter he refers to the Whitehead quote again, and again the range of the quote expands when he substitutes "our Western tradition"[5] for the narrower "the whole Western philosophic tradition." Finally, three paragraphs later, the range of the quote inflates to its proper size when Wilber changes "our Western tradition" to the greatly enlarged "Western civilization." In the space of one page we've moved from "the European philosophic tradition consists of a series of footnotes to Plato" to

---

2 Arthur Lovejoy, *The Great Chain of Being* (Cambridge: Harvard University Press, 1964).

3 Alfred North Whitehead, *Process and Reality* (New York: Macmillan Press, 1929), p. 63.

4 *SES*, p. 319. Although it's true that many misquote Whitehead in this way.

5 *SES*, p. 319.

"Western civilization is a series of footnotes to Plato."[6] Besides being shockingly poor scholarship, this distortion raises an interesting question: Why does Wilber distort Whitehead's quote in just this way?

The answer is that Wilber wants a duality in Plato's thinking to be *the* essential duality driving Western civilization: "the dualism of which all other Western dualisms are merely an incidental subset."[7] To do that, the influence of Plato has to be inflated, hence the changes in Whitehead's aphorism. Wilber contends that the central duality driving Western civilization is between The Path of Ascent and The Path of Descent. According to Wilber, Ascenders believe that the True and the Good are otherworldly phenomena and that the goal of existence is to transcend the mundane world. Consequently, the world of material things and everyday life is devalued and seen as an obstacle to life's goal. The Descenders, by contrast, immerse themselves in the diversity of the mundane world. They see Ascenders as life denying and celebrate the world of everyday life. The materialism of the natural sciences is an example of a descending philosophy.

Yet Lovejoy's history, which Wilber uses to justify this claim, never uses these terms and is much more circumspect in its contentions. In *The Great Chain of Being* Lovejoy traces the history of the idea of the world as a harmoniously interconnected whole or a great chain of being. He starts with Plato, accurately quoting Whitehead's famous aphorism. Lovejoy agrees that Plato has had the greatest influence on the European philosophic tradition, but argues that an aspect of Plato's influence has been neglected. The modern interpretation sees Plato's philosophy as an ascending one concerned with the eternal Ideas of Truth, the Good, and Beauty, which transcend the temporal, mundane world. Lovejoy argues that there is another side to Plato. Plato also tried to explain the origin of and reason behind the mundane world. So Plato sought

6 *SES*, p. 320. These misquotations are retained in the second edition of *SES*.
7 *SES*, p. 321.

not only to explain the nature of the eternal forms, which transcend the world, he also described how they are related to the ever-changing or descended world in which we live. This interpretation coincides with the story of history Wilber wants to tell in which, starting with the Platonic source, there were both ascending and descending historical forces.

How valid, though, is Lovejoy's interpretation of Plato? In an analysis of Lovejoy's history of the great chain of being, Edward P. Mahoney concludes that "there seems little justification for turning Plato's Form of the Good into a God from whom all things flow, unless one wants to reaffirm Neo-Platonism or a variant of it. Lovejoy's reading of Plato's *Republic* and the *Timaeus* is simply mistaken."[8] This reaffirmation of Neo-Platonism is, not coincidentally, an interest of both Wilber and Lovejoy.

Wilber takes this duality of ascending and descending and reifies it, turning this contradiction of ideas into a battle of historical actors. He writes, "The Ascenders and the Descenders, *after two thousand years*, still at each other's throat—each still claiming to be the Whole, each still accusing the other of Evil, each perpetrating the same fractured insanity it despises in the other."[9] But does Lovejoy's text support this hyperbolic historicizing? Lovejoy does say that "the cleavage . . . between otherworldliness and this-worldliness" is "the deepest and farthest-reaching cleavage separating philosophical or religious systems," but he is much subtler than Wilber in his assessment of the effects of this cleavage. Lovejoy refers to otherworldliness as the

> "official philosophy" because nothing, I suppose, is more evident than that most men, however much they may have professed to accept it, and have even found in the reasonings or the rhetoric of its expositors a congenial and moving sort of metaphysical pathos—which is partly

8 Edward P. Mahoney, "Lovejoy and the Hierarchy of Being," *Journal of the History of Ideas*, Vol. 48, Issue 2 (Apr.–Jun., 1987), p. 229.
9 *SES*, p. 521.

the pathos of the ineffable—have never quite believed it, since they have never been able to deny to the things disclosed by the senses a genuine and imposing and highly important kind of realness.[10]

Instead of the "Ascenders and the Descenders . . . still at each other's throat," Lovejoy suggests that "otherworldliness" (or ascension) was "never quite believed" and acted as an "official philosophy." Lovejoy's nuanced and sober discussion of the main cleavage in "philosophical and religious systems" is transformed by Wilber into Western civilization's "battle royale" featuring

> warring opposites, . . . ascetic and repressive and puritanical Ascenders, on the one hand, who will virtually destroy "this world" (of nature, body, sense) in favor of anything they imagine as an 'other world'; and, on the other hand, the shadow-hugging Descenders, troglodytes each and all, who fuss about in the world of time looking for the Timeless, and who, in trying to turn the finite realm into an infinite value, end up distorting 'this world' as horribly as do the Ascenders, precisely because they want —and force—from 'this world' something that it could never deliver: salvation.[11]

This kind of overheated rhetoric would make the prudent Arthur Lovejoy cringe.

The second quote heading Wilber's chapter on the history of Western civilization is also suspect. It is a quote from Plato's Seventh Epistle or Letter, in which Plato says that insight into the Absolute is ineffable, and so "no treatise by me concerning it will exist or ever will exist."[12] Wilber interprets the quote to mean that Plato's message is an essentially spiritual one. He wants this Plato to exist because he wants the history of Western civilization to be

10 Lovejoy, *Great Chain of Being*, pp. 26–27.
11 *SES*, pp. 320–321.
12 *SES*, p. 319.

a spiritual story in which two spiritual forces battle for supremacy. This aspect of Plato's thought is important because Wilber wants to counter the heavily intellectual Plato that dominates Western philosophy. It is also a side of Plato that Arthur Lovejoy emphasizes in his book *The Great Chain of Being.* The quotes tendentiousness is further evidenced by its doubtful authenticity. In *The Cambridge Dictionary of Philosophy*[13] Richard Kraut, in his entry on Plato, writes, "the authenticity of the Seventh Letter is a disputed question."[14]

Lovejoy's history arises from a particular perspective. In a sympathetic review of *The Great Chain of Being,* Daniel J. Wilson, referring to Lovejoy's critics, acknowledges that

> by pointing to the emphasis on creation and the crucial importance of the Romantic period to Lovejoy's own thought, these critics have uncovered the source of the blinders Lovejoy wore when he approached certain texts. . . . When Lovejoy read Plato, Aristotle, Aquinas or any of the other thinkers whom he discussed, he was prepared to find in their work the unresolved, because irresolvable, contradiction between the two conceptions of [an otherworldly and this-worldly] God as creator. We should not be surprised that so careful a scholar as Lovejoy found what he was looking for.[15]

While Lovejoy does the bulk of the work in legitimating Wilber's history, he sometimes lets Wilber down. Lovejoy "passes over those systems—such as that of Plotinus,"[16] so Wilber uses a scholar sufficiently appreciative of Plotinus and continues constructing the history that fits his model. Wilber relies almost exclusively on

13 Robert Audi, ed., *The Cambridge Dictionary of Philosophy* (Cambridge: Cambridge University Press), 1996.

14 Ibid., p. 624.

15 Daniel J. Wilson, "Lovejoy's *The Great Chain of Being* after Fifty Years," *Journal of the History of Ideas,* Vol. 48, Issue 2 (Apr.–Jun., 1987), pp. 195–196.

16 *SES,* p. 628.

W. R. Inge's *Philosophy of Plotinus*,[17] which was published in 1918, thereby disregarding the seventy-five years of Plotinus scholarship published since then. Adam Fox, in his biography of Inge published in 1960, acknowledges that "in the last thirty years more has been learnt about third-century philosophers than Inge could know."[18] Wilber has described why he chose Inge's translation of Plotinus texts,[19] but he does not inform his readers that Inge was an unusual Plotinus scholar. He was unusual in that he was a mystic and a disciple of Plotinus.[20] Fox comments on "the discipleship which is so manifest in the author's attitude to Plotinus the master, as expressed in many places [in Inge's *The Philosophy of Plotinus*]."[21] Of course it is fine to choose scholars who are predisposed to validate your perspective, but when you hope to write an aperspectival integration of knowledge it vitiates your results, making them not aperspectival but decidedly perspectival.

Wilber spends three pages straining to convince us of Plotinus's importance. He gushes: "No other mystical thinker even approaches Plotinus"; "Even Saint Augustine stood back in awe"; "The superlative 'most divine' was always reserved for Plotinus."[22] Yet everyone knows that Plotinus is important, so why does he strain to convince the reader? It is because Plotinus's character, philosophy, and spiritual attainment are Wilber's ideal, and it is not enough for him that Plotinus embodies that ideal; Wilber needs Plotinus's life and work to be The Non-Dual Integration of

---

17 William Ralph Inge, *Philosophy of Plotinus*, (London: Longmans, Green and Co., 1929).

18 Adam Fox, *Dean Inge* (London: J. Murray, 1960), p. 137.

19 Ken Wilber, *The Eye of Spirit* (Boston: Shambhala Publications, 1998), pp. 355–358. Wilber liked: Inge's "deeper spiritual resonance," that Inge was "an accomplished philosopher," and that Inge *"believed in the truth of what Plotinus was saying."*

20 Inge, *Plotinus*, Vol. II, p. 219.

21 Fox, *Dean Inge*, p. 135.

22 This and the two previous quotes are from *SES*, p. 331. The first is Wilber quoting Inge.

The Duality of Western Civilization. Wilber's reasoning appears to be that if Plotinus is the greatest, then his accomplishment is the greatest. If that accomplishment can be described as the integration of a great dualism in Western civilization, then that dualism can be seen as the greatest dualism in Western civilization. Since convincing the reader of his interpretation of Western history would require a great deal more documentation, Wilber resorts to quoting some selected scholars saying that Plotinus was exceptional. But the fact that Plotinus was great and that his Neo-Platonism was very influential doesn't mean that Western civilization is essentially a titanic struggle between Ascenders and Descenders.

The way Wilber uses the concepts of Ascenders and Descenders creates a strange reification of ideas that sharply contrasts with a history writing that regards individuals and social groups as the historical actors. This reification of ideas is one of the main symptoms of viewing history from above and effaces the lives of flesh and blood people in favor of the bloodless interaction of rarified ideas. For example, take the rise of reason and science in opposition to the dominance of Christian religion and faith. Enlightenment reason and science are examples of descending approaches, while Christianity is an ascending path; a seemingly classic example of Wilber's central dualism. But is the nature of the conflict between these two sides essentially a battle between ascending and descending, with all other differences "incidental subsets" of that main duality? Were the power struggle and conflicting interests between differing political-economic groups incidental subsets of the larger duality? What of the role of population movements from the country to the city? Or technological changes? So much more goes into historical changes than is summed up in whether belief-systems can be characterized as this-worldly or other-worldly.

The difference between the other world and this world, or the sacred and profane, or ascenders and descenders, is certainly one useful way of interpreting the history of Western thought, but Wilber needs to have it be *the* duality of Western civilization so he

can justify his spiritual retelling of history and anticipate a transcendence that integrates the Ascenders and Descenders.

With the rise of Enlightenment reason and science in the eigh-
teenth century, the Descenders win out over the Ascenders. The
other-worldly, the Transcendent, and paths beyond this world
are labeled superstitions, myths, and illusions. Two descending
approaches to self and world arise and dominate. Wilber names
them "the Ego" and "the Eco." The Ego refers to those lines of
thought that remove the ego from the rest of the world and then
use that disengaged ego to gaze upon the world with an objective,
scientific eye. The scientific eye sees the world as a causal mechanism with interacting parts. The world is explainable and control-
lable through rational means. The ego is a free, rational entity
able to control its destiny amid the mechanical world of things
in which it exists. The relationship between this free ego and the
determined world remains problematic.

In contrast to the Ego, the Eco criticizes the Ego as too detached. The Eco says that the Ego reduces nature to a mechanical
thing and represses the life forces of sentiment and imagination
surging through both nature and man. The Ego's view represses
emotion in the name of reason and cuts European humanity off
from its proper place within the flow of life. This historical split
plays itself out today in the conflict between those who champion
instrumental reason and technology, and those who believe a new
ecologically connected outlook is needed to solve the problem of
humanity's relationship to nature.

Wilber's story of modern Western history is largely derived
from Charles Taylor's *Sources of the Self* and the first chapter of
Taylor's *Hegel*. In the course of his larger study, Taylor does refer
to what Wilber makes the central duality of modernity. Although
Wilber doesn't quote the following passage from Taylor, it sums up
Wilber's argument quite well. Instead of Wilber's neologisms Ego

and Eco, Taylor uses the conventional categories of instrumental reason and Romanticism respectively. He writes,

> Although the Romantic religions of nature have died away, the idea of our being open to nature within us and without is still a very powerful one. The battle between instrumental reason and this understanding of nature still rages today in the controversies over ecological politics. . . . One sees the dignity of man in his assuming control of an objectified universe through instrumental reason. . . . The other sees in this very stance to nature a purblind denial of our place in things. . . . The battle between these spiritual outlooks, which starts in the eighteenth century, is still going on today."[23]

Taylor's *Sources of the Self* is a brilliant historical work lauded by secularists like Quentin Skinner and Richard Rorty. The general view that the modern world has been characterized by a loss of religiosity, if not spirituality, seems undeniable. So why, if he relies on Taylor, is Wilber's telling of modern history problematic? It's because Wilber wants to use Taylor to say more than Taylor's work allows. Problems occur when Wilber goes beyond Taylor's more modest assertions and tries to use Taylor to validate his vision of modern Western history. There are three main problems. First, Wilber extracts this one duality between the Enlightenment and Romanticism and promotes it to the great dualism of the modern Western world. These two already large categories are subsumed within the even larger categories of the Ego and Eco, respectively. His overheated rhetoric turns them into the battling titans of modernity. "They were in fact locked into a battle royale that, in many ways, was the archbattle, and remains the archbattle, of modernity and postmodernity."[24] "The two camps, in other

---

23 Charles Taylor, *Sources of the Self* (Cambridge: Harvard University Press, 1989), p. 384.

24 *SES*, p. 433.

words, were completely and mutually incompatible (this they both happily—and aggressively—acknowledged)."[25] "The Ego camps and the Eco camps lined up as mortal enemies, each accusing the other, once again, of being the essence of Evil."[26] This attempt to create a dramatic antithesis between the "two camps" contrasts sharply with scholarship that questions both the division between the Enlightenment and Romanticism and the idea of a monolithic Romanticism. The historian Crane Brinton, writing in *The Encyclopedia of Philosophy* on "Romanticism," says,

> Both Enlightenment and Romanticism shared much—a belief in process, change, if not actually progress, a belief in the possibilities of manipulating the environment, indeed a fundamental and very modern relativism never really transcended in the search for eternal verities. Both, whatever their metaphysical position on the problem of determinism, in practice displayed a firm conviction that things not only change, but that they can be changed by human effort. Of many specific doctrines—primitivism, for instance, or individualism in ethics and politics—it is hard to decide whether they are more characteristic of enlightened or of romantic thought. [27]

In politics, Brinton writes, "Probably in the balance Romanticism has worked toward . . . much . . . that gets its start from the rationalists of the Enlightenment."[28] More recently, in his introduction to *Romanticism*, Aidan Day writes that

> many of the preoccupations that are frequently associated with Romanticism—a perception of the stultifying effect of an unthinking imitation of tradition, the emphasis on

25 *SES*, p. 432.

26 *SES*, p. 432.

27 Crane Brinton, "Romanticism," in Paul Edwards, ed., *The Encyclopedia of Philosophy* (New York: Macmillan Publishing Co., Inc., 1972), Vol. VII, p. 207.

28 Ibid., p. 208.

the political rights and the psychological capacities of the individual, the emphasis on feeling not to the exclusion of but *as well as* on reason, the emphasis on primitive simplicity and naturalness, on the importance of nature itself— were fundamentally Enlightenment preoccupations.[29]

Day also cites approvingly Wilber's purported source for his history of Ascenders and Descenders, Arthur O. Lovejoy, who, in his article "On the Discrimination of Romanticisms," counters the idea of a monolithic Romanticism when he writes "that any attempt at a *general* appraisal even of a single chronologically determinate Romanticism—still more, of 'Romanticism' as a whole—is a fatuity."[30]

The second problem with Wilber's Ego/Eco duality is his reification of these abstract categories. After setting them up as mutually exclusive concepts, Wilber allows them to take on the characteristics of living beings. We learn: that "the Ego and the Eco battle for the good life, doomed as they are to mutual repugnance"[31]; that it is "small wonder that both the Ego's view of nature as the fundamental reflected reality and the Eco's attempt to glorify nature as spirit would both meet in an absolute obsession with: sexuality"[32]; that "the Ego and the Eco . . . will remain forever the great Devil in the other's eyes"[33]; and that "however much they went at each other's throats, they were still fighting over the same anemic territory, the territory they both called 'nature.'"[34] When even a large conceptual category like Romanticism, which is a subset of Eco, contains many conflicting tendencies, how can one speak of something like Eco and Ego as having any sort of unified motivation or

29 Aiden Day, *Romanticism* (New York: Routledge, 1996), p. 76.

30 Arthur O. Lovejoy, *Essays in the History of Ideas* (Baltimore: John Hopkins Press, 1948), p. 252.

31 *SES*, p. 433.

32 *SES*, p. 472.

33 *SES*, p. 472.

34 *SES*, p. 468.

concerted action? It is a strange, grandiose anthropomorphizing of conceptual categories.

The third problem with Wilber's history is his de-spiritualization of Romanticism. He wants to see the Enlightenment and Romanticism as descending philosophies that have forsaken any ascending or transcending paths. Their abandoning of ascent leaves them with "flatland ontologies" (i.e., no conception of transcendence). While it does appear true that the Romantics did not have Wilber's version of spirituality, in which we develop through levels of consciousness and finally embrace the All, is that the only spirituality worthy of the name? Richard Tarnas writes in his *The Passion of the Western Mind* that

> religion itself was a central and enduring element in the Romantic spirit, whether it took the form of transcendental idealism, Neoplatonism, Gnosticism, pantheism, mystery religion, nature worship, Christian mysticism, Hindu-Buddhist mysticism, Swedenborgianism, theosophy, esotericism, religious existentialism, neopaganism, shamanism, Mother Goddess worship, evolutionary human divinization or some syncretism of these. Here the "sacred"remained a viable category, whereas in science it had long since disappeared. God was rediscovered in Romanticism—not the God of orthodoxy or deism but of mysticism, pantheism, and immanent cosmic process.[35]

Tarnas is saying that Romanticism included the very same types of spirituality that Wilber regards as countering the flatland ontology.

Bernard M.G. Reardon summarizes his study *Religion in the Age of Romanticism* as follows:

> The essence of romanticism—if determination of its 'essence' be possible at all—lies in the inexpugnable feeling that the finite is not self-explanatory and self-justifying, but

---

35 Richard Tarnas, *The Passion of the Western Mind* (New York: Ballantine, 1993), pp. 372–373.

that behind it and within it—shining, as it were, through it—there is always an infinite 'beyond', and that he who has once glimpsed the infinity that permeates as well as transcends all finitude can never again rest content with the paltry this-and-that, the rationalized simplicities, of everyday life. As William Blake puts it:

> To see a world in a grain of Sand,
> And a heaven in a Wild Flower,
> Hold Infinity in the palm of your hand,
> And Eternity in an hour.

Again and again in Romantic thought we encounter this sense of the coincidence of the finite and the infinite. In all things finite the infinite is present, latent, and the part is meaningless without the whole.[36]

While perhaps not reaching the transcendent heights that Wilber requires of it, Reardon's study demonstrates how integral an ascendant spirituality or other-worldliness was to Romanticism's great interest in nature and history's this-worldliness. This directly contradicts Wilber's characterization of it as mired in "flatland ontology."

Wilber's need to de-spiritualize the modern Descenders causes him to make statements that contradict his main source's central contentions. Whereas Wilber contends that the modern Descenders' "holistic flatland world left no point of insertion for the *subject with depth* (no room for interiors, for I's or we's, for genuine depth in any holons anywhere, animal, human, divine, or otherwise),"[37] Charles Taylor charts the historical growth of individual inwardness and the great self-exploration and discovery of depth that

36 Bernard M.G., Reardon, *Religion in the Age of Romanticism* (New York: Cambridge U. Press, 1985), p. 3.
37 *SES*, p. 431.

the unfolding of our modern history has allowed. Taylor writes that "only with the [Romantic-] expressivist idea of articulating our inner nature do we see the grounds for construing this inner domain as having *depth*, that is, a domain which reaches farther than we can ever articulate, which still stretches beyond our furthest point of clear expression."[38] Because this inner depth and self-exploration was not directed toward the only spirituality worthy of the name, all the depths of self Taylor so patiently charts, culminating in the modern Romantic-expressive self, are dismissed by Wilber as mere flatland ontologies, as having no depth.

While Wilber's source disagrees with him on the previous point, Wilber and Taylor do share an affinity of perspectives, which the historian Quentin Skinner describes. After listing some of Taylor's secular solutions to some of our modern ills, such as "reaffirming the values of everyday life," "the 'epiphantic' powers of art and literature," and "committing ourselves to a life of public and political activity," Skinner writes that

> Taylor's diagnosis of our ills, however, enables him to insist that none of this will be enough. As long as we limit ourselves to values and projects of this character, we shall still be operating entirely within the framework of 'a stripped-down secular outlook' (p. 520). This will prevent us from seeing that life is a quest, and that what we are in quest of, as part of 'our telos as human beings', is a scale of values that will 'command our awe', not merely our admiration or respect (p. 20). As Taylor repeatedly puts it, what we are looking for is something 'incomparably higher' than we can hope to find in any of our individual or even our communal enterprises.[39]

Taylor's spiritual aspirations do not leave his telling of history unaffected. "He incorporates the need for just such a the-

38 Taylor, *Sources of the Self,* p. 389.
39 Quentin Skinner, "Who are 'we'? Ambiguities of the modern self," *Inquiry,* Vol. 34, p. 146.

istic solution into his way of describing our civilization and its discontents."[40] Skinner writes that "it is sometimes hard to resist the suspicion that Taylor is prompting his leading characters to speak the lines that the thrust of his narrative imposes on them."[41] Since Taylor thinks a "theistic solution" is necessary for our contemporary society he, according to Skinner, secularizes Locke and Rousseau, two of the main originators of the descended Ego and Eco perspectives, in order to dramatize the contrast between a secular past and its effect on the present, and our need for Taylor's "theistic solution." Correcting Taylor's secularization of Locke and Rousseau, Skinner writes:

> As Locke explains at the start of the *Two Treatises*, his own view of how we learn our moral duties is that we do so by consulting the law of nature, the normative force of which is said to derive from the fact that it is also the will of God. Consider, similarly, Taylor's treatment of Rousseau, whom he presents as the leading harbinger of the romantic view that 'the inner voice of my true sentiments *defines* what is the good' (p. 362). Rousseau would surely have been no less horrified by such an interpretation, especially as the Savoyard Vicar expends so much eloquence in seeking to persuade us that the only reason why the voice of sentiment can hope to guide us is that it is at the same time the voice of nature and of God.[42]

Skinner also describes Taylor's "account of evolving consciousness,"[43] in which history's

> story is one of 'epistemic gain' (p. 313). A declared foe of relativism, [Taylor] goes so far in the opposite direction as to insist that the proper attitude to adopt in the face of our

40 Ibid., p. 146.
41 Ibid., p. 136.
42 Ibid., p. 136.
43 Ibid., p. 143.

own moral evolution must be strongly affirmative. Despite the barbarism of the present century, we should recognize that we have built 'higher standards' into 'the moral culture of our civilization' than ever before (p. 397).[44]

Just as Taylor believes that "the fullest 'affirmation of the human' can only be achieved with the aid of the divine," Wilber believes that it is the loss of any connection to the divine or ascension that has caused the Ego and the Eco camps to be mired in their "flatland ontology," which offers only the descending manyness of this-world, without the ascending oneness of the other-world. And, like Taylor, Wilber believes it is part of our "telos as human beings" to see "life as a quest" for spiritual realization. Wilber, in his description of the evolution of consciousness and his opposition to relativism, uses Kohlberg and Habermas to affirm a "strongly affirmative" vision of the West's moral culture. These affinities of perspective mean that in Taylor, as in Lovejoy in a different way, Wilber will find the history he is looking for.

This perspectival bias for a progressive history that Wilber and Taylor share results in the loss of loss. Wilber's history telling, while not deterministic, is strongly affirmative. The West's egoic-rational culture is, despite its faults, the morally highest development of human culture. It is a transcendence and inclusion of the essential social structures of the past. In Wilber's history you do not get the impression that anything essential was lost. It is a very un-tragic view of history and reflects Wilber's aversion to negativity and loss in general. Charles Taylor shares similar historical assumptions. Quentin Skinner contrasts Taylor's mode of intellectual history with a different mode of history that describes "the causal story." The causal story describes why particular conceptions of the self and morality disappeared in favor of other conceptions of the self and morality not because of a progressive developmental logic but because it was in the interests of certain social actors that they do

44 Ibid., p. 143.

so. Skinner uses the example of "the triumph of 'everyday' values centering on family life and the ethic of work"[45] that Taylor describes. Skinner describes how this shift of interest and values to the private sphere of home and family allowed absolutist rulers to concentrate more public power in fewer hands. On this view, new moral values win out not because they are better but because they meet the interests of those with the power to put them in place. The whole "Clausewitzian story of conflict"[46] is lost in Taylor's storytelling, and Wilber's use of it allows him to depict Western history as a transcendence and inclusion of all that came before. Skinner concludes that the causal story of history "makes us aware of just how much was lost as well as gained in the course of that process itself. Far from being 'distinct' and 'independent' in the way that Taylor maintains, the causal story tends to undermine the very moral he wishes to draw from his own account of evolving consciousness."[47]

Telling the history of Western civilization is a daunting task, even for a team of historians; so it's not surprising that Wilber's account should be problematic. While the division between this-world and other-world, or the sacred and the profane, is a useful duality for characterizing opposing forces in history—and more commonly in anthropology—the documentation that Wilber provides falls far short of proving his case that the conflict between ascending and descending forces is "the dualism of which all other Western dualisms are merely an incidental subset." In addition, the reader's doubt is enhanced by the reification of this duality into strange, personified forces that are said to be fighting "a battle royale" for supremacy. Wilber's hope for a grounded spirituality that integrates ascending and descending approaches is attractive, but he hasn't demonstrated that Western civilization is driven by those forces and heading towards that resolution.

45 Ibid., p. 144.
46 Ibid., p. 142.
47 Ibid., p. 145.

CHAPTER 7

POSTSTRUCTURALISM
AND POSTMODERNISM

Wilber's integral project can be read as a reaction to what he sees as the fragmenting effects of poststructuralism and postmodernism. Wilber tries to create one great Kosmic narrative that incorporates poststructural truths while not succumbing to the relativism and nihilism he diagnoses in extreme postmodernism. In contrast to his attempt to create one, great, all-encompassing story, poststructuralists emphasize that essential differences between people and ideas are effaced through totalizing historical metanarratives such as Wilber's. By extracting some concepts that can be associated with a poststructural perspective and incorporating them into his integral synthesis, Wilber avoids the fundamental challenges that poststructuralism poses to his system and to knowledge acquisition in general. Wilber's depiction of postmodernism is more varied than his picture of poststructuralism, but it too is limited. He sketches a view of postmodernism as dominating academia and culture, which I show is not the case.

POSTSTRUCTURALISM

Poststructuralism is a broad term for a loose agglomeration of theorists and ideas that arose in the mid-sixties as a reaction to the prevailing intellectual approach of structuralism. The structuralism of Claude Levi-Strauss, Louis Althusser, and Jacques Lacan was itself a reaction to the subject-centered philosophies of phenomenology and existentialism. Structuralism is a social scientific method that uncovers the universal individual and social structures that people unconsciously enact in their everyday behavior. For example, the myths told within given societies can be broken down into their elemental parts and the relationship between the parts mapped. These maps can then be compared cross-culturally and the deep structures of the human psyche revealed.

   Jacques Derrida became a central figure in the poststructural reaction to structuralism with his critique of Levi-Strauss.[1] His deconstructive method takes the very idea of "a structure" and shows how it is built on contradictions that it represses in order to appear consistent. The concept of "structure," like all concepts, derives its meaning not from a self-identity or a one-to-one correspondence to what it describes but from its subterranean relationship to what it is not. Structures are supposed to be fixed, motionless, and synchronic as opposed to the opposite qualities of play, systems, and the diachronic. But, Derrida would contend, "structure" derives its very sense from both what it is and what it is not. It is dependent for its meaning on the other.

   Derrida's *anti-method* method (i.e., a method that is used to show what is problematic in other peoples' methods) does not provide a clear-cut positive program to replace what has been deconstructed. Likewise, Michel Foucault, in his poststructural phase, used a method of social history writing that told a version of the past while simultaneously raising the question of the very possibility of

---

1 Jacques Derrida, "Structure, Sign and Play in the Discourse of the Human Sciences," in *Writing and Difference* (Chicago: University of Chicago Press, 1978).

history writing. He adapted Nietzsche's concept of the genealogy to trace the convoluted twists and turns that particular ideas and practices go through as now this or that group appropriates them for their differing needs. The idea of history as genealogy undermines the positive evolution and developmentalism that Wilber promotes.

The poststructural critique asserts a number of radical propositions: differing perspectives are not reconcilable into some larger scheme; no unproblematic intellectual foundations validate knowledge-claims; the natural sciences offer no epistemological certainty; words themselves—the tools of thinking and writing—are not transparent windows on reality; our era's taken-for-granted humanism, which places "man" at the center of all things, is an intellectual and historical fiction; and metanarratives, which attempt to describe the history of humanity or existence, crush differences and are exclusive while trumpeting integration and inclusion.

Wilber sidesteps this critique and reduces it to the idea that poststructuralism essentially agrees with his holarchic view because "a close look at their work shows that it is driven precisely by a conception of holons within holons, of texts within texts within texts (or contexts within contexts within contexts), and it is the sliding play of texts within texts that forms the 'foundationless' platform from which they launch their attacks."[2] Wilber's "contexts within contexts" refrain undermines the radicality of the poststructural critique. Poststructuralists aren't just showing that there are always contexts within contexts. Poststructuralism is a multifaceted critique that throws the essentials of Wilber's entire system into question. His system exemplifies the intellectual excesses that poststructuralism arose to attack: the centrality of Man; the simplistic historical story-telling; the unproblematic use of language as transparent conveyor of truth; the purported creation of an inclusive system of integrated partial truths that denies profound differences; his unexplained role as teller of the Kosmos's story; the

2 *SES*, p. 38.

essentializing of the subjective realm in the face of the decentering of the subject in structuralism and deconstruction. All of this cuts to the heart of Wilber's project, but when he periodically mentions poststructuralism he repeats a "contexts within contexts" mantra and counters any relativistic difficulty by saying these "sliding contexts" slide in regular patterns.

Wilber extracts one piece of the poststructural critique—the contextualized nature of knowing—and reinterprets it in such a way that he can use it as an authoritative source to confirm an aspect of his system. This gives the impression that he is integrating another partial truth into his inclusive synthesis. He thereby avoids the most difficult philosophical questions in contemporary thought.

Constructivism and Mysticism

The poststructuralists' emphasis on the mediation of knowledge by language has engendered an intellectual approach called *constructivism*. Constructivism suggests that if language mediates our knowledge of the world and is a historically contingent, socially constructed, cultural variable, then we can conceive of our knowledge of the world as a construction rather than as a discovery of what is simply there. This is why Wilber sometimes refers to "creating/discovering" knowledge. The use of the word "creating" is his nod to the poststructural critique.

Constructivism creates a great obstacle for Wilber. He needs to be able to argue that mystical insight delivers knowledge of the spiritual core of existence. In Wilber's view, this Spirit is the animating force and telos of the Kosmos. Humanity is on an evolutionary journey to the realization of Spirit. Spirit's revelation and embodiment by man would be the culmination of the Kosmos's unfolding. The most advanced four stages of consciousness are the proper unfolding of human spirituality, culminating in the realization of the non-dual essence of existence. This deepest of human insights into the nature of Reality is confirmed to be as Wilber describes it because the separate mystical traditions have all found the same Truth at the core of existence. This belief in a common core to mystical experience is the part of the perennial philosophy to which Wilber still adheres.

The philosophy of mysticism was dominated by the perennial philosophy view for many decades. With the rise of the linguistic turn in the twentieth century, deconstruction and constructivism brought a new critique and understanding to the philosophy of mysticism. Steven Katz's *Mysticism and Philosophical Analysis* is the best-known collection of constructivist or anti-perennial philosophy views on mysticism. Constructivists argue that it is language that allows us to have a conscious experience of what we conceive of as reality. Language arises from socio-cultural contexts, one aspect of which is religious tradition. Mystical practices are embedded within the particular worldviews of various religious traditions. These contexts determine the content and form of the mystical experiences that spiritual practitioners have. In contrast to the perennial philosophy, which sees the similarities between seemingly different mystical traditions, constructivism demonstrates the essential differences between differing traditions through a close analysis of the writings of mystical practitioners.

While within academia Katz's book was being published and the philosophy of mysticism was moving away from the perennial philosophy tradition, outside academia Wilber was just making a name for himself with his updating of the perennial tradition in his successful first book, *The Spectrum of Consciousness*. Part of Wilber's task in that book was to resurrect the perennial tradition by arguing that the differing experiences of Reality reported by the world's mystics are actually pointing to the same Reality, and so serve to confirm their individual approaches. If all the major traditions keep seeing the same Reality, that is evidence for the scientific validity of the approaches. Katz's constructivism stands in the way of Wilber's validating mysticism as an actual perception of Reality and as the pinnacle of evolution's movement towards manifesting Spirit.

In two long footnotes Wilber tries strenuously to defeat the constructivists. In so doing he twists himself into such an intellectual knot that it is hard to disentangle his thinking. This in itself is an indication of trouble because Wilber is generally a clear and consistent writer; if his writing is this confused, then something probably isn't working. Wilber's initial statement of Katz's position is mostly accurate. All experiences are mediated by language, cultural background, mental concepts, etc. Since all experience is mediated, it cannot be claimed that mystics attain a direct, unmediated, experience of Reality. Wilber quotes Katz: "there are NO pure (i.e., unmeditated) experiences."[3] Wilber misleadingly omits that Katz states that the previous statement is his "single epistemological assumption."[4] Katz does not claim it is an absolute truth. By failing to mention this Wilber can later claim that Katz contradictorily states that it is absolutely true that there are no absolute truths and gets caught in the relativist self-contradiction paradox.

Wilber also overstates the degree to which Katz does not allow for cross-cultural similarities. He describes their position as maintaining "there can be no commonalities (or cross-cultural similarities) in mystical experiences."[5] This is too strong a statement of the constructivists' position. They can certainly allow "similarities." It is *identities* that they say we cannot be sure of. Wilber needs to exaggerate the constructivist position on this point in order to catch them later through an argument he has devised to counter the "no commonalities (or cross-cultural similarities)" position they have tendentiously been assigned.

In beginning his response Wilber surprisingly tries to out-constructivize the constructivists by asserting that they do not go far

3 *SES*, p. 599.

4 Steven Katz, "Language, Epistemology and Mysticism" in *Mysticism and Philosophical Analysis* (New York : Oxford University Press, 1978), p. 26.

5 *SES*, p. 599

enough. They, he says, make a distinction between raw experience and how it gets mediated by language, culture, etc. But since "every holon—and therefore every experience—is always already situated, mediated, contextual,"[6] the whole experience/meditation dichotomy breaks down. "Everything is always already *a* context *in* a context."[7] Wilber appears to be saying that by even using the concept of experience the constructivists undermine their assertion of total mediation, because it is all mediation. This kind of radical deconstruction is quite suggestive, but it is not a position that Wilber adopts.

Wilber then launches into a convoluted argument that ends in a contradiction. After having said that "every experience . . . is always already situated, mediated, contextual," and that "it is not that 'original experiences' arrive to be reworked by mental concepts; the original experiences are not original,"[8] he then says, a page later, that "in short, experience is immediate prehension of whatever mediated contexts are given, and that is why all experience is *both* pure (immediate) and contextual."[9] Wilber is contradictorily asserting that, on the one hand, experience is wholly mediated and, on the other hand, has elements of mediation and unmediation.

Wilber seems to think that mediation means separation and that if all is mediated we could not know anything without a point of immediacy or touching. He writes, "At the moment of touch, there is no mediation; if there is mediation, there is no touching."[10] But mediation needn't be thought of like this. Mediation is generally understood as the way in which we know or touch things. For example, the mass media is the filter through which we get the news and know what is occurring. Yet because it is composed of

6 *SES*, p. 600.
7 *SES*, p. 600.
8 *SES*, p. 600.
9 *SES*, p. 601.
10 *SES*, p. 600.

interested institutions that have a variety of agendas it is arguable that it never tells us what is really going on.

Wilber then leaves off with this line of attack and returns to his old standby, the self-contradiction argument. "Katz claims that *all* experience is mediated and that this is true for *all* cultures . . . thus he is claiming to be in possession of a non-relative truth that is true cross-culturally and universally."[11] Wilber concludes that Katz, like all strong constructivists, contradicts himself. This argument is easily countered though. Matthew Bagger argues that Katz's "assumption" or "intuition" need not be understood as an *a priori* assumption or absolute proclamation made before the facts. It can be understood as an *a posteriori* working hypothesis that will rely for its validity upon the empirical evidence Katz adduces in support of his view.[12] The works Katz has collected in his three anthologies of writing on mysticism are, in part, an effort to show the efficacy of that assumption for mysticism studies. If a scholar wants to argue against the constructivists' view, he or she must show how these empirical analyses of differing mystical texts are faulty.[13]

Wilber then twists the argument in a strange way in order to attribute an even more extreme claim to the constructivists. Through a number of unjustified leaps in argument he claims that the constructivists are in the position of denying that "individuals from different cultures (or even the same culture) . . . [can] even talk

---

11 *SES*, p. 601.

12 Matthew Bagger, "Ecumenicalism and Perennialism Revisited," *Religious Studies*, 27, pp. 399–411.

13 A recent entry into this debate that should be of interest to those wanting counterarguments to constructivism is Paul Marshall's *Mystical Encounters with the Natural World* (Oxford: Oxford University Press, 2005). Marshall bypasses Wilber's and the constructivists' use of mystical texts and instead uses accounts of spontaneously occurring spiritual experiences of bliss, expansive love, Oneness, and the like. He sees a commonality among these experiences as suggestive of the validity of the perennial philosophy's emphasis on a common core to mystical experience, but claims they avoid social, cultural, and historical mediation because the people having these experiences were not doing any spiritual practices and had no knowledge of mystical traditions.

about *anything.*"[14] Because the constructivists must claim that there are no "transcendental signifieds" (i.e., no shared supra-linguistic understandings that transcend the signifiers we use in spoken and written communication), they cannot account for the fact that people communicate at all, claims Wilber. In other words, there must be some trans-linguistic common ground that people share (i.e., a transcendental signified) in order for people to be able to translate their language into another person's language. In support of this, Wilber claims that even Derrida, the intellectual father of constructivism, admits there are transcendental signifieds. This is surprising because it runs counter to Derrida's famous statement: "There is nothing outside the text"—no signifieds that escape the play of signifiers. Wilber is even able to find a quote where he thinks Derrida affirms the existence of the transcendental signified. However, in the quote and its context Derrida is clearly arguing for the opposite of what Wilber says he is. He quotes Derrida, adding his own brackets: "This does not prevent it [the transcendental signified] from functioning, and even from being indispensable within certain limits. For example, no translation would be possible without it."[15] Derrida appears to be arguing for the necessity of a transcendental signified, but when the relevant page in the book by Derrida from which Wilber quotes him is consulted we find that the "it" which Wilber says refers to "the transcendental signified" actually refers to "this opposition or difference" between "the signifier and the signified."[16] Derrida is actually showing his agreement with Katz when in the same section he writes

---

14 *SES*, p. 601.

15 Quoted with bracketed clarification by Wilber from Jacques Derrida, *Positions* (Chicago: Chicago University Press, 1981), p. 20, in *SES* p. 602.

16 Derrida, *Positions*, p. 20. Just to be clear the entire quote reads: ". . . nor is it a question of confusing at every level, and in all simplicity, the signifier and the signified. That this opposition or difference cannot be radical or absolute does not prevent it from functioning, and even from being indispensable within certain limits—very wide limits. For example, no translation would be possible without it."

"a 'transcendental signified,' . . . in its essence, would refer to no signifier, would exceed the chain of signs, and would no longer itself function as a signifier."[17] In other words, it's outside the verbal loop. There is no way to refer to a transcendental signified because there can be no signifier attached. This is the same argument that mystics make when they say their transcendent experiences are ineffable. Their transcendent experience cannot be put into words; their transcendent signified has no signifier. Katz writes: "It is *not* being argued either that mystical experiences do not happen, or that what they claim may not be true, only that there can be no grounds for deciding this question, i.e., of showing that they are true *even* if they are, in fact true."[18] The mystics may be touching Reality, but we linguistically-bound beings cannot know whether they do or not.

On two other occasions Wilber uses Derrida to counter Katz and makes reference to this one misinterpreted quote as his justification for doing so.

The problems Derrida poses for Wilber go beyond his mistaken interpretation of Derrida's words. At many key points in the text, Wilber relies on Saussure's distinction between the signified and the signifier, assuming the distinction is unproblematic. But one of the crucial deconstructive moves that Derrida makes is to deconstruct that very distinction. Derrida writes,

> If this difference [between signified and signifier] is never pure, no more so is translation, and for the notion of translation we would have to substitute a notion of *transformation*: . . . We will never have, and in fact have never had, to do with some "transport" of pure signifiers from one language to another, or within one and the same language, that the signifying instrument would leave virgin and untouched.[19]

17 Derrida, *Positions*, pp. 19–20.
18 Katz, "Language, Epistemology and Mysticism," p. 22.
19 Derrida, *Positions*, p. 20.

In other words, the spoken and written words we use always leave their marks on the translations made, and we never gain a pure unmediated idea of what the linguistic other says. Just as Katz argues.

Derrida's poststructural critique of Saussure is problematic for Wilber in another way. His deconstruction of the very distinction between signifier and signified that Wilber uses demonstrates that the two are not really distinct entities but necessary ingredients of each other. Can we imagine a signified—a pure concept—by itself? Think of the signified *dog*. Isn't there always the signifier—the image or word—"dog" present? Alternatively, can there be a signifier without a signified? One might say, yes, there are many signifiers—heard or written words—of which we don't know the meaning or signified; they are signifiers without signifieds. Yet when you look that word up in a dictionary, of what does its definition—meaning or signified—consist but a bunch of signs—signifiers and signifieds—strung together? So that meaning or signified you don't know is actually a bunch of signifiers and signifieds and not a pure, isolable meaning. It's just a trick of language that makes you think it is a pure meaning, because we commonly say, "I don't know what that word means (don't know its signified)." This is Derrida's critique of Saussure's description of the sign and just one of the problems Wilber encounters when he uses it.

Wilber's transformation of Derrida into an intellectual ally, against the evidence of the very quotes he is using, to make his case shakes one's confidence in Wilber as a scholarly reporter. Wilber unconsciously manifests his displeasure with his own arguments when he keeps repeating them and resorts to silly invectives. In summing up Katz's position in general and his relation to Habermas in particular, Wilber writes that

> Katz's position is a blunder of half-baked neo-Kantian aphorisms, pressed into the service of a deconstructive atmosphere of self-contradictory (and self-congratulatory) rhetoric. It is shot through with aperspectival mad-

ness, the dominant form of intellectual insanity for the postmodern mind. As therapia, let Katz answer Habermas; we'll talk with the winner.[20]

But not if it's Katz; him we'll misrepresent to serve our own purposes. A similar example occurs toward the end of the book. Wilber refers to the poststructural literary critic Stanley Fish as "that dimmest of the postmodern dim bulbs."[21] People call Stanley Fish a lot of names, but I have never heard anyone, not even those who strenuously disagree with him, call him a dim bulb. He may be wrong, but he *is* brilliant.

Wilber resorts to these kinds of silly statements because he senses that he really can't defeat his opponents with superior arguments. He hides, from the reader and himself, behind a discourse of confident triumphalism as the deep problems poststructuralism poses for his thinking are denied. The questions and problems raised by the poststructural critique go to the heart of Wilber's synthesis: Can one speak truth to power if truth is a construction of power? Should the social and natural sciences be seen as discovering or creating knowledge? In what sense are differing worldviews of historical epochs incommensurable with each other? How do we legitimize truth-claims when there appears to be no foundation from which to legitimize truth? How is the idea of the subject a social construction? Are metanarratives defensible anymore?

Wilber's use of Nagarjuna offers an important illustration of a number of the problems with advances in poststructuralism that I have just explained. Alongside Plotinus in the West, Nagarjuna in the East stands as an exemplar for Wilber of both mystical insight and philosophical excellence. Of Plotinus and Nagarjuna, Wilber writes: "Thus, around the world, East and West, North and South—it is only a slight exaggeration to say that all Nondual

---

20 *SES*, p. 603. The last sentence was excised in the second edition of *SES*.
21 *SES*, p. 722. This line too was removed from the second edition.

roads lead to these two most extraordinary souls, world heroes in the truest sense."[22]

As is often the case with Wilber, the scholar he uses to derive and justify his interpretation is problematic. Wilber uses T.R.V. Murti's study *The Central Philosophy of Buddhism* as his authority on Nagarjuna. Murti's study was published in 1955 and belongs to what Andrew Tuck, in his study of Nagarjuna scholarship,[23] places in the second of four phases of western Nagarjuna scholarship. Wilber extols Murti's study as "generally regarded as the finest treatment of Nagarjuna in English."[24] While he does acknowledge drawbacks and some disagreements with Murti's interpretation, he neglects to inform the reader of the large debate surrounding Nagarjuna interpretation. In Tuck's study we learn that the type of interpretation that Murti and those like him practiced has been criticized by recent poststructural interpreters. These recent interpreters point directly to an ambivalence and contradiction in Murti's Nagarjuna, centering on the very point that Wilber accepts uncritically from Murti. That point is the status of the Absolute in Nagarjuna and its relation to the relative or conventional world of everyday life.

Nagarjuna used skeptical questioning and argumentation to demonstrate the inadequacy of all views of the nature of reality. He showed that the world of conventional reality, which we all share, and the absolute world claimed by mystics to be hidden behind it are both empty of inherent existence or essence. Nagarjuna did not assert the view that there was nothing there, for this would be another view. He claimed that all existent things are empty of a persisting substance, including the very emptiness used to describe reality's essence. Left with no thing to grasp, nor even an idea of nothingness to grasp, the spiritual practitioner is

---

22 *SES*, p. 639, n. 7.

23 Andrew Tuck, *Comparative Philosophy and the Philosophy of Scholarship* (New York: Oxford University Press, 1990).

24 *SES* p. 630, n. 2.

freed from the delusion of a view or substance to hold onto. The experience of freedom from such attachment is the way to Buddhist liberation.

Wilber, who says he has an experiential insight into the nondual or empty nature of reality, is at great pains not to reify that insight and to convey how it is unutterably unlike what words can express. He, like Murti, wants to fully appreciate the ineffability of the Absolute, but still wants there to be some sort of transcendental something that can act as a referent or Ultimate. But influenced by Murti, and with his own need to have the mystic's transpersonal experiences thought an advance over the personal experience of the modern consciousness, he still preserves the non-dual as a something that provides a foundation and a telos for his intellectual project. This use of Murti ignores the large Nagarjuna scholarship of the last fifty-five years and misleads the reader by making it seem as if the weight of academic scholarship supports Wilber's position. But when we consult that recent scholarship we find subtle interpretations of Nagarjuna's philosophy deeply influenced by the very poststructural thinking that Wilber criticizes and, supposedly, integrates. This contemporary scholarship comes to the surprising conclusion that Wilber's spiritual and philosophical exemplar propounded a *non*-self-refuting relativism.

Tuck explains that Murti was caught in a dilemma. He wanted to rescue Nagarjuna from the charge of nihilism that the scholarship previous to his had leveled at Nagarjuna's philosophy, but he also wanted to be true to the radically skeptical nature of Nagarjuna's argumentation. While Murti could claim that Nagarjuna asserts no view of his own, he had to argue, to counter charges of nihilism, that there was some sort of absolute in Nagarjuna's philosophy. Wilber follows Murti in asserting that there is an ineffable something, which one realizes as the empty essence of reality, while trying his hardest not to turn it into a thing. Later Nagarjuna scholarship, however, influenced by contemporary analytic and continental philosophy, feels no compunction in dispensing with talk of an absolute, because they have no fear that nihilism need result. But these scholars, not averse to relativism as Wilber is, can acknowledge Nagarjuna's relativism.[25]

Spiritually, Wilber basks in the paradoxical nature of Nagarjuna's philosophy, and realizes fully that any description of the Absolute, even a negative one, deludes as it seeks to clarify. But intellectually, he feels the need to defeat what he sees as a rampant and destructive relativism, and so must rail against it while having no way to avoid it since the bases of his intellectual system are as subject to it as any intellectual system. Jay Garfield's interpretation (as well as others)[26] demonstrates that a poststructurally informed interpretation can realize the relativistic qualities of Nagarjuna's thought without the dire consequences that Wilber imagines.

POSTMODERNISM

Poststructuralism is one aspect of what may be a larger societal shift called postmodernism. Postmodernism is a new cultural, social, and economic shift in Western societies, in which fundamental aspects of the older modern world have changed to such a degree that a new historical world is upon us. But that the phenomenon of postmodernism even exists, let alone what its nature is, is highly debatable and it has spawned an enormous literature mainly in social and cultural studies.[27] Wilber takes for granted that our current social world is postmodern, but, unlike those who try to describe and explain this world, he tends to think of postmodernism as naming a worldview or, more specifically, a belief about the nature of knowledge. For him the "ism" on the end of

25 See chapter 9 for my views.

26 Jay Garfield, *Empty Words* (Oxford: Oxford University Press, 2002). See also C.W. Huntington, *The Emptiness of Emptiness* (Honolulu: University of Hawaii Press, 1989).

27 See Fredric Jameson's classic account in "The Politics of Theory: Ideological Positions in the Postmodernism Debate," *New German Critique*, No. 33, pp. 53–65.

the word postmodernism suggests a belief-system like the words
Marxism or Judaism. While postmodernism is not such a belief-
system, it is true that accompanying the reports of a change to a
postmodern culture are descriptions of a change in philosophical
assumptions about knowledge. It makes sense that Wilber would
see this one aspect of postmodernism and emphasize its importance. His project is defined as an attempt to weave together the
world's scientific knowledge and create a vast integral synthesis.
So his concentration on postmodernism as a kind of knowledge
makes sense. However, since he's also trying to describe a societal
shift as a shift in consciousness he needs to appreciate the current
understandings of what society is like. This may be what he will
do in volumes II and III of his *Kosmos Trilogy*. For now, his understanding of postmodernism is quite thin and is designed to make
it fit within his larger vision regardless of whether it captures postmodernism or not.

Wilber describes three insights of postmodernism that when
taken to extremes create problems. He tries to incorporate these
insights while identifying and criticizing the extremes, and offering
a remedy through his integral synthesis. First, postmodernism has
shown us that reality is a construction as well as something that is
given. Its emphasis on the degree to which interpretation affects
our description of reality is an advance over modernity's unthink-
ing realism. This emphasis on interpretation has countered the
subtle reductionism of modernity's emphasis on the right hand
side of the holarchy, thereby promoting the integrity of the left
hand side, the knowledge that is dependent on interpretation to
be known. This insight into the constructed nature of knowledge
Wilber terms *constructivism*.

The second insight of postmodernism, for Wilber, is that the
meanings that we interpret to understand the world are context-
dependent. Language and its meaning are not simply derived from
a one-to-one correspondence with the things in the world. Meanings are intersubjective creations that arise from nested personal,

social, cultural, and material contexts. There is no ultimate context that is the guarantor of the one proper meaning, because these contexts are boundless. Wilber terms this truth of postmodernism *contextualism*.

Thirdly, because no context is ultimate there is no one perspective that is ultimately privileged. A particular type of relativism prevails. Wilber sees one of the great achievements of postmodern consciousness as pluralism, or the respect for multiple perspectives. So in postmodern thought there is a great emphasis on difference and the need to respect the *other*. He terms this *integral-aperspectivalism* borrowing the term from Jean Gebser.

Each of these understandings is an historical advance over the modern rational consciousness and allows a further advance in consciousness beyond the postmodern. But postmodernism has a dark side. Each of these three advances has been taken too far by some, and the resulting extremism has dire consequences for society's evolution if not corrected.

Constructivism, or recognizing the role interpretation plays in our knowledge of the world, has been taken to extremes by those who say there is nothing but interpretation and deny reality to the right hand side of the holarchy. Wilber writes that "objective truth itself disappears into arbitrary interpretations."[28] An example of this is Derrida's famous quote about there being nothing outside the text.

Contextualism, or the boundlessness of contexts, can combine with the insight into the relativity of perspectives and lead to a destructive relativism and nihilism in which no perspective is thought to be any better than any other. The aperspectivalism that recognizes the legitimacy of all other perspectives degenerates into an "aperspectival madness" in which it is thought no ranking or hierarchy of perspectives is possible. This extreme relativism effaces all depths because the depths of one perspective can be seen as the mere surface of another. For example, the depths of individual

28 Wilber, *Integral Psychology*, p. 163.

consciousness can be seen as a socially created illusion of modernity and nothing more than crisscrossing societal forces. When everything known becomes a linguistic construction everything is reduced to the surface of the text. Just as modernity effaced individual depths through scientific reductionism, postmodernity effaces depths through a linguistic reductionism.

There are a number of problems with this critique of postmodernism. Wilber accuses extreme postmodern thinkers of denying reality to the objective world and of asserting that no view is better than any other, contradictorily assuming that their view is better then all others; yet he never quotes any postmodern thinker asserting these extreme views. In a *New York Times* op-ed piece after the 9-11 attacks, Stanley Fish—who Wilber labels an extreme postmodern thinker—explicitly denies anti-realism and moral relativism and explains why. He writes, "The only thing postmodern thought argues against is the hope of justifying our response to the attacks in universal terms that would be persuasive to everyone, including our enemies."[29] Wilber, commenting on that op-ed piece, lazily reasserts his relativist self-contradiction criticism and conveniently avoids Fish's quite reasonable distinctions.[30] Wilber needs these "extreme postmodernists" to exist in order to have a societal pathology that his synthesis can remedy, but because no established thinkers actually hold these views he cannot quote anyone asserting them.

Wilber contends that extreme postmodernism completely denies reality to right hand objective facts. The philosopher Richard Rorty is perhaps the most famous of those said to advocate an extreme postmodernism, but if so, what do we make of his

---

29 Stanley Fish, "Condemnation Without Absolutes," *The New York Times,* Oct. 15, 2001, Section A, p. 19, col. 2.

30 Wilber, "The Deconstruction of the World Trade Center," part III, section entitled "Boomeritis Uber Alles, at www.wilber.shambhala.com/html/books/boomeritis/wtc/part3.cfm/.

arguments for a "non-reductive physicalism"[31] in which the reality of causation and the language of the natural sciences are preserved without reducing the mental to them? As for relativists' supposed loss of objectivity, Fish notes that Rorty "is fond of saying, 'Objectivity is the kind of thing we do around here.'"[32] The difference here hinges on the meaning of the word "objectivity." If objectivity refers to a demonstrable relationship to some ahistorical epistemological ground, then no one is objective, for no one has yet provided such a ground. But if objectivity is what Rorty says it means, which is the validity-criteria discussants share, then objectivity *is* the kind of thing these so-called "extreme postmodernists" do around here. This is true of Wilber himself. As I pointed out in the discussion of his three strands of knowledge, Wilber, like Rorty, makes "community consensus" the arbiter of valid knowledge and claims for his system a relative, as opposed to an absolute, objectivity.

There *are* non-postmodernists who deny reality to the objective world. They can be found in mainstream American and British philosophy departments, and methodically use the tools of analytic philosophy to argue for what's currently termed *anti-realism*.

In addition to his caricature of imaginary extreme postmodernists, Wilber also exaggerates the extent that extreme postmodernism has taken over the university and culture in general. He adopts wholesale the picture of the university and culture concocted by cultural conservatives for political purposes in the late '80s and early '90s. He claims:

> At this point in Western history (basically, an amalgam of traditional, modern, and postmodern currents)— and specifically at this time in America (circa 2000)— we are going through a period of an intense flatland

31 Richard Rorty, "Non-reductive Physicalism," in *Objectivity, Relativism and Truth* (Cambridge: Cambridge University Press, 1991).

32 Stanley Fish, "The Ignorance of Our Warrior Intellectuals," *Harpers* Magazine, 7/02, p. 33.

cascade, a combination of rampant scientific materialism (the orange meme) and the "nothing but surfaces"
of the extreme postmodernists (the green meme).[33]

In making the culturally relative surface features the *entire* story, extreme postmodernism (and boomeritis) has
devastated human and spiritual understanding, which
often includes a universal/transcendental component.[34]

The green-meme dominates virtually all of conventional
academia AND countercultural academia.[35]

In contrast, Russell Jacoby charts the course of a different and
more important trend in university education. That trend is away
from degrees and classes in the humanities and social sciences and
toward degrees in business, accounting, communications, computers, and marketing. This is a fundamental and pervasive shift away
from the traditional idea of a liberal education that teaches critical
thinking to a vision of college as vocational education. In addition, the cultural courses that students do take are predominantly
introductory courses in which students probably never even hear
of postmodernism, relativism, or multiculturalism.[36] Stanley Fish
notes that the English Department of Duke University—thought
to be a hotbed of postmodernism—

requires a major author course in Chaucer, Shakespeare,
Spenser, Milton, and Pope, a specified number of courses in literature before 1800, and an introductory course
in the techniques of literary analysis, New Critical style.
There are no multiculturalism requirements (perhaps
there should be), no seminars in sensitivity training, no

---

33 Wilber, "Waves, Streams, States, and Self."

34 Wilber, "Endnotes to Boomeritis," Chapter 9, http://wilber.shambhala.com/
html/books/boomeritis/endnotes/ch9.cfm/.

35 Wilber, "On Critics," part III."

36 Russell Jacoby, *Dogmatic Wisdom* (New York : Doubleday, 1994), pp. 8–10.

harassment of instructors presenting traditional courses in traditional ways (if there were, I would be one of those harassed).[37]

Wilber has adopted a convenient conservative fiction regarding the university instead of doing the important sociological work of uncovering what is really going on beyond the fashionable cultural politics and sensationalized news stories.[38]

Wilber's characterization of modernity is on firmer ground than his critique of contemporary postmodernism. According to Wilber, the most important achievement of modernity is the distinction between the "Big Three" spheres of existence: the "I," or the subjective; the "We," or the intersubjective; and the "It," or the objective. He contends that this differentiation allowed the end of slavery, the rise of feminism, the establishment of liberal democracies, advances in medical sciences, and ideals of equality, freedom, and justice. While a simplification, it is plausible to contend that these increases in individual liberty were dependent upon the delineation of the three separate spheres of value each with their own integrity. Wilber, following Weber and Habermas, also describes modernity's dissociation and disenchantment and the dominance of a scientific materialist reductionism. These negative aspects are what Wilber calls "the flatland ontology" of modernity. To support these claims he refers to Weber and Habermas, but gives no citations. In checking Habermas's major work on this question,[39] we find that the extraction of the Big Three is a fair interpretation of Habermas's gloss on Weber, although Habermas's discussion is much subtler and more complex than Wilber acknowledges.

37 Stanley Fish, *There's No Such Thing as Free Speech . . and it's a Good Thing, Too* (New York: Oxford University Press), p. 54.

38 John K. Wilson's *The Myth of Political Correctness* (Durham: Duke University Press, 1995) demonstrates the mythical nature of what Wilber assumes to be facts.

39 Jurgen Habermas, *Theory of Communicative Action* (Boston: Beacon Press, 1984).

While his use of Habermas here is defensible, Wilber's periodiza-
tion of modernity and postmodernity is confusing. He states that
we can date the beginning of the "postmodern mood" to Hegel,[40]
presumably because Hegel used history to contextualize earlier
epochs, showed the constructed nature of knowledge, and used
vision-logic to create an all embracing system. But if Hegel, at the
start of the nineteenth century begins the postmodern mood, then
what are we to make of historical periodizations of postmodernity
that date it from the mid- to late twentieth century and routinely
refer to late nineteenth- and early twentieth-century thinkers such
as Nietzsche and Bataille as proto-postmodernists? Adding to the
confusion is the constructivism of Hegel's predecessor Kant, who
created his influential rendering of human subjectivity by seeing it
as constitutive of the spatio-temporal world. So either we accept
Wilber's broad definitions of constructivism and contextualism,
which lead to an odd overlapping of the modern and postmodern, or we reject these definitions as too general, which requires
a wholly different way of characterizing the differences between
modern and postmodern thought.

This confusion of modern and postmodern thought is mirrored
in Wilber's description of modern and postmodern social changes. He contends that the strength of postmodernism is pluralism,
multiculturalism, and the respecting of all voices.[41] Yet isn't democratic pluralism, minority rights, public discussion, free press and
religion, and the rational assessment of views a pluralistic part of
modernity? The political theorist Robert A. Dahl published his
classic theory of democratic pluralism in his book *Who Governs?*
in 1961, well before most periodizations of postmodernism. The
strengths that Wilber assigns to postmodernism could easily be
seen as the strengths of modernism. By misattributing qualities to
postmodernism that could just as easily be seen as aspects of modernism, Wilber avoids the stronger and more undermining aspects

40 Wilber, *Integral Psychology*, p. 274, n. 10.
41 Ibid., p. 159.

of postmodern thought. He says that vision-logic, like postmodern thinking, privileges no perspective and weaves them together into an integral-aperspective. Yet Wilber's integral synthesis privileges key ideas that postmodern thought criticizes: evolutionary progress, a telos, anthropocentrism, essences, the division between inner and outer, realism, and a vocabulary that is binding on other times, persons, and places. He never adequately confronts the fundamental problems that poststructuralism and postmodernism raise for his theory of everything.

CHAPTER 8

METHODOLOGY AND PHILOSOPHY

This chapter examines the methodological and philosophical foundations of Wilber's model. In *SES*, the *orienting generalization* is the primary methodological approach. Wilber asserts that orienting generalizations avoid the problem of postmodern relativism and that his method transcends the all-perspectives-are-valid pluralism that postmodern reason has created. In divorcing fact and value, postmodern reason cannot offer fact-based value hierarchies and so advocates an unstructured holistic heap instead of a structured holarchical (hierarchical plus holistic) whole. Wilber contends that with his methodological and philosophical foundations "values and facts are no longer automatically divorced," which means we can now "realign facts and values in a gentler embrace."[1]

ORIENTING GENERALIZATIONS

In Wilber's diagnosis of contemporary intellectual life, modernity's rational level of consciousness contains both a positive respect for other perspectives and a negative postmodern relativity of perspectives. This rational consciousness does not have the capacity to transcend and integrate the multiple perspectives of

1 *SES*, p. 31.

our increasingly interconnected world. An intellectual and social fragmentation results, along with the danger of directionlessness and relativism. To combat this fragmentation of knowledge and society, and the resulting relativism of postmodernity, Wilber proposes an integration of knowledge that transcends and includes the welter of perspectives in the natural, social, and spiritual sciences. He acknowledges that the sciences appear to be an irreconcilable series of specialized debates, but asserts that behind the disagreements within diverse fields of knowledge are what he terms *orienting generalizations.*[2]

Orienting generalizations are the "already-agreed-upon"[3] knowledge that debating scholars take for granted to be true as they debate the relevant issues in their fields. For example, in developmental psychology debates rage about the details of the developmental stages that people go through as they grow to adulthood, yet the fact that people do develop, and the general stages they pass through, is largely agreed upon, says Wilber. He contends that there is a great deal of this already-agreed-upon knowledge in the diverse debates throughout academia. He will gather these orienting generalizations, or partial truths, and weave them together to show that they create a consistent developmental-evolutionary story of the Kosmos. He claims he is inclusive, in that he respects all perspectives, but also critical, in that he sees that each perspective is partially false as well as partially true. The method of orienting generalizations is the most important way that Wilber will validate his evolutionary theory, and is the central methodological point that he makes in his introduction to *Sex, Ecology, Spirituality.*[4]

2 In response to my critique, Wilber implied that the method of orienting generalizations has been superseded by his new Integral Methodological Pluralism. In an appendix to this chapter, I explain why I think the method of orienting generalizations remains relevant.

3 *SES*, p. ix.

4 In addition to the importance attributed to the method in both editions of *SES*, Jack Crittenden extols the method in his laudatory foreword to Wilber's *The Eye of Spirit*. Wilber then reprints Crittenden's foreword in his journal, *One Taste*.

In the preceding chapters I demonstrated that Wilber does not use the "simple but sturdy"[5] and "already-agreed-upon" knowledge of the natural, social, and spiritual sciences. He does not really use the orienting generalizations of knowledge, and as a consequence an *ad hoc* methodology results. Instead of finding the orienting generalizations of knowledge, the reader is often told what famous writers say. Wilber makes statements of fact and validates them by attributing them to a few great thinkers. The assumption is that if a great and influential thinker asserts something, then it should carry authority. For example, Wilber uses Ferdinand de Saussure's distinction between the signifier and the signified without any mention of Derrida's critique of the distinction or other approaches to the sign that followed Saussure's. The assumption appears to be that if a great thinker like Saussure says it, that's validation enough. In another example, he spends an entire page convincing us of the precocity, brilliance, and great influence of the German philosopher Friedrich Schelling, as if these traits have some bearing on whether what he said was true or false. The same is done with Jurgen Habermas, A. O. Lovejoy, and Charles Taylor. It's a curious pre-Enlightenment way of validating statements by reference to authority and is contrary to Wilber's post-Enlightenment desire to rely on science as the arbiter of truth. The reason reputation replaces orienting generalizations is that the method of orienting generalizations is unworkable.

Throughout this book I have shown that Wilber does not use orienting generalizations. But here I argue further that the orienting generalizations methodology is unworkable at all. The methodology is unworkable because the "simple but sturdy" background knowledge that the participants in a given academic debate presuppose appears "simple but sturdy" only because the participants in *that* debate do not happen to be debating the validity of *that* background knowledge. Why aren't they debating that knowledge? Because it's not their job; it's the job of other scholars

5 *SES*, p. ix.

in some other academic discipline to debate what their colleagues are taking to be true.

Let's take the important field of developmental psychology. The participants within the debate assume there is a process of development and that it does follow identifiable and relatively invariant stages. But that's just because they don't happen to be debating those assumptions or orienting generalizations at the moment. It doesn't mean they are not debatable. In *Value Presuppositions in Theories of Human Development*,[6] some of the most respected names in academia—Jerome Kagan, Jerome Bruner, Carol Gilligan, Richard Bernstein, and others—debate the values lodged within developmental descriptions of cognition, and whether it is valid to speak of stages and structures at all. Needless to say, no consensus is reached. Although, the participants do assume, as an orienting generalization, that their words represent reality. Is this a piece of "simple but sturdy" knowledge? Not according to contemporary debates in epistemology, where the representational theory of truth is criticized quite vigorously. And on it goes; one person's orienting generalization is someone else's point of contention.

Natural scientists might object that this is true for the "soft" social sciences but not true for the "hard" natural sciences. The natural sciences definitely have more agreement about facts, explanations, and methods. Scientists do not debate whether biological evolution occurs. It does; it's a fact. They do debate the details of how it occurs, but this we can envision them coming to agreement upon in the future. What they will not come to agreement upon is what it *means* that it occurs. And this is the kind of question that Wilber needs to answer if he is going to weave together disparate fields of knowledge and tell a coherent story about the evolution of matter, life, and mind. This is because to move from describing facts to telling a story is to move from facts to values.

Hayden White, in his book *The Content of the Form*, shows that

6 Leonard Cirillo and Seymour Wapner, eds., *Value Presuppositions in Theories of Human Development* (Hillsdale, N.J.: L. Erlbaum Associates, 1986).

telling a story necessarily entails morals or values.[7] Without the moral, one's facts are just a list, what historian's call a chronology of events. This is why historians cannot avoid having values infuse their history writing. Wilber does not want to just catalogue human knowledge and say there is similarity here and dissimilarity there, he wants to tell "a brief history of cosmos, bios, psyche, theos,"[8] or "a chronicle of what you have done, a tale of what you have seen, a measure of what we all might become."[9] Of course, it's fine to tell a story, but if you want your story to be sanctioned by the orienting generalizations of the natural sciences you are going to have a problem because the facts and explanations that science provides do not tell you how to put those facts together into a coherent narrative. For that, as White shows, one needs values, a morality. And as the thousands of pages expended on moral philosophy attest, a consensus on morals is not coming any time soon. This is why I claim there are no natural scientific orienting generalizations that tell you what ought to be.

If Wilber does not use orienting generalizations, then how does he determine what will go into his synthesis and what will not? He must use the ongoing academic debates in diverse fields of knowledge to determine what is true. But it is the participants within those debates who are trying to determine what is true by debating. By not knowing the details of the contemporary intellectual debates on which his synthesis depends, he tramples on the very debates that determine the truths he needs to construct his integration. His actual practice is to reach into a debate, pull out the work of an author he can use, and then neglect the thicket of ongoing arguments and counter-arguments in which the truths he needs to build his system are being thrashed out.[10] Instead of an

7 Hayden White, *The Content of the Form* (Baltimore: John Hopkins University Press, 1987).

8 *SES*, p. viii.

9 *SES*, p. xi.

10 My description of his actual scholarly practice coincides with Wilber's own

integration of the already-agreed-upon knowledge in each field of study, he ends up taking one side of an ongoing debate, and so builds his synthesis with debatable and debated knowledge. The result is that Wilber's method of inclusion is actually a practice of exclusion; an exclusion of all the perspectives and facts that do not fit into his synthesis.

An illustration of how Wilber's apparently neat integration of major contemporary intellectual perspectives is actually a fundamentally problematic disregard for the integrity of each perspective occurs in the following passage. He is describing how diverse approaches to knowledge can be integrated by being contextualized, one within another:

> The autonomous ego of the Enlightenment is not *that* autonomous because it is actually set in the context of its own organic drives (the psychoanalytic critique of the Enlightenment), and these previously unconscious drives must be integrated for true autonomy to emerge. But even the entire integrated and autonomous person of psychoanalysis is not *really* autonomous, because that individual is actually set in contexts of *linguistic structures* that autonomously determine meaning without the individual even knowing about it (the critique launched by structuralism, archaeology). But linguistic structures aren't really *that* autonomous, because they exist only in the context of pre-articulate worldviews that use language without language ever registering that fact (the critique by Heidegger, Gebser). But further, worldviews themselves are merely a small component of massive networks and contexts of social practices

description of his reading habits. He says, "I usually try to go through two to four books a day, which means I skim through them very quickly, making a few notes where necessary. If I find a really important book, then I'll slow down and spend a week or more with it, taking extensive notes. Really good books I'll read three or four times." (*One Taste*, p. 122.) I surmise that Wilber skims a lot of books looking for the ones that agree with his intellectual preferences. He then studies those books carefully and fits what they say together to create a picture of the world to his liking.

(in various ways, Marx, Habermas, the later Foucault). And further yet, theorists from Kierkegaard to Schelling to Hegel would insist that those social practices only exist in and because of the larger contexts of Spirit.[11]

Yet, wouldn't the autonomous ego of the Enlightenment defend its autonomy against the psychoanalytic unconscious by arguing that psychoanalysis is unscientific and unproven? And doesn't the integrated ego assert its autonomy against the supposedly determining linguistic structures by continually creating novel linguistic structures? Do "linguistic structures . . . exist only in the context of pre-articulate worldviews," or does the idea of "pre-articulate worldviews" require linguistic structures even to exist, since a worldview cannot exist prior to linguistic structures? Is Spirit the "larger context" or an epiphenomenon of an essentially naturalistic world? And aren't the first mentioned "organic drives" what evolutionary psychologists take to be the crucial determining context structuring the character of human individual and social life? Each perspective is a different worldview that constructs the world in different ways. Wilber neglects these differing perspectives by assuming there is one world—which happens to be the one he sees—and that they are all describing different aspects of *it*. But to take them seriously, to plumb the depths of their thought, to formulate them as powerfully as possible and to not efface their fundamental differences we need to keep present before our minds the problem of relativism or perspectivalism. Wilber thinks he is creating an integration that extracts what is true from differing perspectives, but he is actually disrespecting the profound differences in radically divergent constructions of "reality" and avoiding the great intellectual problem of our time: *difference*.

Hiding behind Wilber's belief that all partial truths must fit together is the debatable assumption that all the partial truths correspond to one true world. If all the truths of all the sciences can

11 *SES*, pp. 72–73.

form a coherent whole it is because they share something in common. That common thing is the world, reality, the way in which things are. Yet the philosopher Nelson Goodman has made a strong argument that there are contradictory truths that cannot be assimilated into one coherent picture of the world.[12] Goodman uses the example of the sun's motion. The statements "the sun moves through the sky" and "the sun is stationary" are both true. The first is easily verifiable by our daily observation, while the second is a cornerstone of our heliocentric understanding of our solar system. The clever response that from one perspective the sun moves but from another perspective it is stationary appears to set things aright. But Goodman then asks, what is the sun's motion apart from all perspectives? What is its motion like in and of itself? The mind goes blank. There is no one way the sun *is* independent of all perspectives, as far as we can tell. There is no one world guaranteeing the coherence of all true versions, as Wilber assumes; or if there is, we cannot demonstrate when we are in contact with it. The philosopher Andrew Blais has elaborated Goodman's work and argued that there is a plurality of actual worlds.[13] This is not a dominant view in philosophy, but the power of this kind of argumentation gives us an indication of the problems with the philosophical underpinnings of Wilber's project.

In the introduction to *SES*, Wilber calls the orienting generalizations "beads of knowledge."[14] All we have to do is string them together to get a grand synthesizing necklace. It's a nice image, but where do we get the thread? In what order should the beads go? Why a necklace and not a beaded curtain? Contrary to the popular maxim, the facts do *not* speak for themselves. Likewise, orienting generalizations do not speak for themselves; we must interpret what they say.

12 Nelson Goodman, *Ways of Worldmaking* (Indianapolis: Hackett Publishing, 1978), pp. 2–3.

13 Andrew Blais, *On the Plurality of Actual Worlds* (Amherst: UMass Press, 1997).

14 *SES*, p. ix.

I think Wilber sensed these difficulties, because he says in his introduction to *SES* that "in addition to being composed of broad orienting generalizations, I would say this is a book of a thousand hypotheses."[15] Yet instead of informing the reader what parts are the "simple but sturdy" orienting generalizations and what parts make up the "thousand hypotheses," he then says, "I will be telling the story as if it were simply the case (because telling it that way makes for much better reading)."[16] Much better reading but much worse scholarship.

RELATIVISM

The method of orienting generalizations is Wilber's way of gaining valid knowledge in order to counter what he sees as a rampant relativism. He also confronts relativism directly in several different contexts, but his argument against it is quite weak. This is due, in part, to his crude formulation of the relativist position. In Wilber's mind, relativists make an absolute statement by saying there are no absolutes and all is relative. Wilber then condescendingly states over and over—sometimes three times within the same discussion—that this is a contradiction because the relativists' statement that "all is relative" is stated absolutely, and so is self-contradictory. In reply to simplistic formulations of relativism such as this, Richard Rorty states that "no one holds this view. Except for the occasional cooperative freshman, one cannot find anybody who says that two incompatible opinions on an important topic are equally good."[17] This is why Wilber never quotes any of his so-called relativist opponents actually asserting the view.

Anyone who reads a lot of academic writing develops *straw man radar*. The reader senses when the arguments attributed to the

15 *SES*, p. iv.

16 *SES*, p. x.

17 Richard Rorty, *Consequences of Pragmatism* (Minneapolis: University of Minnesota, 1982), p. 166.

author's opponents are being weakly formulated. With Wilber, weak formulations of opponents' views are common. What he typically does in *SES* is: refer to some general group of authors such as "the ecophilosophers" or "the multiculturists," caricature some part of their views he doesn't like, and then repeatedly "prove" that they are wrong about the caricatured point. While reading these pages, the reader wonders who these people are and do they actually believe such simplistic things? Most of the time, after pages of debate, the reader never learns the names of Wilber's opponents, the books they've written, or reads their own words. While Wilber never ceases to delight in chopping his straw man relativists down, the reader grows frustrated having to sit through such a self-serving display. The problem is, as Rorty says, "such neat little dialectical strategies only work against lightly-sketched fictional characters."[18] I referred to this weakness of argumentation as a problem, but it is only a problem for those serious about argumentation. For Wilber it is not problematic but functional. By deploying his self-contradiction argument he can avoid the real difficulties that serious scholars present for his position.

The philosopher Michael Krausz has edited two well-regarded texts on relativism and published, with Rom Harre, *Varieties of Relativism*.[19] Harre and Krausz survey the whole philosophical debate between absolutism and relativism and state, "In no case do we think that we have found arguments of overwhelming strength on either side of the debate. Perhaps there is no final resolution in rational terms of this great schism in people's attitudes to existence, knowledge, meaning and values."[20] Yet Wilber resolves the "great schism" in one simple stroke. In contrast to Wilber's easy dismissal of relativism, Krausz and Harre write that the

---

18 Ibid., p. 167.

19 Rom Harre and Michael Krausz, *Varieties of Relativism* (Oxford: Blackwell, 1996).

20 Ibid., p. 33.

diversity [of relativisms] will serve both to cure anyone of the idea that relativism can be defended or attacked briefly and easily, or on one basis alone, and to define the complex challenge to provide an adequate exegesis and commentary on the gamut of philosophical consider-ations that have or could be adduced in defence of or at-tack upon this or that variety of relativism.[21]

Varieties of Relativism is a condensed catalogue of the wide variety of relativisms and their intricate arguments with a wide variety of opposing absolutisms.

Wilber claims that postmodern relativism results from the valu-able postmodern insight that everything is contexts within con-texts. There is no autonomous God, no autonomous ego, no au-tonomous ground of knowing, nothing without a context. The postmodernists, though, carry this too far into relativism. Wilber's solution is to acknowledge that everything is contextualized, but not in any old way. "Thus, that everything is relative does not mean nothing is better; it means some things are, indeed, relatively bet-ter than others, all the time."[22] But this is mistaken. If something is "relatively better" that means it can also be relatively worse. If one wants to contend that the relatively better cannot be seen as relatively worse from some other perspective, then one would have to show how it is *always* relatively better; but if it's always relatively better, then it is absolutely better. The whole point of qualifying "better" with the word "relatively" is because it is not "absolutely better." The awkward inclusion of "all the time" at the end of the previous quote suggests the need to bolster the problematic point. If it is relatively better "all the time" then it is absolutely better, not relatively better.

Wilber offers no example to support the point I just quoted, but instead illustrates the problem I am describing. He writes,

---

21 Ibid., p. 23.
22 *SES*, p. 202.

"Neither atoms nor molecules are final or ultimate constituents of the universe; nonetheless *wherever* they appear, molecules *always* contain atoms in a deeper embrace."[23] But that fact does not prove that molecules are "better" than atoms. "Better" is a value judgment not a statement of fact. We have seen that Wilber does have a reason for calling a molecule better—greater depth and inclusion—but that value system does not stand on a firm foundation.

I think that Wilber unconsciously understands that he has not subdued the relativist menace. For all the bluster with which he confidently declaims his self-contradiction riposte, the fact that he repeats it over and over, even though the point is abundantly clear, indicates he doubts his own argument.

WILBER'S STANDPOINT AND THE VALIDITY OF THE SYSTEM

Wilber's oft-repeated exposing of the relativist's supposed self-contradiction raises a problematic question: How does Wilber think he escapes relativism? How does he absolutely or objectively validate his intellectual foundations using reason? Where does Wilber stand intellectually in order to give us a broad orienting map of existence and distinguish true from false?

There are two avenues to truth claimed in Wilber's work: a pragmatic avenue based on the agreement of the expert community, and a realist avenue that justifies truth through contact with "the pre-given," reality, or the world as it is in itself. Neither of these is extensively argued, nor do they provide the philosophical foundation which would validate Wilber's system. The pragmatic avenue is described in Wilber's three strands of knowledge: first, the injunction, or directions for attaining knowledge; second, the apperception, or seeing for oneself using the injunction; and third, communal confirmation, or the validation of the knowledge by the members of the relevant community.[24] The dominant criterion of

23 *SES*, p. 203.
24 The three strands are examined more fully in Chapter 4.

validity for Wilber is the degree of agreement among the experts. We look to the already-agreed-upon knowledge of the community of inquirers and extract what they agree upon.

Wilber even uses this approach for the spiritual sciences. A mystic has an overwhelming insight into the truth, but that is just the second or apperceptive strand of determining validity. The apperception has to be validated by the relevant community. Although, while the mystic's relevant community may agree that the mystic did experience the Absolute, other communities who also deal with reality—philosophers, let's say—may not agree. Wilber would say that they have not followed the injunctions and had the apperception; but they would critically question the injunctions and their effects on the apperception. The community of philosophers has a different mode of investigating reality, and so has different criteria they apply. They would use the criteria of rational consistency, logic, and evidence. What if two communities disagree? Who decides? Which community's criteria will prevail? Wilber could try to argue that widespread agreement among the major mystical communities is confirmation of the validity of an individual's mystical insight, but then he would have to engage those who disagree that there is such widespread agreement. I show in Chapter 7 how his arguments against the constructivists—who argue there is disagreement among differing mystical traditions—fail.

If orienting generalizations are understood to be the knowledge confirmed by the relevant expert communities then it's no different from a pragmatic approach to validation and would be as acceptable to certain so-called relativists (e.g., John Dewey's "warranted assertability"; Richard Rorty's "justified belief"; Stanley Fish's "interpretive communities") as it is to Wilber. So the orienting generalization cannot be the foundation for knowledge that distinguishes Wilber's system from the relativists.

The realist avenue is argued in a couple of uncharacteristically convoluted footnotes in which Wilber appears to be saying that there is a way to know reality because there is a "pre-given" world and an "immediate touching" that guarantees contact with this world. His arguments, though, are contradictory and take no account of the extensive history of philosophical debate that addresses these questions and has come to no satisfactory resolution.[25] In the first footnote Wilber asserts that humans do have a way to connect to a reality beyond language and conceptuality. He writes, "The general features of the sensorimotor world are ...already laid down by evolution prior to the emergence of rational reflection," and "Fundamental aspects of sensorimotor holons are 'pregiven.'"[26] But in the very next footnote he contradicts this by stating that "'rational commonsense' *took entirely for granted,* and thus it *failed* to see that its 'common and obvious' world supposedly open to simple 'empirical viewing' was in fact a *particular* and generated *worldspace,*" and "the intersubjective created worldspace, which itself allows the disclosure of individuated subjects and objects, was ditched in favor a [sic] mindless staring at the *end result* (mistaken as pregiven)." So in the first footnote there is a pregiven, which we have access to before interpretation intrudes, and in the second footnote "the intersubjective created worldspace . . . allows the disclosure of . . . subjects and objects." This contradiction appears irremediable.

Wilber is left with communal confirmation and the orienting generalizations that supposedly follow from it. My examination of the major areas of knowledge Wilber employs shows that the sciences do not agree as Wilber contends: that there is disagreement where he suggests there is agreement; that there are facts and alternative interpretations that do not fit his map; that if he insists on trying to validate a mystically infused but rationally argued vision of the Kosmos, he will be subject to the criteria used in rational argumentation and his vision's validity will be undermined; and that his effort to reconcile all perspectives into one big map

25 Richard Rorty gives an account of this debate in his *Philosophy and the Mirror of Nature* (Princeton, N.J.: Princeton University Press, 1979).
26 *SES*, p. 653.

of the Kosmos will be dashed upon the ultimately irreconcilable, irreducible difference of perspectives.

THINKING VS. BEING

Another way Wilber tries to validate his system is through a distinction between thinking and being. The thinker uses the criteria of reason to evaluate claims to validity and asks: Does the claim correspond to the evidence? Does it cohere with other things we know? Is it internally consistent? These are the criteria I use in this book. The mystic, who is primarily interested in an alteration in being, will use words to express his or her insight, convince others of its validity, and help others to gain the insight for themselves. The validity of the mystic's insight rests on the convincingness of the experience and on the confirmation of the insight by the mystic's teachers or sacred texts. If an analytic philosopher poked holes in the mystic's assertions regarding the nature of reality, the mystic should be unaffected since the truth of his or her insight rests in the experience not the conclusiveness of the argumentation. It's the mystic's seeing through all conceptuality—conceptuality being the philosopher's stock-in-trade—that leads to the mystic's insight.

Wilber is a mystic and a thinker, and so inhabits both worlds. The bulk of his written work uses the criteria of the thinker: arguments and evidence. But his vision and its understanding of the Kosmos's goal is inspired by his experience of and faith in the mystic's insight. These two sides of thinker and mystic exist uncomfortably within him, as my chapter on his psychology (Chapter 10) describes. This uneasy alliance is also present in his recent use of Spiral Dynamics, which has its origins in the work of Clare Graves and has been popularized by Don Beck and Chris Cowan.[27] The question raised is: what criteria are we going to use to evaluate

27 Don Beck and Chris Cowan, *Spiral Dynamics* (Cambridge, MA: Blackwell Business, 1996).

the validity of Wilber's view? Wilber is of two minds. On the one hand, he uses a phalanx of footnotes and the idea of orienting generalizations to legitimate his assertions; but, on the other hand, in his book *A Theory of Everything,* he acknowledges that the nature of his system makes this kind of rational, academically-oriented validation problematic. He states that "many arguments are not really a matter of the better *objective* evidence, but of the *subjective* level of those arguing." Because of the differences between subjective levels, "'cross-level' debates are rarely resolved." As a consequence "nothing that can be said in this book will convince you that a [theory of everything] is possible, unless you already have a touch of [transpersonal insight] coloring your cognitive palette."[28] More recently, Wilber has asserted this view more strongly and described it with the concept of *altitude*.[29] In other words, having an advanced consciousness is necessary to gain greater intellectual insight into how the Kosmos works. By allowing a superior vantage point, it allows a superior seeing of the whole. Rational argumentation is not enough.

This is a problematic conflation of intellectual and spiritual insight. Wilber uses Spiral Dynamics and his own developmental scheme to merge intellectual and spiritual attainment. But what of thinkers like Habermas, Max Weber, Foucault, and Piaget? Did they have any distinctive spiritual attainment? Not that I can find evidence of. And what of contemporary spiritual adepts like Ramana Maharshi, Ramesh Balsekar, or Poonjaji? Did they create great social analyses? No. Profound spiritual adepts do not necessarily have superior social scientific theories. This assumption of a confluence between superior thinking and spiritual attainment is the reason Wilber advances Plato, Plotinus, and Aurobindo as individuals and scholars. He implies that the validity

---

28 Wilber, *A Theory of Everything*, p. 14.

29 Wilber, "What We Are, That We See," Part I, at www.kenwilber.com/blog/show/46.

of their philosophical work is connected to their spiritual attainments, but there is no necessary correlation between the two.

This problematic way of thinking has its dangers. For on what basis does one accept Wilber's ranking of levels of consciousness in the first place? Is the ranking accepted because of its accuracy validated by arguments and the evidence, or is it accepted because the system intuitively appeals to the hearer? If it is appealing to the hearer, then the hearer is one of the spiritual elite (or an elite wannabe); if it doesn't appeal to the hearer, the system will be dismissed. This threatens to make it a closed system. Those who "get it" will work within it and not question the foundations. By getting it, one joins the spiritual-intellectual elite and, as Wilber's critiques of those lower on the developmental hierarchy shows, this can easily slide into condescension However, those who don't "get it" will ignore it, unless it gets too powerful to ignore. Wilber implicitly understands this, as his savvy strategic use of his own work indicates. He repeatedly condenses his ideas into user-friendly forms that help to promote them widely, even awkwardly inserting them into his heart-wrenching book about his wife's death. And, in his attempt to set up an Integral Institute in which young scholars taken with his system can get money to employ and promote it he shows that he understands that new intellectual ideas often prevail by replacing, rather than proving wrong, reigning intellectual perspectives.

This distinction between thinking and being raises a more subtle point regarding Wilber's entire project. While he wants his thinking to validate and promote an essentially spiritual insight, all of Wilber's work takes place in the realm of thought. The writings are ideas written in language and argued with reasons. He argues for a spiritual insight that grasps the essence of existence, yet the arguments and the whole of his system is a thought that owes its existence to the realm of thinking. While Wilber uses language to claim that spiritual experience grasps the whole, it is, in practical reality, his thinking that attempts to grasp the whole in the form of his system. Without the printed page, the spoken word, the thoughts that create them, and the language that allows them all to exist, there is no integral synthesis, no understanding at all. In Wilber's work it is mind that grasps the Kosmos not spirit.

VALUES AND HIERARCHY

The values underlying Wilber's system are often assumed rather than argued. If, as he says, "some things are, indeed, relatively better than other things, all the time," what is the criterion of value that determines better and worse? Oddly, for all Wilber's emphasis on higher consciousness, fact/value connectedness, and the qualitative uniqueness of subjectivity, his criteria of better and worse is quantitative: more is better. The more emergent properties a holon embraces the more complex it is. The more complex a holon is, the higher or better it is in Wilber's holarchy. Increasing complexity is claimed to be nature's evolutionary tendency. The molecule includes the atoms within it and adds new properties; it is therefore more complex. The cell does the same to the atoms and the molecules within *it*. Why is more better? There is no explanation; it is just assumed. This assumption does not say anything about the Kosmos, but it does tell us about Wilber's bias. By valuing in this way, human beings are judged to be the most advanced entities in the Kosmos. Wilber's criterion allows him to mold, out of the vast multiplicity of evolutionarily created entities, a vision in which it appears that the whole Kosmos is geared toward producing us humans. It seems an incredible coincidence that out of the millions of types of entities that exist, the ones who are constructing the value scheme for placing everything into a hierarchy happen to determine that they themselves are highest on that value scheme.

In addition to his species bias, Wilber's criteria of valuation also imply a positive valuation of his project and of himself. If largeness of inclusion is the standard by which one judges what is better and worse, then Wilber's intellectual project—a theory of everything—is the greatest project to attempt and to have accomplished. The same goes for Wilber's spiritual accomplishments. As described in his journals, he has tasted, and mostly resides in, the highest, most inclusive state of consciousness. So by his own standard of inclusiveness his intellectual work and his level of consciousness are the greatest to do and to be.

VALUES AND DEVELOPMENTAL MODELS

Values are also latent in the developmental approach that Wilber uses. Models of individual and societal development appear to be purely descriptive and so appear scientific and value-neutral. But every model of human development carries a prescriptive aspect within its descriptions. Since any phenomenon to be studied is a variegated multiplicity, any developmental model must abstract from this multiplicity those aspects of interest to the researcher. The aspects of interest must then be linked together and seen as unfolding in a developmental pattern. The most important aspect is the goal or final stage of the developmental sequence, which organizes the selection of phenomena to be included or excluded from the model. The model itself is an abstraction from the actual multiplicity of empirical reality and implicitly becomes a norm of development. In defining the developmental pattern, the researcher implicitly labels those aspects of the phenomena that do not follow the pattern as precocious, regressed, stagnated, or anomalous. Yet precocities, regressions, stagnations, and anomalies are only seen as such in relation to the developmental norm, which was defined by what the researcher chose to abstract from the multiplicity of phenomena in the first place.

Wilber's ignorance of the value-laden character of all developmental models is demonstrated in his most famous paper, "The Pre/trans Fallacy."[30] In that article, Wilber distinguishes the prerational spirituality of children, primitives, and those immersed in

30 Wilber, "The Pre/Trans Fallacy," *ReVision*, Vol. 3, No. 2., 1980, pp. 51–73.

mythic religion from the trans-rational spirituality of mystical adepts. Wilber argues that pre-rational and trans-rational states have been confused, resulting in either a reduction of the trans-rational to the pre-rational, as in the "oceanic feeling" of Freudian psychoanalysis, or an elevation of the pre-rational to trans-rational status, as in aspects of Jungian psychology. In the introductory section of that article Wilber writes:

> Since the world of time is the world of flux, all things in this world are in constant change: change implies some sort of difference from state to state, that is, some sort of *development*; thus all things in this world can only be conceived as ones that have developed. The development may be forward, backward, or stationary, but it is never entirely absent. In short, *all phenomena develop*, and thus true phenomenology is always evolutionary, dynamic, or developmental."[31]

These sentences contain a subtle and problematic shift. Change, a fact of existence, is equated with development, even though the word *development* has the connotation of directed or patterned change through time. Change and development cannot be equated, because we can certainly imagine random change, such as the change in numbers that a random number generator creates, that show no development. We are told that development can be stationary; and while there can be stationary development, can there be stationary change? It sounds like a contradiction in terms. This difference between change and development is due to the value-laden character of the word *development*, which suggests a change over time, the character of which is deemed to advance, regress, or stay the same. All things change, as Wilber says, but to assess development we need some criterion of advance and regress in order to make a value judgment.[32]

31 Wilber, *Eye to Eye*, p. 202.

32 Wilber and Michael Washburn have debated the merits of Wilber's idea of the pre/trans fallacy. See Rothberg and Kelly, *Ken Wilber in Dialogue*.

CONCLUSION

Orienting generalizations are the already-agreed-upon back-ground knowledge that scholars in specific fields take to be true as they debate the issues on which they differ. Wilber claims that his integral synthesis is constructed out of this "simple but sturdy" background knowledge, and so has the validity that the natural, social, and spiritual sciences can provide. The research in this book demonstrates that Wilber does not use the orienting general-izations of the sciences as he claims. As a replacement method he quotes some great names in science. Because he does not have the authority of the orienting generalizations, Wilber tends to carica-ture perspectives different from his own, and thereby not confront the problems they would pose were they strongly formulated. He creates his synthesis by weaving together the ideas that he finds congenial to his outlook and fits them together to make his syn-thesis. This is problematic because his synthesis is supposed to be a transcendence of all less inclusive correct views, yet, actually, it excludes those arguably correct views that do not fit his particular integration.

This problem with the method of orienting generalizations goes beyond the improper use of the method; this chapter shows that the method cannot work at all. This is because the already-agreed-upon background knowledge of the diverse scientific disciplines is only agreed upon to be true by those within the given discipline. There can always be other academics in other disciplines who take as their problematic debating point the agreed upon knowledge in a neighboring discipline.

On an even more fundamental philosophical level, Wilber as-sumes that all true statements should fit together. This assumption presupposes that all true statements share something in common, such as a connection to the world as it is in itself. But it's clear that there are true statements that contradict each other and are not reconcilable by appeal to some larger more inclusive perspective.

Wilber collects the agreed upon knowledge of the sciences to tell the story of the Kosmos. To tell a story, a moral is always required. The facts of science will not tell their own story, and so the value system of the teller must be brought to bear. Wilber acknowledges the role of values in his integral synthesis but gives the impression that his story gains its legitimacy from the weight of scientific knowledge and that the value-system he uses arises from the facts. This is important to Wilber's entire project because he is offering his integral synthesis as a transcendence and inclusion of the partial truths of all the scientific disciplines. While the partiality of all other disciplines is subject to the undermining effects of relativism, Wilber's integral synthesis is offered as a solution to relativism. The traditional solution to relativism is some kind of absolute knowledge. Wilber tries to incorporate the true part of relativism by offering a relatively absolute knowledge as a synthesis.

The idea of relatively absolute knowledge is found to be contradictory, and his criticism of what he takes to be the implications of relativism is shown to be weak. His method of validating knowledge using communal consensus is no different from a pragmatic justification of knowledge agreeable to a Richard Rorty or a Stanley Fish—thinkers who, it is said, have succumbed to the contradictions of relativism because of their pragmatic justification of knowledge.

The question of values is as vexed as the question of knowledge within the synthesis. The fundamental value underlying Wilber's criteria for determining differing levels of advancement in his integral hierarchy is a simple one: more is better. The more emergent features a holon has, the higher it is in his hierarchy. Yet it is never explained why more is better and leads suspiciously to a supreme valuation of humanity.

Unacknowledged values are embedded in all developmental models. Values do not arise from the facts and impose themselves on the theorist, as Wilber implies. The theorist's values come first and allow the theorist to organize his or her developmental

scheme and decide what is normal, abnormal, and anomalous development. This fact of developmental models is hidden within
their scientific-sounding jargon and undermines their claims to
value-neutrality.

An alternative criterion of validity is found in Wilber's assumption that increases in the development of one's consciousness or
being allows a superior vision of how things work. Yet the criterion
for distinguishing superior from inferior visions must still be determined by deciding which vision is most correct using the standard
criteria of rational argumentation. Wilber offers no new criteria.
That a person has a more advanced consciousness does not mean
their understanding of the world is superior.

APPENDIX

In response to my criticisms, Wilber has implied that the method
of orienting generalizations has been superseded by his new Integral Methodological Pluralism.[33] He doesn't defend the assertion
(making it difficult to respond to), but I will say that in the latest
version of his theory he asserts the validity of the four-quadrant
(*AQAL*) model first elaborated in *SES*, which I've examined here.[34]

In excising the concept of orienting generalizations from his
most recent theory, the question arises as to how Wilber constructs
and justifies the AQAL model. We're told that "AQAL, then, is a
metatheory that attempts to integrate the most amount of material from an integral methodological pluralism, thus honoring the

33 As Wilber colorfully states: "Hey, did you see the one where a critic said that
my methodology consisted of 'orienting generalizations,' and then attacked
the shit out of orienting generalizations? Or rather, gave a really embarrassing,
green, performative-contradiction attempt to do so. I wonder if his [sic] guy has
ever heard of Integral Methodological Pluralism, which uses at least 8 different
methodologies." Ken Wilber, "What We Are, That We See," Part I.

34 Wilber defines AQAL (pronounced ah quil), which is short for "all quadrants,
all levels, all lines, all states, all types.'" "Excerpt B: The Many Ways We Touch.
Part I" at wilber.shambhala.com/html/books/kosmos/excerptB/part1.cfm.

primary injunction of an integral embrace: Everybody is right."[35]
"Everybody is right" means that every perspective, that's not purely idiosyncratic, has some truth that needs to be acknowledged
and integrated. The "Everybody" refers to "the ingredients of the
AQAL metatheory [which] are the phenomena (subjective, intersubjective, objective, and interobjective) enacted and brought
forth by literally dozens of time-honored methodologies, injunctions, paradigms, and practices."[36] The missing piece, however, is
how the many results from the "time-honored methodologies" will
be culled to separate the truths from the falsities and so construct
his AQAL model. This is the work that the method of orienting
generalizations did in the *SES*-era, or Wilber-4[37]. We still have the
familiar AQAL, four-quadrant model but have lost the methodology supposedly used to construct and justify it.

Mark Edwards has made a different and more effective critique
of my argument.[38] He points out that Wilber's methodology is that
of systems thinking and evokes the tradition of systems theory. A
systems approach focuses on the interrelationship between wholes
and parts as opposed to an analytic, atomistic and highly specialized approach that focuses more narrowly on the workings of individual entities. To understand a forest we could treat it as an "eco-
system," a variety of interrelated parts that create a whole. Each of
the varying-sized parts as well as the whole itself affect each other
through a variety of feedback loops. There's a pattern to the interactions of parts and parts with the whole which can be likened
to the patterns of other systems in other domains. Wilber's special
ability is to link common patterns in differing domains inquiry.

35 Ibid.

36 Ibid.

37 Wilber has divided the progression of his thought into five phases, Phase 4
is notable for the four quadrant model, Phase 5 for his Integral Methodological
Pluralism and post-metaphysics. See Alan M. Kazlev at www.kheper.net/topics/
Wilber/Ken_Wilber.htm.

38 Mark Edwards, "Meyerhoff, Wilber and the Post-Formal Stages," at www.
integralworld.net/index/html?edwards25.html.

In my reply to Edwards, I accepted the correctness of his point that the systems framework crucially informs the construction of Wilber's model despite Wilber's not explicitly acknowledging the methodological role that systems thinking plays in his work, treating it instead like another type of knowledge to be integrated. Wilber's use of Arthur Koestler, Erich Jantsch, and Ervin Laszlo demonstrates the structuring role that systems thinking plays in the construction of his four-quadrant model. I added, however, in my response to Edwards that the method of orienting generalizations is also used and that the two methods are in conflict. The evolutionary-developmental systems framework is assumed even when the orienting generalizations from academia don't support it. I offered as one example the lack of scholars who believe in the kind of human social evolution that is crucial to Wilber's model.[39]

So while Wilber's Integral Methodological Pluralism is a change in form, the content of the system—the factual assertions about developmental stages, the nature of the mind, the social development from village to nation-state, etc.—still relies on findings from the various academic disciplines that Wilber surveyed in *SES*.

39 Jeff Meyerhoff, "What's Worthy of Inclusion?," at www.integralworld.net/meyerhoff3.html.

CHAPTER 9

A Different Path

My critique of Ken Wilber's project demonstrates the continually contrary nature of intellectual debate. In chapter after chapter I show the legitimate alternative perspectives and arguments against what Wilber presents as the "simple but sturdy" truths of academia. Even the natural sciences—thought of as the royal road to reality—can now, since Thomas Kuhn and Paul Feyerabend and their historicizing of the natural sciences, be seen as one among many worldviews. To object that this is a misinterpretation of Kuhn, and that Feyerabend goes too far, is to become part of the ongoing debate in the philosophy of science, epistemology, and science studies.

Wilber champions a false consensus in the sciences. In contrast, I show the profound differences in perspective in many areas of study, such as cultural psychology, poststructuralism, mysticism, and sociology, that are excluded or tendentiously interpreted in order to create a false inclusiveness that masks the radically perspectival nature of knowing.

Wilber believes that one characteristic of the postmodern era is the proliferation of multiple and conflicting perspectives on the world, and that carrying this postmodern perspectivism too far leads to a pernicious, self-contradictory relativism because no perspective can claim ultimate authority. The result is an inability to rank perspectives according to their validity. This self-contradictory, "anything goes" relativism is the shadow side of the "contextualism" that Wilber sees as one of the important contributions of postmodern thinking.

His solution is an integral transcendence and inclusion of this seemingly irreconcilable multiplicity of perspectives. Wilber's purported transcendence and inclusion of perspectives is accomplished through the use of a reason-transcending mode of thinking and being called *vision-logic*. Vision-logic is a further cognitive stage beyond reason—in academia, called the postformal stage—in which the limits of postmodern reason are transcended by a new mode of thinking/being. Vision-logic requires an experiential shift, but it is not only a mystical transcendence of thinking, since its product is, most prominently, discursive; Wilber's system being one example.

A crucial difference between Wilber's position and mine is that I don't believe that vision-logic is a new mode of cognition. Wilber describes historical developmental changes in modes of knowing from mythic faith to modern rationality to postmodern vision-logic. While I agree that there are fundamental differences between faith and reason as modes of knowing, I do not agree that there is a fundamental difference between rationality and vision-logic.[1] As described in Chapter 3, since there is no new criterion of judging validity between reason and vision-logic, there is no fundamental difference in the knowledge they produce. To say there is no difference in the *mode* of knowing is not to say that there is no difference in the *content* of knowledge between rationality, as conceived here, and vision-logic. Vision-logic describes a thinking that attempts to

---

1 But see Steven D. Hales, *Relativism and the Foundations of Philosophy* (Cambridge MA: MIT Press, 2006). Here, an analytic philosopher argues that there is no neutral way to demonstrate the superiority of rational philosophy over Christian revelation or hallucinogenic-induced native beliefs. He argues that their fundamental methods of knowledge acquisition are different and that there is no neutral or non-question-begging way to demonstrate the superiority of one over the other.

synthesize diverse fields of knowledge into coherent systems, but the evaluation of these systems is still done in the usual, rational way.

I offer a different approach to the postmodern multiplicity of perspectives. Instead of trying, as has been tried many times throughout intellectual history, to make all of knowledge cohere, we should accept the ultimate irreconcilability of diverse perspectives and inquire into its nature. I describe a new area of inquiry and method of investigation that uses the postmodern reinterpretation of the constructed character of knowledge to show how acknowledging the limits of reason opens a door to another type of inquiry beyond reason. This inquiry forces reason to integrate its suppressed shadow-side in opposition to which it constitutes itself. I will justify doing this type of inquiry and provide illustrations of it. We will see that this inquiry is both a mode of knowledge acquisition and self-development, similar in this way to Buddhism and ancient Western philosophical practices of the self such as Epicureanism and Stoicism. The validity of this approach is supplemented by recent work in cognitive science and psychological research that show the crucial role that emotions and the unconscious play in perception, belief, and knowledge creation.

Background

The dominant image of post-Enlightenment reason has been constructed through the exclusion of aspects of the psyche seen as arational hindrances to reason. Emotions, passions, desires, subjectivity, personal biases all stand as what reason is *not* and what it strives to avoid in order to realize its ideals of objectivity, universality, truth, knowledge, and certainty. Reason wielders are expected to adhere to the norms of rationality in order to gain unbiased knowledge.

The dominant societal character type of *rational man* has such contemporary subtypes as "the disinterested judge," "the neutral reporter," and "the detached scientist." It is commonly thought that the more disinterested the judge the fairer the decision; the more neutral the reporter the more truthful the story; and the more detached and objective the scientist the nearer his or her findings will be to reality. These character types are assumed to play a zero-sum game: the less subjectivity entering their work the more objectivity that results. More objectivity means a more objective view of the world, which is supposed to be: a view of the world as it really is; the world as it is whether humans see it or not; the world as God sees it; the world as it is in itself, not as it's seen from a particular perspective. By applying a detached and neutral rationality in concert with others we should be able to determine the way things are and should be. For knowledge acquisition in the natural and social sciences and ethical decision-making in everyday life emotions and subjectivity are generally seen as sources of bias.

The field of philosophy, and specifically Anglo-American analytic philosophy, has the cultural task of justifying and explicating the methods and products of reason. Its questions inquire into the nature of knowledge and morality by asking: What is reality? What is the good? What is the right thing to do? What is knowledge? How do we know when we have knowledge? In contrast to continental philosophy, mysticism, and religious faith, analytic philosophy has tried to emulate the natural sciences because of their enormous success in prediction, control, and explanatory power. While philosophy's subject matter is not just the physical world, it still uses the natural sciences' successful methods to solve meta-physical problems. These methods of inquiry require taking the stance of the rational man, which means: detachment from emotion, particularities, and subjectivity; rigor in argumentation and logic; appeals to evidence; thought-experiments; and value-neutrality. It was thought that the great successes of the natural sciences would be repeated by emulating the natural scientific method.

Yet a curious thing has occurred as Western thinkers have employed reason to determine true knowledge. Reason users find that they can and do come to irresolvable rational disagreements.[2] Yet if reason users share both a method of inquiry and a world, then shouldn't they be able to come to agreement about all issues, at least in principle? Shouldn't their rational procedures and the corrective effect of reality lead them all to the one truth? Popular expression like "try to be objective," "do the right thing," and "be reasonable" perpetuate the impression that there is, at least ideally, one objective, right thing found by using reason. In academia and in everyday life there is a largely unexamined presupposition that there is *a* or *one* way in which things are. Those who are "right" know it or are closer to it, and those who are wrong are further from it. But when this presupposition is examined we find it to be very elusive; reason gives out and the ideal evaporates. Foucault evocatively described this goal of inquiry as, that "shimmering mirage" of truth.[3]

THE ARGUMENT

We justify our beliefs by giving reasons; if there are no reasons, then there is no justification. The strength or weakness of our reasons determines the validity of our beliefs. This is true for all reason givers. Yet the most accomplished practitioners of reason commonly state that when we try to ground our beliefs using reason we all reach a point where we have no reasons left.[4] If reasons

---

2 Richard Feldman has discussed the problem of "reasonable disagreements" and ends with "A Skeptical Conclusion" in "Epistemological Puzzles About Disagreement" in *Epistemology Futures*, edited by Stephen Hetherington, (Oxford: Oxford University Press, 2006). Robert Fogelin has reinterpreted Pyrhonnian Scepticism in *Pyrrhonian Reflections on Knowledge and Justification* (New York: Oxford University Press, 1994) and sparked a debate in *Pyrrhonian Skepticism*, edited by Walter Sinnott-Armstrong (New York : Oxford University Press, 2004).

3 Michel Foucault, *History of Sexuality* (New York: Vintage, 1990) p. 59.

4 In analytic philosophy these are called our "rational intuitions." See Gra-

are what justify what we believe, and if at the end of our chain of reasons there is no reason, then the validity of our beliefs is thrown into question. *In this sense*, all our beliefs are equally justifiable.[5] Each of us is floating in our rational boat on a shared sea, imagining that *we* are the ones solidly on land guiding the wayward to shore. If it is not reason, what is the nature of our connection to our beliefs?

By examining our reasons for believing what we believe beyond the reason giving we do to defend our beliefs, we find the animating core that motivates us to have the foundational beliefs that we have and deploy the reasons that we do. The reasons we give for believing as we do are not the real reasons we believe, because they always ultimately end in circularity, regress, or assumptions.[6] Since all belief-systems, if pursued long enough, will end in circularity, regress, or assumptions, we cannot say that it is reasons that ultimately cause us to believe. There must be something else that causes us to adopt our particular reasoning chain or web of beliefs. Since in terms of their *ultimate* rational validity our belief-systems are only as good as opposed belief-systems, there must be something else that causes us to choose, and that holds us to, our particular belief-system. What is characteristic of us is not only the combination of beliefs we have woven together—since everyone does that with greater or lesser originality—but also why we adhere to this rather than that belief-system. In our rational discussions there is a way in which we miss the point, since it is not the reasons we are deploying that cause us to believe. If we are trying to convince another person or challenge our own beliefs, then we should, for more efficiency, go to the source of the belief, which is

ham Priest, *Beyond the Limits of Thought* (Oxford: Oxford University Press, 2002), Hales, *Relativism*, and, for a debate on the topic, Michael R. DePaul, and William Ramsey, *Rethinking Intuition* (Lanham, MD: Rowman & Littlefield, 1998).

5 But see Michael Williams in "The Agrippan Argument and Two Forms of Skepticism," in Sinnott-Armstrong, *Pyrrhonian Skepticism* for an alternative view.

6 Priest, *Beyond the Limits of Thought*.

the emotional and psychic need to have the world be the way we or they believe it is.

THE EMOTIONAL SUBSTRUCTURE OF BELIEF

The structure of belief has two levels. The upper level has the array of beliefs that we hold in more or less conscious and coherent groupings, and that flow through our minds or are activated when appropriate inputs come from visual, written, or aural sources. We take in information and ideas, react to and evaluate it, decide what we think, and perhaps assert our view. All of this takes place on the upper level of belief. Underneath this upper level is a lower level containing *the emotional substructure of belief*. After reason giving comes to an end we can begin to see how we are attached to our beliefs for emotional and psychological reasons. This attachment routinely reveals itself when we get agitated during supposedly purely intellectual discussions; when we easily get defensive if cherished beliefs are questioned; when we overlook contradictory information; when we formulate opponents' arguments weakly; when we keep having unwanted doubts about a point we believe is settled; and when we feel an unusual urgency to make our point.[7] This substructure of belief is the realm of our complicated psychological and emotional ties to our beliefs. It's the neglected subjective side of our belief-system; the side that has been denied in order to emulate the natural scientist and maintain the fiction of the rational man.

RATIONAL DISAGREEMENTS

This is not an argument for abandoning reason. If we share enough foundational beliefs with our discussion partners,

---

7 Of course there are other reasons for the urgency to be heard. We may be bringing to light an injustice or trying to get what we want. I am referring here to purely intellectual discussions.

then we can come to rational agreements. Most of our discussions don't require uncovering our basic levels of belief and can be conducted within the realm of reason. In fact, most discussions I encounter don't have *enough* reason, as people routinely make comments off topic, bad analogies, misunderstand their opponents' positions, and avoid evidence that contradicts their views. As long as we have not reached bedrock rational assumptions—"rational intuitions"—in our debates, applying well the rules of reason is all that's needed.

When we have reached bedrock rational assumptions this approach provides a way to pursue debate beyond disagreement. The purpose of rational argumentation is to determine what is true or good. When people debate, the goal is to gain agreement; if they come to agreement they are done. This often does not occur. If the debate ends in disagreement, what are the debaters to do? They must agree to disagree. I am proposing that there is more to be done. Intellectual impasses could be shifted or, if not shifted, at least brought into view. So often discussants don't understand what the real difference is between their views. In principle, this could be done together with the two discussants examining the bases of their beliefs. In practice, it would be hard for two people disagreeing on fundamental issues to reveal the bases of their beliefs without fearing that their opponent will take advantage of their revelations, but two exceptionally aware people could do it.

Fortunately, two people are not necessary. One person with the cultivated ability to mindfully see the emotional substructure of belief can gain some insight into, and freedom from, the controlling and enabling affects of the arational world with which reason is entwined. The examples below will illustrate this process.

The reality of the difficulty of two people engaging in this type of inquiry reveals a disjunction between the ideal of rational argumentation and its reality. Ideally, rational inquirers have the same goal and are on the same side because rational argumentation is supposed to be bringing them to the one right answer we all share.

But so often in rational debates, the discussants act like enemies instead of allies in a common project. I think this has to do with the falseness of the rational assumption that we are getting the one true world right through our rational discussions. While our method of inquiry may be similar in its use of the norms of reason, the arational values held dearly can be, or seem to be, diametrically opposed.

So the practice I'm advocating does not even come into play unless the discussants reach an impasse in their rational discussions. If two people can settle their rational disagreement using reason, then what need is there for any other method? What I'm proposing is only used if a rational impasse occurs, as a way to explore beliefs further.

Reaching the Point of Undecidability

When a true impasse is reached the discussants have reached *the point of rational undecidability*. This occurs when the discussion participants have reached their bedrock assumptions. Often more reasons can be given, but these turn out to be circular and of no help in making a rational justification for belief. For example, in debating the merits of capitalism the discussants could reach a point where one person says, "I just think people are basically selfish." And the other person could say, "I think human nature is malleable." Or in a debate about abortion, one person believes that "the rights of the unborn child trump the rights of the mother," while the other person believes that "the right of the mother to control her body trumps the rights of the fetus." The difference in these positions cannot reach a rationally adjudicated terminus.

Another example of reaching the point of undecidability is described by Richard Rorty in his essay "Daniel Dennett on Intrinsicality." Rorty gets to the nub of the disagreement between Dennett and the philosopher Thomas Nagel. The question for Dennett in

Consciousness Explained is how is the subjective experience of human consciousness—the "Cartesian Theater"—connected to our brains; or, what is the relationship between a seemingly immaterial mind and the material matter of the brain? Dennett explains—or, perhaps, explains away—our subjective experience of consciousness using his quasi-scientific multiple drafts model, which describes how the material brain produces the seemingly immaterial effects of consciousness. Our subjective experiencing is not as purely *there* as we like to think. For Nagel, subjective experience is the self-evident reality that *is* immediately there; what could be more obvious? An explanation such as Dennett's that explains why it *seems* to be there is not explaining it at all; for Nagel it's an avoidance of the problem. As Rorty writes: "At the depth of disagreement that separates these two philosophers, both their spades are turned [i.e., they can go no further]."[8] So a question arises: if reason has reached an endpoint for each thinker, why does Dennett hold his view of the subject and Nagel his opposing view? Why isn't it the other way around? What causes each thinker to hold his view?

THE PSYCHOLOGICAL ANALYSIS OF BELIEF

Inquiring into this substructure of belief can be as simple as recovering or acknowledging the emotion behind a belief or as complex as developing a portrait of the psychological work that a certain complex of beliefs does to maintain our *psychic economy*.

A psychological analysis of belief can be a self-analysis or an analysis of another. Robert Stolorow and George Atwood do the latter kind of analysis in their *Faces in a Cloud: Subjectivity in Personality*

---

8 Richard Rorty, "Daniel Dennett on Intrinsicality" in *Truth and Progress* (Cambridge: Cambridge University Press, 1998), p. 104

Theory.[9] There they interpret the theories of Freud, Jung, Reich, and Rank in relation to their psychobiographies. In the next chapter I interpret Ken Wilber's integral theory in terms of his substructure of belief. Here I will use a subject closer-to-hand to give some illustrations of a psychology of belief.

Within me is an uneasy mix of a dominant Chomskyan-Marxian, socialist, political-economic worldview and a subterranean and unintegrated Ayn Randian libertarianism. The appeal of socialism has part of its psychic origins in a childhood familial structure that allotted the intrinsic good of attention unfairly. I was in a rigged competition with an older sibling in which I didn't get the goods. My older brother was intellectually brilliant at a young age, and intellect was something my parents valued highly. I quickly resigned myself to a second-class status and developed a defense of idolization and trumpeted his exploits as a substitute for having my own. I gained narcissistic satisfaction only vicariously. The resulting unconscious frustration and anger caused me to be relentlessly critical of any status quo. The socialist ideal of a non-competitive, fair distribution of goods acts, in adulthood, as a political corrective to a personal need, as well as being a standard by which to measure the current competitive political-economic reality that never measures up to an ideal of non-competition.[10] Marx's impassioned writings against capitalist competition offers an inspiring social and economic ideal and, on another level, a symbolic relief from a sibling competition I was resigned to losing. I continually have to "win" in fantasy what I actually lost in reality.

This same situation produced a shadow political-economic vision. The lack of familial rewards caused disappointment and withdrawal. A false self-sufficiency was created since caregivers could not be relied upon and healthy dependency was seen as

9 Robert Stolorow and George Atwood, *Faces in a Cloud: Subjectivity in Personality Theory* (New York: Jason Aronson, 1979).

10 Alfie Kohn's classic *No Contest* (Boston: Houghton-Mifflin, 1986) makes the case for the detrimental effects of competition.

a danger. This false self-sufficiency thinks of itself as a healthy autonomy. The need to not need anyone and to "pull myself up by my own bootstraps" laid the foundation for an anti-socialist, uncompassionate libertarianism that believes "it is every man for himself."

Notice that the shadow libertarian worldview is described negatively as a pathological outcome. It wouldn't describe itself in that way as evidenced by those who hold such views as their dominant belief-system. So a further exploration here would be how one political-economic vision gained ascendancy and the ways in which the dominant vision holds sway through an invidious characterization of the subordinate worldview. The speculation then suggests itself: what would it be like experientially to actually be that shadow self?

These two political-economic outlooks could be integrated into a libertarian socialism of the kind Chomsky has described. And they are integrated, to a small degree, on the level of political ideals and when forming opinions on current political events. But on a deeper level they remain largely unexamined. The emotional substructure of belief animates the political beliefs and holds them within certain bounds. The political views can be refined and broadened on the intellectual level through the usual means of reading, discussion, and political action. But an additional method is to explore the psychic terrain from which these beliefs grew and upon which they are still dependent. As long as this is not done these beliefs will repetitively have to do the psychic work of satisfying primary needs in never-quite-satisfying secondary ways; the never-completed Sisyphean task of the repetition compulsion. The examination of the shunned Randianism may release new energies and create a novel political integration, or it may just allow a deeper more sympathetic appreciation of the character of an alien view. There's no guarantee that an integration of the other may result.

A different use of this approach occurred in an exchange with Mark Edwards over my critique of Wilber's work.[11] In his rebuttal to my work Edwards made the point that Wilber's method was not, as I claimed, that of the orienting generalization but derived from systems thinking. He described the tradition of systems thinking and showed how Wilber's work was in keeping with it. Since my book is centered around orienting generalizations as Wilber's method, and he himself describes it as his method in his weightiest work, *Sex, Ecology, Spirituality*, I had good grounds for believing Edwards was wrong. Wilber does write about systems thinking, but I could have argued—and initially intended to argue against Edwards—that he does not treat it as his method, instead treating it as one more area of knowledge he culls for its partial truths. So I should have been fine with that; Edwards is wrong and I'm right. But the point kept nagging at me, even though it had been decided. I tried to dismiss it as mistaken, but it wouldn't go away. Then one morning, upon waking, before my everyday consciousness had a chance to reassemble itself and take control of who I am, I simply accepted the fact that even though I was right and Wilber doesn't *explicitly* say that systems thinking is a method he uses, Edwards is also right and it's obvious that that is what Wilber's whole integral *system* is. Yet that doesn't mean he doesn't use orienting generalizations; so the question arises: how are the two methods related? Now that I could accept the fact of Wilber's systems methodology I could ask this question. What I concluded is that they have an uneasy relationship in Wilber's theory, with systems thinking providing the form and orienting generalizations providing the content. But what if the content doesn't fit the form, as I've shown in this book? Wilber's solution is to selectively extract content from the sciences and mold them in such a way that they

11 This book appeared previously online at www.integralworld.net/index. html?meyerhoff-ba-toc.html. Regarding Edwards's criticism, see *Bald Ambition*, Chapter 3 and Mark Edwards, "Meyerhoff, Wilber and the Post-formal Stages" at www.integralworld.net/index.html?edwards25.html.

fit into the evolutionary-developmental system he is convinced is true. By recognizing a defensive and emotional attachment to a certain view, I was able to detach from that view, accept a new fact, and create a more satisfying integration of views.

The cognitive scientist George Lakoff, a political liberal, examined the roots of both liberal and conservative beliefs and gained a newfound understanding of why conservatives believe as they do and why he, a liberal, believes as he does. He writes:

> Every day, I have had to compare my liberal beliefs with conservative beliefs and ask myself what, if any, reason I had to hold my beliefs. . . . I find that I now can consciously comprehend my old instincts. I can give names to things that I could not clearly articulate before, things that were part of a vague sense of what was right.[12]

In delving into the substructure of belief Lakoff developed a new way of characterizing the differences in worldviews between conservatives and liberals. This caused him to be more sympathetic toward conservative views, fear them more for their dangers, and to feel even more committed to his liberal political outlook.

And finally, one theme I've pursued in this book and in two responses to Ken Wilber, is a critique of developmentalism in psychology. I've stressed the value-laden character of any theory or description of individual consciousness development. Those analyses, like Wilber's or anyone else's, stand on their own without any need for a psychological analysis of belief as I am proposing here. This kind of investigation into the psychology of belief says nothing about the validity of the beliefs held. Their validity depends on their coherence, plausibility, agreement with the evidence, and all the other criteria of rational knowledge claims. And yet, at the same time, this type of analysis affects truth and objectivity.

---

12 George Lakoff, *Moral Politics* (Chicago: University of Chicago Press, 1996), pp. 335–336.

So apart from the legitimacy of my critique of developmentalism, why do I find myself on that side of the issue? Why aren't I a person who agrees with Wilber? Since my constructivism doesn't allow me to claim a superior perspicacious relation to the final arbiter of truth—reality—how do I come to hold the view that I hold (beyond the strength of the argument I can muster for it). I trace my critical orientation toward development to my lack of success in personal development. I've felt let down by development. It doesn't seem to work for me. Of course, I have the cognitive skills necessary to do sophisticated intellectual work, but I have hoped, ever since I became aware of practices of self-development, that I could unblock developmental obstacles and grow emotionally, socially, and spiritually. But it hasn't happened that way, or has happened much less and much more slowly than I anticipated. I'm a discouraged developmentalist, and I think part of the motivation for my suspicion of developmentalism comes from this discouragement. The criticality acts as a defensive posture to make sure I "won't get fooled again." In contrast, Wilber has had a great deal of success in his intellectual and spiritual development, and, perhaps not coincidentally, is a champion of development.

There are two mistaken reactions to my description of the psychological background of my critique of development. The first commits the genetic fallacy and dismisses my arguments critical of developmentalism because they are thought to come from personal frustration with development. This is a mistake because the strength of the arguments has nothing to do with the reason I choose to make them. Just as nothing in Wilber's psyche and personal history have anything to do with whether his arguments for his integral theory are valid. That's why the great majority of my book is about arguments and evidence. This first mistake would typically be made by the Wilber loyalist who wants to avoid my arguments to protect his or her attachment to Wilber's views.

The second mistake is to think that uncovering the psychological causes of belief has nothing to do with the determination of truth and the creation of knowledge. This mistake would be made by the person who thinks that because of the genetic fallacy the genesis or origin of a person's beliefs plays no role in the determination of truth and knowledge. This person believes that truth and knowledge are representations of reality and are determined by the application of rationality and empirical experience. While it is a common way of looking at things, this conceptualization, after centuries of attempted grounding by philosophy, is no closer to being justified and actually looks further from validation. This person would be tempted to dismiss my views as a pernicious relativism. Yet, the relativist bogeyman is an odd creature. Universalistic, foundationalist, and absolutist philosophers and others decry constructivist and relativist accounts of truth and knowledge that have arisen in the last forty years. Yet part of the origin and legitimation of constructivist and relativist approaches to knowledge and morality come from inquiries and results within analytic philosophy itself. Typically, analytic philosophers combating the relativist threat will appeal to concepts of *truth, knowledge, justification,* and *norms,* which are themselves contested concepts in their own areas of specialization.

The Role of Truth and Objectivity

This kind of examination in the psychology of belief can be interesting in itself, but it is commonly thought to be irrelevant to the truth or falsity of the beliefs examined. But this is not the case. This kind of self-analysis affects truth and objectivity.

When this kind of *ad hominem* analysis is used to undermine the validity of a thinker's beliefs it's said that the analyzer commits the *genetic fallacy.* The genetic fallacy says that the origin of a person's intellectual views plays no role in determining the validity of those views. The validity lies in whether the views are valid according to the criteria of valid knowledge claims such as agreement with the facts or consistency. The philosopher John Wisdom's analysis of the psychological origins of Bishop Berkeley's idealism—regardless of its accuracy—says nothing about the validity of Berkeley's philosophy.[13] The philosopher Ben-Ami Scharfstein writes in his psychological analysis of some great philosophers' ideas that "nothing in the truth or value of an idea is affected by the circumstances of its origin. These circumstances help to explain just how the idea was arrived at and what its contemporary nuances were, but in themselves they have no bearing on its truth or falsity."[14] Likewise, the reasons for Wilber's allegiance to certain ideas say nothing about the validity of those ideas. So in this light, my psychological analysis of the reasons for Wilber's beliefs in the following chapter will be seen as an interesting, yet inappropriate, invasion of another's psyche.

The genetic fallacy assumes that there is a correct representing that some beliefs do and that we can determine which beliefs represent correctly and which do not; that reality impresses itself upon some people, making their beliefs true, and is missed by others, necessitating finding another origin for their mistaken beliefs. Yet, in philosophy it is readily admitted that we do not have a theory of truth, or an epistemology, that has been conclusively proven to be true.[15] Moreover, the very project of explaining our connection to, and knowledge of, a reality beyond us has been brought into serious doubt. If we take seriously this historical failure to explain our connection to reality and the current lack of an agreed-upon theory, we have to conclude, for now, that it is false to compare an imagined correct relation to reality that makes some

13 John Oulton Wisdom, *The Unconscious Origin of Berkeley's Philosophy* (London: The Hogarth Press, The Institute of Psycho-Analysis, 1953).

14 Ben-Ami Scharfstein, *The Philosophers* (Oxford: Basil Blackwell, 1980), p. 380

15 In Roger Scruton's mainstream account of philosophy he describes five major competing theories of truth. *Modern Philosophy* (New York: Penguin Books, 1994), pp. 97–111. Joseph Margolis gives a short history of philosophy's lack of success in these areas in *The Unraveling of Scientism*, (Ithaca and London: Cornell University Press, 2003), pp. 1–18. And there is also the position that truth is not the kind of thing we should hope to have a theory about.

beliefs true with a mistaken relation that makes other beliefs false. We cannot know the world outside of any given person's perspective on the world, or, if we can know, we can't know that that is what we know.

The predominant way of thinking regarding rational debate is that the debate participants share the same objective world, which is the guarantor of reaching truth. If the debaters follow rational procedures of argumentation in an unbiased fashion then they should eventually come to agreement about whatever matter they are discussing, because all participants should agree that the most rational understanding of the issue will represent best the one reality that the participants are trying to get right using their reason.

For those non-realists who believe there isn't one independent reality we all share, another neutral guarantor of correctness is thought to be our criteria for valid knowledge claims. It may be hoped that our criteria of valid knowledge claims, such as simplicity, plausibility, consistency, adherence to the facts, and coherence, could provide a neutral criteria of validation, but here too a rational foundation for these values is missing. Hilary Putnam, one of the foremost analytic philosophers, argues that even seemingly neutral rational criteria such as simplicity, plausibility, consistency, and coherence are themselves values—*epistemic* values—which cannot rationally ground their primacy as standards for evaluating thought.[16]

As a contrast to rational worldviews, which apply the criteria of consistency, we can think of Walt Whitman's poetic worldview, which exalts contradiction—"Do I contradict myself? / Very well then I contradict myself, / (I am large, I contain multitudes.)"— in order to more truly grasp the world by transcending reason. Another example of paradoxical wisdom occurs in the *Tao te Ching*, which contradictorily speaks of that which cannot be spoken of. Here are alternative visions and ways of living that reveal the

---

16 Hilary Putnam, *The Collapse of the Fact/Value Dichotomy and Other Essays* (Harvard: Harvard University Press, 2002).

*a*rational choice of consistency inherent within seemingly neutral rational criteria for evaluating truth-claims.

The philosopher Steven Hales has recently employed the fact that rationalist thinkers must rely upon "rational intuitions"—propositions that feel intuitively or self-evidently true—and that there is no getting around the rational groundlessness of these intuitions. He argues that a rational worldview, based as it is on rational intuitions, cannot demonstrate its superiority to other approaches such as the two he examines: Christian revelation and tribal beliefs gained through the ritual ingestion of hallucinogens.[17] We do not have to side with Putnam, Hales, and others to acknowledge that the mere existence of their strongly argued positions within the Anglo-American philosophical debate suggests a lack of rational consensus in the field. This situation suggests that classical notions of truth and objectivity, which we commonly take for granted, are still radically contested.

Barbara Herrnstein Smith has made a strong synthesizing defense of a broad range of these contemporary counter-intuitive intellectual currents, which she loosely groups under the term *constructivism*.[18] She calls this constructivist grouping *post-classical theory* and opposes it to the more traditional and still dominant *classical theory*. Some of this post-classical theory includes the usual suspects from postmodern continental philosophy such as Derrida and Foucault and the contemporary Neo-Pragmatism of Stanley Fish, Richard Rorty, and others who have described a coherent-enough philosophical foundationlessness. But it also includes much else. Herrnstein Smith refers to the constructivism arising out of systems theory and cybernetics that's associated with Heinz von Foerster, Ernst von Glaserfeld, and others.[19] There is the attempt to

17 Hales, *Relativism and the Foundations of Philosophy*,

18 Barbara Herrnstein Smith, *Belief & Resistance* (Cambridge: Harvard University Press, 1997) and *Scandalous Knowledge* (Durham: Duke University Press, 2005).

19 Bernhard Poerksen, *The Certainty of Uncertainty: Dialogues Introducing Constructivism* (Charlottesville: Imprint Academic, 2004).

bypass the nature/nurture dichotomy not through a compromise between the two but through an analysis of the multiple causal components of an inherently contingent evolutionary process.[20] In the sociology and history of science there is a substantial tradition demonstrating through micro-analytical case studies the constructed character of scientific knowledge.[21]

Classical theory so understood asserts or assumes a vision of our world that will appear to most to be so intuitively and obviously true as to not need any defense. There is a way in which the world is, in and of itself, which we humans try to know through perspicuous representations. Science and reason are the best modes of depicting and explaining the world and the various results of the differing scientific disciplines provide true knowledge of the world or lead us steadily in that direction. The nature of the world acts as a corrective to errant views through our empirical testing of our hypotheses and the reactions of our peers. The result of this kind of inquiry is justified true belief, or knowledge of the world. Because this is a trial and error process, there have been, and certainly still are, many erroneous beliefs; these errors have been and will be discovered in time, as the rational-scientific process is applied to the results of our inquiries and our mistakes are corrected. True knowledge is objective knowledge because it represents the world as it is in itself, even if no humans were around to perceive it. Those whose views are closer to the world's true character are thinking more objectively. What could be more obvious?

In many everyday situations this conceptualization meets our needs. But in many other everyday and philosophically reflective situations it does not. We are commonly cautioned (in the U.S.) not to discuss religion or politics in polite company because such discussions can too easily lead to irreconcilable conflict instead of rational consensus. Another common quandary in our culture is

---

20 Susan Oyama, Paul E. Griffiths, and Russell D. Gray, *Cycles of Contingency* (Cambridge: MIT Press, 2003).

21 Mario Biagioli, ed., *The Science Studies Reader* (New York: Routledge, 1999).

whether the cause of peoples' aberrant behavior is biological or psychological or a mixture of the two. The assumption behind this quandary is that reality is one way and not another. There is assumed to be the (one) way that it is, but this may not be the case. Instead, the biological and the psychological explanations could be seen as alternative ways of living, to which could be added the poetic, the spiritual, or the martial approaches to deviancy and living in general; each with their own costs and benefits. And adding to the puzzle is the commonly held belief that our biology or brain matter produces our psychologies, which makes it difficult to understand how our psychology could produce any behavior without the workings of our biology.

Philosophically, when this classical view is confronted by critical questioning, we find: that there may not be a way the world is in and of itself, or, if there is, we can't know when we know it; that there are social, historical, cognitive, and psychological factors in knowledge creation; that language is what allows specifically *human* knowledge but is not a window on the world as it is; that the concepts of *truth, knowledge, belief, good, bad*, and *objectivity* are notoriously difficult to define and make cohere.

So despite this reflective and experiential inquiry into psychological and emotional subjectivity, the goals of truth and objectivity will still play a crucial role in our discussions. But they won't be the usual concepts of truth and objectivity as absolute existents or ideals. Instead, because we will continue to employ shared criteria for evaluating ethical and knowledge claims we will continue to have a use for the notion of objectivity. Objectivity within a discussion will be gained through the overlap of the participants' criteria of validation. If two or more people share criteria of validation, then they can determine what they take to be objectively true. Two people who share no criteria of validation (if this is even possible) could not even have a discussion, since they would share no objective world in common. This way of thinking allows us to see the way in which we fashion our worlds and why worlds often collide.

If truth is understood to be determined and re-determined in an ongoing fashion in the vast number of discussions occurring both publicly and privately every day, then a method such as the one I am describing, which alters the character and resolution of such discussions, will also alter what is thought to be true. In that way, contrary to the genetic fallacy, the investigation of the psychological causes of beliefs affects what is determined to be true and false.

In the above example in which I reported my experience confronting Edwards's criticism, my self-examination led to a new understanding and altered my response. Of course, this is just one small incident, but multiplied many times these kinds of changes alter discussions, and so alter what is understood to be true (and false) and what we call knowledge. Does this mean that the truth is what anyone says it is? No, but the question itself needs to be examined because it presupposes that there is a truth that is not just what people inquiring together believe is the truth. The question implies that there is the objective truth, the real truth, but I've already said that I'm presuming that until philosophers can determine what that is we will accept that objective truth does not now exist for us, and work on that basis. But even without the idea of the objective truth, what anyone says is the truth is not the truth, because you or I or someone else may not believe that truth and will believe something else is the truth. So someone else's "truth" will be what I call a falsity. We don't give up our strongly held beliefs just because we've uncovered our arational ground of believing. The truth is always being forged and maintained in the ongoing social discussions in society. This is why a vigilance regarding our (as opposed to their) deeply held truths is necessary, because truth does not have a power or existence apart from our collective social construction of truth. We must be its champions, but we must also recognize that those we oppose will be opposing our truth with what they call the truth, and if there is a shift in power, those whose truth procedures are currently institutionally dominant could have their truth overthrown, at which point they would have to wage a guerilla war for (their) truth.

For example, in contemporary Western societies what Max Weber called the rational-legal view prevails. Modern bureaucratic institutions justify their existence by giving reasons and citing the law or rights. The rational-legal view displaced the traditional worldview that dominated Western societies when the Catholic Church and Christianity held sway. The Church's authority was founded on tradition and the Word of God. Things were justified, in part, because "that is the way they've always been done" or because The Bible or Aristotle said so. Contemporary rational, liberal pluralists like to think they treat all religions and views equally by allowing freedom of speech and worship. But for a Christian fundamentalist who knows God's Truth, to allow the methods and results of a Godless Reason to be the dominant mode of institutional organization is wrong and an offense. Why should falsity and immorality prevail? Shouldn't our institutions be structured by knowledge of (God's) Truth? There's no proving the superior connection to reality and morality of the rational-scientific worldview, as philosophers have shown. The rational-legal worldview is dominant in the advanced industrialized countries, and that dominance must be maintained through rhetorical skill and control of the cultural and educational institutions of society. The minds of each new generation will be molded by conflicting cultural forces; those that hold the reins of hegemonic epistemic legitimacy will have an advantage in inculcating what anyone who wants to be regarded seriously must believe is the truth.

The truth will be a function of what each person and group thinks human beings are, can be, and should be; and how each person and group thinks we should live both collectively and individually.

RESISTANCES

It makes perfect sense that this understanding of and inquiry into the psychology of belief creates discomfort. After all, we wouldn't expend so much individual and cultural energy avoiding the emotional substructure of belief if doing so weren't something unappealing and potentially painful. But there is also something painful about denying what is there—denying what is there being a Buddhist's definition of *suffering*.

One aspect of this discomfort is the squeamishness felt by hard rationalists for "touchy-feely" self-explorations. We feel comfortable explaining why our intellectual opponents are so wrong about what we know is right; but turning our gaze upon ourselves is unpleasant. It's easy to think it will simply create more navel-gazing and psychobabble. Hard rationalists will probably feel revulsion for this kind of inquiry. Yet if rationalists are as hard as they say, then they should carry their rational inquiries wherever they lead. I have made rational arguments for why this inquiry makes rational sense; it would require rational arguments to show how it is wrong. We must replace squeamishness with rational integrity. The resistance that keeps us ignorant can be transmuted into the insight that creates greater knowledge.

SCIENTIFIC VALIDATION

One intellectual expression of this feeling of squeamishness is a strong doubt of the validity of the psychoanalytically oriented introspective method that would be used to examine the emotional substructure of belief. Yet ironically, in contrast to the image of rational man in contemporary intellectual life, we find that the most rational and scientific of our inquiries has offered some confirmation of the image of ourselves that I am describing. Despite the strong criticism of Freud's ideas and the so-called "Freud Wars" that flared in the U.S. in the mid-nineties, the empirical confirmation of the unconscious in general, and Freud's postulated unconscious in particular, is surprisingly strong. The hard rationalist rightly believes in the high value of scientific results. This research runs from strong confirmation of the existence of vast areas of unconscious cognitive processes to demonstrations of the arational basis of beliefs.

The Nobel Prize winner and neuroscientist Gerald Edelman writes:

> The postulation of an unconscious is a central binding principle of Freud's psychological theories. Since his time, ample evidence has accumulated from the study of neurosis, hypnotism, and parapraxes to show that his basic theses about the action of the unconscious were essentially correct. As he used it, the term unconscious referred to elements that can be easily transformed into conscious states—"the preconscious"—as well as those that can be transformed only with great difficulty or not at all—"the unconscious proper." . . . Freud's notion of repression is consistent with the models of consciousness presented here.[22]

The psychologist Drew Westen writes in his survey of research in psychology that

> ironically, at a time when the prestige of psychoanalysis is at a low ebb in both psychiatry and academic psychology, an explosion of experimental research on several psychological fronts (much of it conducted by researchers with little interest in, or knowledge about, psychoanalysis has now documented conclusively that Freud was right in this central tenet [i.e., that much of mental life is unconscious]."[23]

22 Gerald Edelman, *Bright Air, Brilliant Fire* (USA: BasicBooks, 1992), p. 145.

23 D. Westen, "The Scientific Status of Unconscious Processes," *Journal of the American Psychoanalytical Association*, 47:1061–1106 (1999), online at www.psych-systems.net/lab/NEW_Sci_Status_Uncon.pdf, p. 3. See also Frank Tallis, *Hidden*

He concludes that "the data are incontrovertible: consciousness is the tip of the psychic iceberg that Freud imagined it to be."[24] These citations show that there is a basis in the conventional scientific literature for the idea that large portions of cognition are unconscious.

Related research in the relationship between emotion and cognition has reversed the intellectuals' common conception of emotion as a hindrance to reason and shown the necessity of emotions for reasoning. The neuroscientist Antonio Damasio has written, "Work from my laboratory has shown that emotion is integral to the processes of reasoning and decision making, for worse and for better."[25] In a collection of essays entitled *Emotions and Beliefs*, the editors state that emotions "can be seen as influencing the content and the strength of an individual's beliefs, and their resistance to modification."[26] In a 2006 publication called *Hot Thought: Mechanisms and Applications of Emotional Cognition*, the well-known philosopher and cognitive scientist Paul Thagard asserts that "contrary to standard philosophical assumptions, reasoning is often an emotional process, and improving it requires identifying and assessing the impact of emotions."[27] Thagard even has a chapter on "The Passionate Scientist: Emotion in Scientific Cognition," in which he "conclude[s] that emotions are an essential part of scientific cognition."[28]

Minds: The History of the Unconscious (New York: Arcade Publishing, 2002) and Dan Stein, ed., *Cognitive Science and the Unconscious* (Washington, D.C.: American Psychiatric Press, 1997).

24 Westen, "Scientific Status," p. 38.

25 Antonio Damasio, *The Feeling of What Happens* (New York: Harcourt Brace and Co.,1999), pp. 40–41. Also, his *Descartes' Error* (New York: Grosset/Putnam, 1994).

26 Nico H. Frijda, Antony S. R. Manstead, and Sacha Bem, *Emotions and Beliefs* (Cambridge: Cambridge University Press, 2000), p. 1.

27 Paul Thagard, *Hot Thoughts* (Cambridge, MA: MIT Press, 2006), p. 3.

28 Ibid., p. 172.

Finally, a recent study by Drew Westen et al. entitled "Neural Bases of Motivated Reasoning" used an MRI to record the parts of the brain used by subjects assessing positive, negative, and neutral information regarding their chosen political candidates. Westen et al. found that

> research on political judgment and decision-making has converged with decades of research in clinical and social psychology suggesting the ubiquity of emotion-biased motivated reasoning. Motivated reasoning is a form of implicit emotion regulation in which the brain converges on judgments that minimize negative and maximize positive affect states associated with threat to or attainment of motives. To what extent motivated reasoning engages neural circuits involved in "cold" reasoning and conscious emotion regulation (e.g., suppression) is, however, unknown. We used functional neuroimaging to study the neural responses of 30 committed partisans during the U.S. Presidential election of 2004. We presented subjects with reasoning tasks involving judgments about information threatening to their own candidate, the opposing candidate, or neutral control targets . . . As predicted, motivated reasoning was not associated with neural activity in regions previously linked to cold reasoning tasks and conscious (explicit) emotion regulation. The findings provide the first neuroimaging evidence for phenomena variously described as motivated reasoning, implicit emotion regulation, and psychological defense. They suggest that motivated reasoning is qualitatively distinct from reasoning when people do not have a strong emotional stake in the conclusions reached.[29]

These studies are just one way of validating the plausibility of the image of belief I am describing here. I offer them because

29 Drew Westen et al., "Neural Bases of Motivated Reasoning," *Journal of Cognitive Neuroscience,* 2006;18: 1947–1958, p. 1947. Thanks to Andy Smith and a reader of my blog for this reference.

the scientific approach is rightly held in such high esteem, and it is significant when one's assertions can be confirmed in that way. Further, it is important to make as much of the knowledge implied by one's worldview cohere as possible. More importantly, though, are the pragmatic benefits of this method of inquiry. Here, ethics is given an edge over epistemology, so the kind of person and world that is constructed by engaging in a given practice is what is crucial. Ideally, the person who engages in the kind of self-reflection I'm describing is gaining greater insight into him- or herself by confronting and expanding their beliefs.

Why Do This?

Through this type of investigation we can gain greater knowledge of self and other by understanding better the roots of our own and others' beliefs. More specifically, blind spots and contradictions, which we work hard to keep from ourselves when we are trying to be rational, can be revealed through this type of investigation. When the psycho-emotional causes for maintaining a contradiction are brought into awareness a loosening of their hold can occur. This insight into our attachment and the possibility of transformation can engender sets of beliefs more congruent with each other and with our selves as a whole. In going through this process with another we can better understand what causes our opponents to hold radically opposed notions. This process and the new understanding of our opponents can lead to a better relationship with our opponents. When our beliefs are better understood we can feel less defensive and can move past argumentative sticking points that occur because one side cannot allow themselves to understand what the other side is actually saying. The better understanding of self and other, the insight into blind spots, and the revealing of contradictions enhance truth and objectivity since these are determined and re-determined in ongoing debates such as these.

Since it's difficult for two people with fundamentally differing views to engage in this type of inquiry, a more likely scenario is an individual engaging in self-examination in order to further their own thought. This furthering will of course be judged by their own lights, although the presentation of their discoveries will provoke responses and judgments from others. One person's furthering of their thoughts can always be interpreted by another as an increase in mistakenness.

This approach will not make knowledge more accurate in the sense of representing reality as it really is. We won't gain an absolutely superior perspective because we integrate a wider amount of views. It assumes the necessity of giving up the notion of finally "getting it right" and grasping "the way it is." There is no way it is (or, if there is we can't seem to determine it definitively).

The whole notion of the ends of inquiry as "finally getting it right" or "grasping the way it is" needs to be repositioned within the larger objective of living rightly and making the world right. Ethics encompasses epistemology; community discussion and agreement undergirds objectivity. In mysticism, the way you act becomes more important than what state you've achieved. In the natural sciences, one powerful way of "getting physical reality right" is offered, but it's not *the* final way, since poetry or sensory awareness training can give us kinds of knowledge of nature that are also helpful for living a good life.

Modern Western philosophy's self-conception has been primarily epistemological with the guiding image being philosophy as a mirror of nature, or a way to get the world right using language, logic, evidence, and rational argumentation.[30] But this is not the only way of understanding what philosophy is. In the Western tradition, philosophy as a spiritual practice or way of life has an ancient pedigree and has an accomplished champion in the great

---

30 See Rorty in *Philosophy and the Mirror of Nature*. While Rorty's conclusions about philosophy are controversial, this basic historical point about the central concern of philosophy is less so.

French scholar Pierre Hadot. In *Philosophy as a Way of Life* Hadot recovers the ancient vision of philosophy as a "spiritual practice" with "spiritual exercises," somewhat similar to ancient Buddhism, which merges metaphysical insight and self-development. We don't just *know* what we think is right, we become and enact it. Similarly, I'm proposing a practice of thinking that attempts to recover all the constituents of our beliefs in an effort to create greater knowledge and better being.

CONCLUSION

I have argued that a psychological inquiry into the origins of belief can uncover the reasons beyond reason that cause us to believe. According to Pascal, "The heart has its reasons, which reason does not know." In contrast, I am arguing that the subterranean psychic world of the heart lying beneath reason that gives our beliefs their animating force can be better known. Richard Rorty, while not referring to this particular approach, states, "The point of philosophy, on this view, is not to find out what anything is 'really' like, but to help us grow up—to make us happier, freer, and more flexible."[31]

The reasons we believe must be supplemented by the reasons *why* we believe. Currently, the reasons why we believe play a hidden role in the creation of belief and knowledge. To ignore or deny these reasons beyond reason hinders our inquiry by neglecting an essential part of the process of knowledge creation. To include what is always going on anyway and gain greater awareness of it is a part of the rational task of gaining clear and distinct knowledge of what is occurring.

Reason cannot do all the work itself, because we do not believe only for rational reasons. The emotional substructure of belief must be brought into our investigations and debates in order to enhance

31 Richard Rorty, "Analytic and Conversational Philosophy," in C.G. Prado, ed., *A House Divided* (Amherst, New York: Humanity Books, 2003), p. 22.

the process of gaining greater consciousness of what's going on.

Neglecting important parts of belief and knowledge creation has costs, because that which is neglected will have its say through indirect means. To paraphrase Jung, when our shadow is not made conscious, it becomes our fate.

CHAPTER 10

PSYCHOLOGICAL ANALYSIS
OF WILBER'S BELIEFS

I present here a psychological analysis of Ken Wilber's theory of everything. This is an unconventional analysis, so I offer three justifications.

In the previous chapter I described and justified a psychological analysis of belief and used myself as an illustration. Here, the success of a psychological analysis of belief can be judged by comparing Ken Wilber's ideas with the published biographical and autobiographical material about him.

Secondly, throughout the book I have provided evidence for the contention that Wilber has created not an all-encompassing integration using an aperspectival vision-logic but a particular perspective that meets particular needs. The profound correlations that I show in this chapter between the character of his system and his life are more evidence for that contention.

Finally, if we assume, as is conventionally assumed, that it is the nature of reality that causes one to have a correct theory of reality, then there must be some other cause, besides reality, for an incorrect theory. I have shown many fundamental flaws in Wilber's theory of the Kosmos. If Wilber's theory is fundamentally problematic, this suggests that it is not the facts of the Kosmos that determine the character of his theory. If Wilber's theory of the Kosmos is not derived from the actual Kosmos, from where does it derive? Why does Wilber construct this particular theory? To answer these questions I will show the way in which Wilber's theory is derived from his psychology and life. As he says "the all-important question when trying to understand artifacts is: what level of consciousness . . . produced the artifact?"[1] Since I think less hierarchically than him, I will modify his question and ask: what *kind* of consciousness produced the artifact that is his system?

Loss

In essential ways the story Wilber tells about the Kosmos is Wilber's story. His life and tasks become the Kosmos's nature and purpose. For Wilber, duality, fragmentation, and separation are repeatedly identified as what is problematic in the world. The dualities such as interior/exterior, subject/object, individual/social, science/spirit, Ascending/Descending, Ego/Eco must be reconciled. So too, Western history, modern life, the individual's spiritual path, conflicting psychological models and therapies, and the big three are all diagnosed as being split, fragmented, or separated, and must be transcended. In each case the solution is integration, whether through a spectrum of consciousness, the four quadrant map, transcendence and inclusion, holons, the centaur, a marriage of sense and soul, or an integral psychology. The problem diagnosed and the cure recommended repeats.

Similarly, the pattern in which problems develop and solutions are found repeats. As far back as *The Spectrum of Consciousness* Wilber's task has been to integrate contradictory but true knowledge claims. This has not been a merely intellectual issue for him, it has been essential for his psychic well-being. In a 1982 article entitled "Odyssey" he stated that:

1 Wilber, "On Critics."

Life for me *was* sour; it was unhappy. And in part I was obsessed with reading all the great psychologists and sages because I was searching for a way out of the sour life; reading was motivated by personal existential therapy, to put it in dry terms. The point is that I had to "read everything" because I was trying mentally and emotionally to put together in a comprehensive framework that which I felt was necessary for my own salvation.[2]

The phrase "necessary for my own salvation" suggests the spiritual and emotional urgency of making everything fit together intellectually. Over the course of his intellectual life, the need to integrate diverse areas of knowledge was his guiding drive. His desire for integration is evident in the series of books he has written culminating in *SES*, his biggest attempt to overcome duality. Similarly, when working on *SES* he "was trying to pull together dozens of disciplines in all four quadrants, and this was a seemingly unending nightmare."[3] Wilber's characteristic "unending nightmare" being one in which there is a chaos of knowledge that he must order. It is as if the world keeps confronting him as a disassembled jigsaw puzzle which he feels compelled to assemble.

I wondered about this pattern for some time. Not everyone sees the world in this way or experiences this as one of their central issues. What does it mean to him? Why the pattern of focusing on dualities and feeling driven to reconcile them? Even the ground and ever-present essence of the universe is, in Wilber's terms, "*non*-duality." Then, an image hit me and it all coalesced. Early in *Grace and Grit* he and his late wife are awaiting the doctor's prognosis on her test for cancer. When told that she did indeed have cancer, Wilber says, "It felt like the universe turned into a thin paper, and then someone simply tore the tissue in half right in front of my eyes." Later in the same paragraph he returns to this

---

2 Wilber, "Odyssey: A personal inquiry into humanistic and transpersonal psychology," *Journal of Humanistic Psychology*, Vol. 22, No. 1, p. 60.

3 Wilber, *One Taste*, p. 122.

image, stating that "our universe had just been torn right down the middle."[4] The universe that had been whole was now split into two parts—a duality. This duality arose out of the prospect and premonition of a tremendous loss. Here the loss was of the person who completed him, who allowed him to go from being a part to a whole.

> I will always be at home in ideas, Treya will always be at home in nature, but together, joined in the Heart, we were whole; we could find that primal unity which neither alone could manage. Our favorite Plato quote became: "Men and women were once whole but were torn in two, and the pursuit and desire of that whole is called love."[5]

Surrounding the same loss we have three references to tearing. Eleven years later, in his novel *Boomeritis* the protagonist, named Ken Wilber, says, "'I wanted to feel that I wasn't being internally drawn and quartered'—that was it exactly. I kept saying that to myself all that summer—I don't want to be torn inside."[6] This image of the universe "torn in two," of being torn as the result of a horrendous loss, is the central metaphor of Wilber's work. To overcome duality and the attendant loss is his primary motivating need. Integration is the method by which wholeness is restored and duality, separation, and loss are deferred.

The loss of his wife in 1988 was probably the most horrible of his life, but the pattern of loss was established much earlier. In Tony Schwartz's *What Really Matters?* there are only a few pages about Wilber's background, but what is striking about them is the central theme of loss in his life. The family's losses began even before Wilber was born. His father suffered the horrible tragedy of losing both his father and mother when he was young. Wilber states, "My father was abandoned by his own father when he was

4 Wilber, *Grace and Grit*, p. 34.

5 Ibid., pp. 307–8.

6 Wilber, *Boomeritis* (Boston: Shambhala Publications, 2002), p. 31.

four, his mother died of tuberculosis soon after."[7] Yet even with these staggering losses his father "never blamed any of life's difficulties on his father's leaving him or his mother's death." A noble stoicism, but a means of coping that suggests these tremendous losses were not worked through and so acted out. This is partially confirmed when we learn from Wilber that his "father wasn't around a lot when [he] was growing up."[8] A repetition of the father's loss of his father passed down to the son.

Wilber's mother had her own issues with loss, which she transmitted to her son. With her husband absent a lot, Wilber "became not only my mother's darling kid but almost a substitute husband."[9] "When it came time to really let me go, that became a real problem."[10] "I . . . felt overwhelmed. I needed to establish my own space—without feeling that I'd be abandoned [i.e., suffer loss]."[11]

For Wilber's father and mother, abandonment, separation, and loss were central issues. Loss and the terror of loss were transmitted to Wilber as a child in overt and covert ways. While Wilber was growing up, his father's job as a career officer in the Air Force required that "the family move to a new town nearly every year."[12] Wilber acknowledges how painful this was and recounts "sobbing continuously for several days when he had to leave one town."[13] For a child, the pain of moving can be severe; Wilber had to do it "nearly every year."

While loss is a central theme in his childhood, it doesn't seem like enough loss to explain the outsized yearning for a positive wholeness that his intellectual system demonstrates. In addition

7 Tony Schwartz, *What Really Matters?* (New York: Bantam Books, 1995), p. 347.
8 Ibid., p. 350.
9 Ibid., p. 350.
10 Ibid., p. 347.
11 Ibid., p. 350.
12 Ibid., p. 347.
13 Ibid., p. 347.

to the losses themselves is the fact that the losses were compensated for by the security and freedom that his parents provided,
his exceptional abilities in academics, sports, and school politics,
and a seemingly in-born resiliency and good humor. (Although,
in *Grace and Grit* he attributes these childhood accomplishments
to a "fear of rejection"; rejection being another form of loss.)[14] It
seems like a more profound loss would better explain the outsized
need to create such a vast, progressive, un-tragic system. With
only a limited amount of information about his background, I can
only speculate, but one passage is suggestive. In Wilber's words:
"My true passion, my inner daemon, was for science. I fashioned
a self that was built on logic, structured by physics, and moved by
chemistry."[15] This devotion to the natural sciences and the "self
that was built on" them went through a radical change through
his exposure to Eastern mystical literature at the age of twenty.
"Within a period of a few months . . . the meaning of my life, as I
had known it, simply began to disappear." He jokingly and ironically compares it to a marital relationship: "Oh, it was nothing
dramatic; more like waking up one morning, after twenty years of
marriage, with the 'sudden' realization that you no longer loved
(or even recognized) your spouse." "It was a time for separation."
"The old sage [Lao-tse, through the *Tao te Ching*] had touched a
cord so deep in me (and so much stronger due to its 20-year repression) that I suddenly awoke to the silent but certain realization
that my old life, my old self, my old beliefs could no longer be
energized."[16] For a "repression" to occur there must be an event
that necessitated the repression. What caused that "20-year repression" of Wilber's spiritual self? What was that event that had
the power to cause the baby to disconnect from his spiritual self
and adopt the dramatically opposite persona of "a self that was
built on logic, structured by physics, and moved by chemistry"? A

14 Wilber, *Grace and Grit*, p. 240.
15 Wilber, "Odyssey," p. 58.
16 Ibid., p. 58.

dramatic shift, and one Wilber experienced as calling for "a separation," and a "repression" of part of himself.

We see this core issue of duality or separation and the need to integrate played out in many different ways. A central theme in his personal life, his intellectual project, and his diagnosis of society is the split between science and spirit. Both personally and intellectually he needs to validate spirit to science. In Wilber's journal, *One Taste*, one of the rare negative exchanges occurs when Wilber, in his zeal to prove that higher spiritual states are scientifically verifiable, shows his guests a videotape of himself hooked up to an EEG machine that records his brain wave activity as he passes through higher and higher spiritual states. Wilber writes that his good friend Sam Bercholz "says I make a total ass out of myself by showing this, since it seems so self-serving, so braggadocio." But Wilber doesn't care, writing "to me it's just an objective event," and "it also convinced the soon-to-be psychiatrist [in the audience], as it does virtually every scientific type I show it to."[17] He gets to impress people with his spiritual attainment *and* use that attainment to convince a "scientific type" of the validity of spiritual states.

We see this split between science and spirit and the need to prove spirit to science repeatedly in Wilber's intellectual project. Over his thirty-year career he has tried to validate spirituality to science. The convincingness of his integral synthesis depends not on spiritual insight but on scientific evidence and rational argumentation. In books such as *Eye to Eye*, *Quantum Questions*, and many others he tries to bring spirituality into the mainstream scientific fold. His whole Kosmic synthesis in *SES* can be understood as an attempt to gain scientific legitimacy for spirituality and for himself. His personal task to reconcile his scientific and spiritual selves becomes his intellectual task. This need is evidenced in a small but telling comment he makes to his wife in *Grace and Grit*. His late wife quotes his reaction to someone's comment that he

17 Wilber, *One Taste*, p. 76.

is considered the leading theorist in transpersonal studies. This could be received by Wilber in many ways: he could brim with pride, be modest, etc. He responds by saying that "being called the foremost theorist in transpersonal studies is like being called the tallest building in Kansas City."[18] On the surface this comment shows Wilber's good-natured humor and his realism in assessing the marginal status of Transpersonal Psychology. But beneath the surface is the suggestion that being the leading transpersonal theorist is not worth much in comparison to being the leading theorist in some well-regarded academic field. It would be much better to be the tallest building in New York City or London. His mammoth theory of everything, documented with nearly 240 pages of endnotes, and attempting to integrate all the sciences can be read as his attempt to be the tallest building in the largest of academic cities.

This personal and intellectual task becomes contemporary society's task. The need to both reconcile spirit and science and prove spirit to science becomes the culture's need in a book such as *The Marriage of Sense and Soul*. Historically, what Wilber repressed for twenty years is what post-Enlightenment society has repressed for three hundred years and needs to recover. Like him, rational, scientific, post-Enlightenment society repressed its spirituality throughout its "childhood" and must recover its lost spirit. Wilber's main diagnosis of modern society is that it is a "flatland" society (i.e., it has no spiritual sense, because of its excessive devotion to a scientific-materialist reductionism)—a critique the spiritual, adult Wilber could make of his former scientific, childhood self.

Spiritually, each individual's mystical journey and human society's future development follow the same stages as Wilber's personal journey. As described in "Odyssey," Wilber was drawn mainly to Eastern practices. He passed through what he calls psychic, subtle, causal, and non-dual stages of insight. Not coincidentally, he believes that these same developmental stages occur in all mys-

18 Wilber, *Grace and Grit*, p. 22.

tical traditions. More implausibly, though, he contends this could be the natural unfolding of society's evolution. If all goes well, society will pass through each of these four stages of development just as it passed through the magic, mythic, and rational stages. Wilber's culminating non-dual insight is the supreme insight of all the major mystical traditions and describes the essential nature of the Kosmos. It is not just what *he* realized through his spiritual practices, it is the Kosmos's own ground and telos. Of course, Wilber would argue that I have it backwards. He passed through those spiritual stages because everyone does, not the other way around. But this would have to be demonstrated through textual analysis, and, despite Wilber's claims, this has not been done.

An example which brings together the issues of early loss of spirit, insecurity relative to the academic establishment, the need to prove to and conquer that establishment, and the great attachment to themes of development and maturity can be found on the very first page of *SES*. On the surface it appears that Wilber is simply contrasting his work with prevailing attitudes in academia and intellectual culture. But the psychologically suggestive metaphor he chooses to depict the contrast, and his assertive, irritated, and defensive tone indicate the deeper issues that are at play for him.

Wilber asserts that in contrast to the predominant intellectual perspective, which denies any larger order, meaning, or pattern behind the workings of the Kosmos, he believes there is something else going on behind all the appearances, some greater order and meaning. He derogatorily names his opponents' position "the philosophy of oops" because they think that ultimately everything just happens by accident: "oops." The way Wilber expresses this straightforward point is quite revealing. The central metaphor revolves around the issue of development, or who is mature and who immature. He says that in contrast to those, like himself, who want to ask the big questions about why we are here and what's it all about, the philosophers of oops appear "sophisticated and adult" but that their response boils down to "Don't ask!" They contend,

according to Wilber, that "the *question itself* is . . . confused, pathological, nonsensical, or infantile" and that the "mark of maturity"
is to stop "asking such silly and confused questions," much like a
frustrated parent to a precocious child. But Wilber turns the tables
on these maturity poseurs and says that their answer to the big
questions ("Don't ask!") "is about as infantile a response as the
human condition could possibly offer." So it is *they* who are immature and infantile and it *he*, in his metaphysical questioning, who is
mature and adult.

Here we see so many of Wilber's personal issues being played
out on the very first page of his magnum opus. By asking metaphysical questions and seeking answers in spirituality, Wilber sees
himself as "infantile" and like a little boy relative to the dominant
intellectuals who falsely think they are "adult" and dismiss questions such as Wilber's as "silly." He sees himself in the eyes of rational adulthood as a silly boy. But, he is able to turn the tables on
this misguided skeptical rationality and see that it is they who offer
an "infantile" response, and that it is actually he who is "mature"
or developmentally advanced. The little spiritual boy who put his
spirituality away in order to adopt a scientific and rational persona
finally gets his due by devising a seemingly rational and scientific
system that both includes his scientific persona and transcends it in
a larger encompassing spirituality. Despite their societal legitimacy
and authority, Wilber has exposed the "infantile" nature of the
dominant philosophies and assumed the mantle of maturity.

We see here how he couches his struggle in terms of maturity
and immaturity. When discussing individuals' and groups' levels
of development he demonstrates a strong ambivalence toward
those on lower developmental levels, whom he feels compelled to
both condescend to and appreciate. And the same issue is seen in
his overwhelming need to create a theory in which his spiritual
attainment and intellectual synthesis are supreme. Intellectually,
these psychological issues manifest in his well-known pre/trans
fallacy in which what is advanced and what is regressed is sorted

out, and in his powerful need to see the entire Kosmos in goal-directed, evolutionary, and developmental terms despite the undermining that prevailing skeptical approaches threaten. Wilber once quipped to his wife that "kids love him . . . because he's the same emotional age as they are."[19]

An aversion to loss, and a resulting desire for integration, accounts for Wilber's strong favoring of positive system-building theorists. As are his heroes Plotinus, Schelling, and Habermas, Wilber is a positive system builder. His is a grand, all-encompassing synthesis in which nature or a deeper order advances toward greater complexity and higher inclusion and transcendence. His work is about evolutionary progress and developmental advance, which, when unfolding naturally, create a more moral Kosmos. Contrary to the belief that we live in an amoral, relativistic, postmodern miasma, Wilber believes there is a moral order and we can have direct knowledge of the essence of reality through mystical practice. Humans are again on top, reversing the demotions in our standing that the Copernican, Darwinian, and Freudian revolutions wrought. The evolutionary process of transcendence and inclusion means that nothing essential need be lost, because the natural, social, and individual structures that arise retain what is essential from previous stages. As we saw in the chapter on social evolution, the emphasis is on the negative aspects of bygone eras, so that the positive aspects of developmentally later eras can be highlighted. The basic structures of past social systems are preserved in superior, superseding systems. The vast loss of cultures, peoples, languages, and ways of life is neglected. It is an unrelentingly positive philosophy and affirmative history of everything.

The way negative Kosmic occurrences are understood reinforces the positive view. Wilber acknowledges that things can go wrong with development, but the problems of ecological devastation, resource depletion, nuclear war, or a corporatized globalization are rarely mentioned. They are deployed to show his awareness

19 Wilber, *Grace and Grit*, p. 73.

of them and that his system is not deterministic. The horrors of earlier historical eras are used to defend his contention that past eras were worse than ours and so ours can be seen as a developmental advance over them. However bad the social structure or regrettable the suffering of the past, it was the best that humanity could manage at that stage of developmental advance. Negative occurrences are labeled regressions or pathologies, and their status within his system is ambiguous. According to tenet twelve, physical, biological, and mental systems are pulled toward actualization or development; the natural tendency of things is to advance. But if this is the case, how do we understand regressions and pathologies? Are they *not* intended by the larger order? Are they mistakes or chance occurrences? If things go right and greater complexity unfolds through the process of transcendence and inclusion according to the twenty tenets, then things have unfolded according the way the Kosmos is set up. But how are we to understand things going wrong as when destruction, devolution, and extinction occur? How are we to understand the increasing simplification of some species, the destruction of the dinosaurs, the daily extinction of species, or the probable cold death of the universe? Because Wilber's system is fundamentally positive, negative occurrences are unexplained.

The positivity of Wilber's history of everything and his idiosyncratic universalism can be seen clearly by placing it within Hayden White's typology of history writing. In multiple books such as *The Content of the Form*[20] and *Metahistory*,[21] White has demonstrated how history writing, because it is a narrative or story, is forced to commit itself to the literary forms and values that narratives must assume. While Wilber wants his history of the Kosmos to be as inclusive, aperspectival, and universal as possible, its narrative form betrays its bias. Narrative differs from a chronicle, or a list of dates and

20 Hayden White, *The Content of the Form* (Baltimore : John Hopkins University Press, 1987).
21 Hayden White, *Metahistory* (Baltimore : John Hopkins University Press, 1990).

facts, in that it is tied together with a moral. No moral, no story. Value presuppositions must infuse all history written in the story form. Each form of history writing commits itself to a particular narrative structure which is chosen not based on the facts of the matter, but on the values that matter to the writer. The narrative type in which history is written prefigures the "facts" and the world "represented" by the writer. Because Wilber is writing "a brief history of cosmos, bios, psyche, theos—a tale,"[22] he commits himself to one of the types of narrative structure that White describes. By examining Wilber's historical style we can see the particularity of his purported universality. In juxtaposing his style to other possible narrative styles we can see the options Wilber rejected and the other ways the history of the Kosmos can be written.

The first aspect of narrative that White describes is what he terms the narrative's type of *emplotment*. The four main types of emplotment are Romance, Comedy, Tragedy, and Satire. "If, in the course of narrating his story, the historian provides it with the plot structure of a Tragedy, he has 'explained' it in one way; if he has structured it as a Comedy, he has 'explained' it in another way."[23] By unconsciously choosing one plot structure over another the writer has determined the meaning of history. "The Romance is fundamentally a drama of self-identification symbolized by the hero's transcendence of the world of experience, his victory over it, and his final liberation from it—the sort of drama associated with the Grail legend or the story of the resurrection of Christ in Christian mythology."[24] While the story of Wilber's personal journey could be fashioned in this way by reference to his spiritual achievements, it is not the mode of emplotment of his history of the Kosmos. Wilber's history follows the Comedic mode in that it

22 *SES*, p. viii.
23 White, *Metahistory*, p. 7.
24 Ibid., pp. 8–9.

suggest[s] the possibility of at least partial liberation from
the condition of the Fall and provisional release from the
divided state in which men find themselves in this world. . . .
In Comedy, hope is held out for the temporary triumph of
man over his world by the prospect of occasional *reconciliations* of the forces at play in the social and natural worlds.
. . .The reconciliations which occur at the end of Comedy
are reconciliations of men with men, of men with their
world and their society; the condition of society is represented as being purer, saner, and healthier as a result
of the conflict among seemingly inalterably opposed elements in the world; these elements are revealed to be, in
the long run, harmonizable with one another, unified, at
one with themselves and the others.[25]

For Wilber, a non-dual society is far off in the future. Unlike in the
Romantic Marxist vision, we will not be enjoying a classless, com-
munist utopia anytime soon. For now, we can hope that the "divided state in which men find themselves in this world" and "the
conflict among seemingly opposed elements"—the dualities—
will result in "reconciliations"—new integrations—in which the
"seemingly inalterably opposed elements" of science and spirit,
the big three, etc. will be transcended and included and "revealed
to be in the long run, harmonizable with one another, unified, at
one with themselves and the others" in a centauric evolutionary
embrace.

Confirming my characterization of Wilber's work as positive is
his distance from the two negative modes of emplotment, Tragedy
and Satire. "In Tragedy, there are no festive occasions, except false
and illusory ones; rather, there are intimations of states of division
among men more terrible than that which incited the tragic agon
at the beginning of the drama. . . .The reconciliations that occur
at the end of Tragedy are much more somber; they are more in
the nature of resignations of men to the conditions under which

25 Ibid., p. 9.

they must labor in the world."[26] Wilber's work does have some tragic elements, as in his view that the conflicts and challenges humanity confronts become greater as we evolve, but they play a small role in his overall vision.

Satire, the most negative mode, plays no role in Wilber's vision. Satire views "the hopes, possibilities, and truths of human existence revealed in Romance, Comedy, and Tragedy . . . ironically, in the atmosphere generated by the apprehension of the ultimate inadequacy of consciousness to live in the world happily or to comprehend it fully."[27]

The second aspect of White's typology of history writing is the demarcation of four forms of argumentation. Unlike the modes of emplotment, Wilber's argumentative approach falls exclusively within only one of the four forms. The four forms are the Formist, Organicist, Mechanistic, and Contextualist. Wilber uses the Organicist form, which White explains this way:

> *Organicist* world hypotheses and their corresponding theories of truth and argument are relatively more "integrative" and hence more reductive in their operations. The Organicist attempts to depict the particulars discerned in the historical field as components of synthetic processes. At the heart of the Organicist strategy is a metaphysical commitment to the paradigm of the microcosmic-macrocosmic relationship; and the Organicist historian will tend to be governed by the desire to see individual entities as components of processes which aggregate into wholes that are greater than, or qualitatively different from, the sum of their parts. . . . historians working in this mode will be more interested in characterizing the integrative process than in depicting its individual elements. This is what gives to the historical arguments cast in this mode their "abstract" quality. Moreover, history written in this

26 Ibid., p. 9.
27 Ibid., pp. 9–10.

mode tends to be oriented toward the determination of the *end* or *goal* toward which all the processes found in the historical field are presumed to be tending.[28]

Written five years before the publication of Wilber's first book in 1978, this reads, with minor emendations, like a summation of Wilber's central view.

The third aspect of White's typology is the ideological implications of the historian's style. The four are: Anarchism, Conservatism, Radicalism, and Liberalism. Classifying Wilber here is trickier. One clue is what White terms the *elective affinities* between modes of emplotment, argument, and ideological implication. Particular types tend to go together, and it so happens that the Comedic mode and the Organicist mode are most commonly affiliated. Interestingly, though, the type of ideology that they have an affinity to is the Conservative. Wilber's politics are a liberal and conservative mix, but I won't examine those here. For now, we see that Wilber's unconsciously chosen narrative style creates a positive view of history and holds at bay negative views—no less valid—which see history as Tragedy or Satire.

By delineating Wilber's particular type of history writing I undercut his claim to greatest inclusiveness or universality. The narrative form by its very nature imposes upon the historian choices of which he or she is usually unaware. Wilber likes to think that discoveries in the sciences impel him and us to adopt a vision like his own, but, as White shows, this is not the case. The facts do not tell the historian what mode of emplotment to adopt; it is a value judgment. Wilber's selection of the Comedic mode and his avoidance of the Tragic and Satirical modes result from his need to tell a positive and progressive story of history, not from the determining weight of historical facts.

28 Ibid., pp. 15–16.

GRANDIOSITY

The most salient quality of Wilber's work is its grandiosity. It is grandiose in that it is enormously large in scope, and, because it is fundamentally flawed, it is incommensurate with reality. Mistakenly maintaining that one has a valid theory of everything is a sign of personal grandiosity. The great danger for the grandiose person is deflation by the intrusion of the real. For the theory and psyche that are inflated to the breaking point, as for a balloon, every criticism looks like a sharp pin. This ever-present danger of deflation results in a shadow insecurity. The job of the grandiose psyche is to keep from awareness those aspects of reality that could threaten the grandiose vision. Consequently, maintaining a positive, progressive, Kosmic system which redeems all loss is difficult; it requires a lot of mental contortions in order to avoid seeing its flaws. This causes a number of *textual symptoms* to appear in *SES*. Textual symptoms are places in the text where the psyche of the author inserts itself to inhibit rational argumentation and keep the system afloat. These textual symptoms redirect the reader's attention away from the content of the book and motivate the reader to wonder about their cause.

The repetitiveness of *SES* is quite striking. This is not the repetitiveness that sometimes occurs over the course of a long book. This is a repetitiveness that occurs within single sections in which a single point is being made. Wilber simply repeats the point he is making over and over. His tone of absolute conclusiveness is belied by his inability to conclude. There are many examples of this in *SES*. For one, he repeats over and over that those who reject value hierarchies presuppose a value hierarchy.[29] The point is simple, yet he beats it to death. It is similar to the point he makes against so-called cultural relativists who contradict themselves when they assume that their view—that all views are of equal validity—has superior validity. That point is made at least three times over the

29 *SES*, pp. 25–27.

course of the book and rephrased a number of times within each of those discussions. Wilber is a clear writer, yet he seems to think that the point has not been made. Later in the book, four pages are devoted to repeating that the Romantics made nature the source of spirituality. He seems to think that if he repeats the point in different ways he makes it stronger.

Since this happens many times over the course of the book, I started to wonder why. I concluded that despite the tone of conclusiveness, there is an unacknowledged doubt that his argument is conclusive. Because he cannot admit to himself that he has not conclusively won his point, he is compelled to repeat it over and over in a futile attempt to be victorious by other means. But as we know from psychology, repetition compulsions never satisfy, because they do not get to the root of the problem. The root of the problem for Wilber is that he is doubtful about the validity of his own points because somewhere inside he knows that he is arguing, in each of these cases, against a caricature of his opponent's position, and will never gain the victory he craves.

This repetitiveness is one symptom of an overall insecurity that results from the impossible position in which he finds himself. On some level he knows that he is not living up to his own standard of using orienting generalizations, and so is never really making his case with the all-inclusive conclusiveness that he desires. The fundamental flaws that I have pointed out in the course of this book must be kept out of consciousness, and these textual symptoms act as a defense mechanism. He fools himself into believing that repeating a point over and over again is making the point.

Another technique of avoiding threatening counterarguments is the caricaturing of opponents' positions. In the chapter on methodology I note the lack of citations and quotes of opponents, lumping people together in large categories like "the ecophilosophers," "the multiculturists," "the retro-romantics," etc., and using simplistic formulations of opponents' positions.

Sometimes Wilber's insecurity drives him beyond repetitiveness and caricature to the sarcasm and snideness for which he has been criticized. This rudeness has become a topic of debate.[30] Some think it inappropriate. I happen to like polemical invective when used against people who have acted cruelly or hypocritically and are not recognized as such. But Wilber works himself up into a lather against scholars who, to my mind, haven't done anything heinous, like Morris Berman, Steven Katz, or Stanley Fish. Yet others with whom he also disagrees aren't treated derisively. Wilber is respectful of Stanislav Grof, Francisco Varela, and others. I puzzled over this for quite awhile. Why condescend to one set of scholars yet treat another set with respect, even though you have disagreements with both? Was it the degree of disagreement, with those who disagreed most getting the most abuse? That didn't seem to fit, because Morris Berman's views seem similar to Wilber's, yet he is treated derisively. I finally realized that it is not degree of disagreement with himself that Wilber dislikes; it is a thinker's degree of negative critique.

Thinkers can be divided into two groups: system builders and system underminers. Wilber's favorites—Plato, Plotinus, Schelling, and Habermas—are positive philosophers who build intellectual systems. Who Wilber hates are negative thinkers whose basic approach is critical—Stanley Fish, Georges Bataille, and Steven Katz. These thinkers undo systems and dismantle foundations. He has a strong aversion to thinkers who are essentially critical. He equates critical orientation with nihilism and believes it corresponds to those who believe in the "philosophy of 'oops,'" which is that "the universe just occurs, there is nothing behind it, it's all ultimately accidental or random, it just is, it just happens—oops!"[31] Later in the book Wilber angrily denounces "'tenured radicals,' who want to deconstruct all forms of accepted knowledge," and

30 Robert McDermott, "The Need for Philosophical and Spiritual Dialogue," *ReVision*, 19(2).

31 *SES*, p. vii.

who only have "the wits, as it were, to tear down but not create: deconstruction exhausts the limits of their talent."[32]

Psychologically, these thinkers say to Wilber, "You can't repair the universe. You have to live with loss. You can't have your big integration." Wilber cannot stand hearing this, so he avoids their arguments by caricaturing them and then repetitively "proving" that the caricatured argument is wrong.

Derrida and Foucault are considered negative thinkers, but Wilber generally treats them favorably. An apparent anomaly, but easily explained. They have achieved such a level of fame, and their work is so influential that a person such as Wilber, who wants to claim inclusiveness, must incorporate them into his synthesis. He does this by extracting something from them that agrees with his view, thereby misrepresenting them in the process. Another reason for Wilber's respect for famous negative thinkers is that he tends toward hero worship, and so their fame alone insulates them from the derogatory treatment that less famous, but no less negative, thinkers have to endure.

Wilber has defended his snideness and sarcasm by saying that it was a conscious strategy to shake up the most important critics of his system: the postmodern, poststructural, and the politically correct, who he perceives as having taken over academe. I find this unconvincing. As I asserted in a previous chapter, a stronger case can be made that these postmodern enemies have not taken over academe. And his tone in *SES* suggests not a calculated derision but a release of pent up anger.

For a better explanation of his negativity I look to a personal comment he made in *Grace and Grit*: "In my case, when I become afraid, when fear overcomes me, my ordinary lightness of outlook, which generously might be referred to as wit, degenerates into sarcasm and snideness, a biting bitterness towards those around me—not because I am snide by nature, but because I am afraid."[33]

32 *SES*, p. 662.
33 Wilber, *Grace and Grit*, p. 152.

In *SES* fear, in the form of a threat posed by others to the fragile coherence of his grand integration, causes the degeneration into sarcasm and snideness. It is a way to hold at bay those who do not think things ultimately cohere, who see the profound loss and sadness at the heart of life, and who think it illusory to try to affirm an essentially positive telos embedded in nature.

Toward the end of the book these textual symptoms escalate. The first 450 pages of the main text have 140 pages of footnotes, while the last seventy pages require ninety-six pages of footnotes. Footnotes that were merely long in the first five-sixths of the book became short essays in the last sixth. It seems that Wilber just could not bring himself to finish the book. Exaggerated statements and verbal attacks also escalate. It's as if Wilber senses he is not going to make a conclusive case that he has integrated all knowledge and resorts to extreme claims and insults to make what he says so. On page 492, we learn that "The Big Bang has made Idealists out of virtually anybody who thinks about it, and the result is that most philosophers of science now openly admit—and even champion—the fact that evolution has some sort of self-transcending drive" It has?! They do?! On page 722 we get childish name-calling directed at "Stanley Fish, that dimmest of the postmodern dim bulbs." On the final page of the main text Wilber tries to prove by fiat what he has not proven through argumentation: "if today is rationality, tomorrow is transrationality, and there is not a single scientific argument in the world that can disagree with that, and every argument in favor of it."[34] There is a crazy desperation in a statement like that. He cannot admit to himself that he is not confronting the reality of his opponents' positions. This is why he lumps them into big categories like "the ecophilosophers," "the heterarchists," "the multiculturists;" generally doesn't name and quote individuals; and turns his opponents into simple-minded straw men who hold intellectual positions it is hard to imagine anyone with any brains holding.

34 *SES*, p. 524.

While much of himself can be found latently in his system, conversely, Wilber is silent or evasive about the overt place he as creator occupies in his own system. In *SES*, he is the Kosmos's describer, explainer, integrator, and the embodier of its highest spiritual attainment, yet he never acknowledges it. He displays a healthy sense of shame in his discomfort with his role and uses a variety of techniques to avoid it, the most common being omission. In reading *SES*, this omission always becomes noticeable to me when he repeats his argument against the poststructuralists and relativists. He accuses them of being self-contradictory because they say that all views have equal validity while assuming their view is superior to all other views. I always wonder on what basis he feels that *his* view is superior. Of course, he can appeal to the coherence of his entire system, or the orienting generalizations, or its agreement with scientific evidence, or its superior inclusiveness, but none of these satisfy the philosophical demand for a foundation to knowledge, the absence of which makes relativism seem like a valid conclusion. Without it, Wilber is in the same boat as the relativist, except that he does not admit it to himself.

Other examples in *SES* of Wilber's silence about his own position relative to his system come when he repeats the poststructural insight that the world is made up of a dizzying array of contexts within contexts within contexts. He incorporates this insight into his system, but he never contextualizes himself. The contextualization of the author and the author's standpoint are two of the central poststructural contextualizations, yet Wilber simply ignores them and assumes some unexplained standpoint from which to map the Kosmos. To grasp the whole and produce a "theory of everything" he must have a position outside or above it, yet nowhere does he explain it. I assume he believes he has achieved the position of aperspectival vision-logic as Hegel, Habermas, and Foucault have, but nowhere does he state this. And that position is not really outside or above, since it is just one developmental stage within the system.

He doesn't explain his standpoint, because he feels embarrassed by the exalted position he occupies. This embarrassment is apparent when he does make reference to his place in his system. He often uses self-deprecating humor to deflect attention. For example, he was asked by an interviewer his level of consciousness according to an eight-stage model he was using. He jokingly says, "I'm trying to work my way up to beige [the lowest level]."[35] Or, he implies his position without saying it directly, as in *Grace and Grit*, where he states that there are "two types of people who believed in universal Spirit—those who were not too bright (e.g., Oral Roberts), and those who were extremely bright (e.g., Einstein). . . . Treya and I believed in God . . . which meant we were either very bright or slightly dumb."[36] Guess which. And, being "very bright," they were in quite good company, Einstein no less. He entitles a recent interview "On Critics, Integral Institute, My Recent Writing, and *Other Matters of Little Consequence*" (italics added). His joking self-deprecations are the outward manifestation of an outsized self-regard.

Another way in which Wilber demonstrates his discomfort with his position is in his awkward ambivalence when discussing those lower than him on his value hierarchy. He wants to both respect lower developmental stages as appropriate to their time or place and yet judge them as inferior relative to higher stages. At one point in *Grace and Grit* he digresses to insert a distinction between different New Age types. He is part of the twenty percent that is transrational or transpersonal and not of the eighty percent that is prerational or prepersonal. *They* are the ones who make people think that *he* is flaky or goofy, when in reality he is beyond the rational, not below it, as they are. Although these prerational, New Age types use "magical and narcissistic" thinking, Wilber and his transrational ilk "are not against prepersonal beliefs," it's just that it is such a chore, because "in the field of transpersonal psychology, we are constantly

35 Wilber, "On Critics," part III.
36 Wilber, *Grace and Grit*, p. 21.

having to deal as delicately and as gently as we can with the pre-personal [or pre-rational] trends."[37] His whole discussion here is an uneasy mix of smug superiority and a congratulatory tolerance for the less advanced.

Another example is Wilber's treatment of "green memes." This is a social category describing people who have achieved the highest level of social and personal development below a transpersonal breakthrough. The green memes are sensitive selves who mistrust cold reason and emphasize feeling. They are against hierarchies of all kinds and exalt a pluralistic relativism. They are responsible for political correctness and conduct codes, and champion egalitarian and multicultural politics. These are the people most angered by Wilber's nasty endnotes in *SES*, yet they are the group most ready to be shepherded into the transpersonal stage. In a number of interviews Wilber's ambivalent attitude toward them is evident in his movement from superior mocking of this less advanced group to respectful enumeration of their positive qualities.

While Wilber omits himself from his theory, there are ways that he unconsciously inserts himself back into the text of *SES*. Trying to hold at bay the many contradictions and counter-arguments, these unconscious insertions come in the form of a self-critique. It is as if Wilber's psychic shadow had to be given its say through these textual symptoms. Wilber projects this shadow onto his subject matter and unwittingly criticizes his own project. Projection occurs when one projects one's own views onto others and believes that those others actually hold those views. This is how most of us live up to the New Age dictum to create your own reality. Wilber does this a number of times during the course of the book, and it gives a very interesting insight into him when these instances are decoded.

Early in the book Wilber warns us about the concept of wholeness: "'Wholeness'—this is a very dangerous concept . . . dangerous for many reasons, not the least of which is that it is always

37 Ibid., p. 268.

available to be pushed into ideological ends. Whenever anybody talks of wholeness being the ultimate, then we must be very wary, because they are telling us that we are merely 'parts' of their particular version of 'wholeness,' and so we should be subservient to their vision—we are merely strands in their wonderful web."[38] Of course he argues that he avoids this danger, but for those of us who disagree this is an excellent description of a problem with Wilber's grand synthesis. Whole fields of knowledge, distinct spiritual states, and vast historical epochs find that they are "merely 'parts'" in Wilber's "particular version of 'wholeness.'" This might feel to them like being "subservient to [his] vision . . . merely strands in [his] wonderful web."

Later in the book, Wilber unwittingly describes my analysis of his ignorance of his own psyche and the intellectual consequences of it. He writes, "I believe it is a profound truth of human development that one can fully transcend any level only if one fully honors it first (thus allowing embrace/Agape). Otherwise one's 'development' is simply a reaction to, a reaction against, the preceding level, and thus one remains stuck to it with the energy of disapproval—Phobos, not Eros."[39] This is a good description of what has happened to Wilber himself. He has not worked through and embraced his own psychological issues, and so acts them out in his thinking, writing, and behavior. His aversion to loss (Phobos) is transformed into a positive, constructive system-building, and is a "reaction against" negative or critical thinkers rather than an "allowing embrace" of them. His unresolved issues with maturity and immaturity come out as a strongly developmental and progressive program with himself at the spiritual pinnacle (i.e., the most mature). His fear of being a big fish in a small pond, or merely the "tallest building in Kansas City," pushes him to grandiosity. And the insecurity he feels about keeping his big synthesis afloat is compensated for by his repetitive, incantatory, and defensive argumentation.

38 *SES*, p. 36–37.
39 *SES*, p. 375.

Wilber describes his own shadow methodology when writing about the early Christian scholar Origen's method of interpreting Christian myths. Wilber writes,

> The brilliance of this scheme is that it takes a prerational myth (literal) and reworks it at both a rational (ethical) level and a transrational (mystical) level, so that "the myth" can be made to say whatever it is necessary to make it say, quite regardless of how its originators actually meant it. In other words, the interpretation takes the myth quite beyond itself—first into the space of reason, and then into the space of spirit. The myth is thoroughly preserved—and utterly negated. This allows Origen to put into the myths whatever meanings from a higher level he wishes to put into them, so that he can both claim scriptural authority and basically ignore it at the same time.[40]

This is an excellent description of what I claim Wilber is doing with his story of the Kosmos. Wilber takes the "literal" knowledge of the sciences and "reworks it" on a "rational (ethical) level and a transrational (mystical) level" to make everything make sense. Through selective scholarship, the knowledge "can be made to say whatever it is necessary to make it say." The knowledge is "preserved" in that it lives in Wilber's new synthesis, and yet it is "utterly negated" in that it is ripped out of the academic debates in which it is situated and given its larger validity. Wilber's method of culling preferred pieces of knowledge from diverse sciences allows him to give his story of the Kosmos "whatever meanings from a higher level he wishes to put into them." He "can both claim scriptural authority" (by saying he is using our taken-for-granted knowledge and by having 238 pages of endnotes) and "basically ignore it at the same time" (by only really using a select few scholars and misrepresenting those who disagree).

40 *SES*, p. 397

Finally, Wilber's description of the damage done by the Ego (Enlightenment Rationalist) and Eco (Romantic) camps doubles as a compelling, unconscious self-description. Of the Ego camp he writes:

> The rational-ego, hyperagentic and hyperindependent, took its own relative autonomy (which had indeed increased significantly), and blew it up to absolute proportions. In understandably wanting to increase freedom and liberty, it paradoxically left massive road kill everywhere on the highway to rational heaven.[41]

While ostensibly a description of a historical consciousness, this quote is a fitting critique of Wilber's own approach to writing *SES*. Wilber, in his efforts to construct a rational all-encompassing synthesis, raises himself up to an extraordinary height—a "rational heaven"—with no sense of his own contextualization or how it affects his supposedly neutral, aperspectival, "hyperindependent" viewing. He tells his story of matter, life, mind, and spirit, and thinks that it is the Kosmos's own story (i.e., he "blew it up to absolute proportions"). "In understandably wishing to increase freedom and liberty," he leaves "massive road kill everywhere on the highway to rational heaven" when he caricatures opponents, uses knowledge selectively, and claims an inclusiveness that is not there.

Wilber's description of the Eco camp's damage to the world is also an acute self-critique. He writes:

> But the same paradox of damage beset the Eco camps. In starting out with the express intention of *decentering* the Ego, of inserting it back into the larger currents of Life and Love, the Eco camps ended up—inadvertently, paradoxically—championing modes of knowing and feeling that were supremely egocentric and flagrantly narcissistic. In wishing to overthrow the Ego—and still being stuck, with their opponents, in monological flatland—the Eco

41 *SES*, p. 457.

camps introduced the modern world to a glorification of *divine egoism*: the outrageous return and exaltation of that which it expressly set out to overcome.[42]

Wilber's personal Eastern mystical practices had "the express intention of *decentering* the Ego," or "overthrow[ing] the Ego," but, in the search for a theory of everything, "ended up—inadvertently, paradoxically—championing modes of knowing and feeling that were supremely egocentric and flagrantly narcissistic," and so we witness the "outrageous return and exaltation of that which it [his mystical practices] expressly set out to overcome": "a glorification of divine egoism."

CONCLUSION

Ken Wilber's personal experiences of division and loss are compensated for by grandiosity represented in his overwhelmingly positive and massive theory of everything. This in no way undermines the validity of his theory, but it does complete the picture of its perspectival nature, which has been demonstrated in previous chapters. It also provides another illustration of my thesis in the previous chapter that there is a psychological origin to our beliefs by showing the psychological origins of Wilber's view of the Kosmos.

The above analysis received some disturbing empirical confirmation after it was written. In June of 2006 Ken Wilber posted a blog entry in which he appeared to have a spontaneous, raging outburst at critics of his integral theory.[43] (He later said that the piece and its insults were well-considered.) The abrasiveness of the piece forced people to react one way or another, and he later wrote that a purpose of the piece was to separate the integral wheat from the integral (world) chaff. Those who got the

---

42 *SES*, p. 457–458.
43 Wilber, "What We Are, That We See."

Kosmic "joke" demonstrated a higher consciousness from those who missed it and by missing it gave evidence of their lower consciousness.

The piece is filled with the behaviors described in this chapter. There's the grandiosity and outsized self-regard (he refers to his critics as "fleas"), the caricatured rendering of opponents, the defensive reactivity, the creation of fissures and the black-and-white thinking.

Regarding the thesis of this and the previous chapter, it's interesting to see how the rhetoric of inclusiveness and the genuine attempt to include all those lower on the developmental holarchy can be linked to the opposite tendencies in the thinker's psyche. As is true of all of us, Wilber's intellectual edifice and his deeply held beliefs also serve personal psychological purposes which when examined can reveal a determining arational cause of belief. If rational argumentation reaches these bedrock beliefs, an examination of the emotional substructure of belief can create experiential and intellectual illumination and alter our personal and collective understanding of what is true and good.

Conclusion

The theory of the Big Bang tells us that we can trace everything that exists back to a common birth moment. From the singularity of creation we get the multiplicity of existence. How did we get from an infinitely dense speck of matter to all that appears today? What is the unifying story of this interconnected Kosmos? Why is it all here and where is it all going?

It is Ken Wilber's bald ambition to try to answer these questions by explaining how everything came to be, fits together, and what it all means. Not just the theoretical physicist's theory of everything, or the cosmologist's explanation of the cosmos, but a true Theory of Everything: matter, life, mind, and spirit. The fact that this absurdly ambitious attempt cannot immediately be dismissed is a credit to Wilber's knowledge and imagination. But the fact that it does not succeed is not surprising given the enormous diversity of knowledge it must integrate and the unsustainability of much more modest systematic integrations.

This book's initial question regarding Wilber—Einstein of consciousness or New Age pseudo-scientist?—was used for dramatic effect. There is a vast territory between these two descriptions. Wilber is a creative synthesizer whose interests span all types of knowledge in contrast to the narrow specialization prevalent in academia. He has done more than perhaps any other thinker to forge a synthesis of Western and Eastern theories and practices of self-development. His grand theorizing does have real world applications and he is actively trying to institutionalize his work and propagate it to create individual and social change. He is an accomplished mystical practitioner and speaks knowledgeably about both the theoretical and experiential aspects of mysticism. His work shows signs of development as it loosens its grip on problematic notions like linear development and tries to incorporate perspectivism.[1]

However, the deep dualities Wilber's integration seeks to remedy are not resolved. Subject and object, science and spirit, individual and social, are mapped and juxtaposed but not integrated. There is the appearance of integration, but a closer look and an examination of the details yields contrary facts and inconsistencies. If a theory contradicts the facts or is inconsistent, its validity is compromised. These are essential aspects of reason's method that must be satisfied if, as Wilber claims, he has transcended and integrated the rational stage within his larger synthesis.

A common response to this type of criticism is that Wilber is working at a higher level of integration and that the "details" will be worked out in the future. Yet there is good reason it is said, in differing contexts, that God or the Devil resides in the details. God is said to be in the details when one experiences the sublime in concrete particulars; and the Devil is in the details when one encounters the anomaly whose stubborn factuality threatens one's seamless theoretical unity. And details don't only refer to those stubborn little bits. There is also the detailed examination of a large-scale theory, which reveals whether there is or is not consistency. In Chapter 1, I described Andrew Smith's criticism of Wilber's tenet 9, which was the apparently clear-cut rule that

---

1 See his notes, "Excerpt D: The Look of a Feeling," for the forthcoming volume in the Kosmos trilogy at http://wilber.shambhala.com/html/books/kosmos/excerptD/part1.cfm/.

determined where holons rank developmentally. By examining whether it worked in detail, Smith showed the inconsistencies in the tenet and how, if applied consistently, it would not rank holons as Wilber's model does.

Wilber's strength as an imaginative synthesizer flying high over the "details" is also his downfall. Those so-called "details" are the debated and debatable knowledge from the various academic specialties. They are not, what Wilber calls, "already-agreed-upon," "simple but sturdy" knowledge. The present state of knowledge does not provide the validation he needs to ground his speculative theorizing. Wilber's synthesis is creative and his life philosophy attractive, but there are too many anomalies for it to be considered a valid theory.

Previous chapters examined the academic literature Wilber does and does not cite and show fundamental debates by the leading experts where Wilber contends there is consensus around orienting generalizations. The chapter on holarchy demonstrates the fundamental problems with the concepts and definitions Wilber uses to create his ontology and tenets of the Kosmos. Chapters on consciousness, social evolution, mysticism, postmodernism, western history, vision-logic, philosophy, and methodology, and investigations into topics such as epistemology, the perennial philosophy, human violence, the Enlightenment, and Romanticism show Wilber's mischaracterization of debates and the falseness of his contention of an academic consensus around his views.

Wilber and I offer different solutions to the problem of opposed perspectives. Wilber tries to solve it on the level of intellect; I try to solve it on the level of relationship—relationship to our own beliefs and to our opponents'. Wilber contends that he takes the truth in the other's perspective and incorporates it into his perspective, but what is deemed true in the other's perspective is dependent upon the character of the perspective doing the choosing. Wilber obscures this fact by claiming he's using the consensus knowledge or orienting generalizations of the sciences, yet I demonstrate that they don't exist or don't exist in the way he needs them to exist. The truth we take from others—the places where we agree—are dependent upon the character of our perspectives. While we will certainly value things differently and have our particular hierarchies of value, the way to mediate the differences in perspective is not through the creation of an illusory mega-perspective but through the way we relate to the person holding the opposing perspective in the moments in which we are engaging that person. This approach would be problematic for Wilber, we can infer from his numerous acrimonious discussions with, or avoidance of, people who oppose his views too fundamentally.

A fundamental assumption of Wilber's particular perspective is that there is one truth or way in which the world is. Consequently, for Wilber, if we take all the confirmed truths in all the different fields of knowledge and integrate them, they should fit together because they are all pieces of one big puzzle. But there are many criteria of truth and so many different kinds of truth; some fit together, some overlap, and some contradict. People today have to deal with this diversity of truths. The approach I advocate recognizes the postmodern insight of these many truths and surrenders the desire to be in possession of the one truth. We are then still left with differing perspectives, the people who hold them, and the problem of how to get along. It is our relationship to the truths we hold dear and the nature of that dearness that I suggest we examine.

ACKNOWLEDGMENTS

Scott Parker thought this should be a real book as well as a virtual one and donated his skillful editing, excellent judgment, and dedication to the project.

Frank Visser first published the book on integralworld.net and has maintained it on his fine website.

Andy Smith wrote an appreciative review of the book and gave it needed respectability. His penetrating analyses were crucial to Chapter 1.

Our dog Callie, my little buddy, who died in December of 2004, was with me during the years of research and writing.

My family provided the environment and support that allowed me to become the person I am. My father, who died on May 18, 2009, provided the model of reasoning that I try to emulate.

Rivka has been with me for the last twenty years and still, inexplicably, loves me. I, explicably, am still trying to express my boundless love for her.

INDEX

ABOUT THE AUTHOR

Jeff Meyerhoff, M.A., L.S.W., is the author of *Bald Ambition: A Critique of Ken Wilber's Theory of Everything* and many essays on integral theory, several of which are available at www.integralworld.net. His weekly radio show, *The Ruminator*, is archived at www.wmfo. org. Please visit his blog: www.philosophyautobiography.blogspot. com.